# A True Fisherman's Tail

Spiderwize
Remus House
Coltsfoot Drive
Woodston
Peterborough
PE2 9BF

www.spiderwize.com

A CIP catalogue record for this book is available from the British Library.

The views expressed in this work are solely those of the author and do not necessarily reflect the views of the publisher, and the publisher hereby disclaims any responsibility for them.

ISBN: 978-1-911596-58-5
eBook: 978-1-911596-59-2

# A TRUE
# FISHERMAN'S TAIL

## J. KEITH *(Kipper)* LYNCH

SPIDERWIZE
Peterborough UK
2018

# Contents

# ACKNOWLEDGEMENTS

If it had not been for the encouragement, support and companionship of many special people, coupled with numerous personal encounters experienced over a period spanning close on 50 years of angling, the subject of this book would not have been possible.

Family, friends, fellow anglers and members of the general public associated with the sport have most definitely provided me with the ammunition and the memories to fill the following pages. For this, I will be forever grateful and indebted to them.

However, I feel I must indulge and make no apology to single out just a few to whom I feel I must pay particular and special thanks.

My mother, for being so patient in my early years of angling, when I would return home with my clothes soaking wet, covered in mud and not really appreciating the extra work I was bestowing upon her (she had to wash, clean and iron them). For returning home long after tea-time, only to find my dinner (a dinner which she had spent time preparing and cooking) in the dog.

For explaining to neighbours "Our Keith? Prowling about your lovely cut lawn late last night, in all that rain? Och, he was only looking for dew worms for the fishing."

My Father, for whom at times it must have felt he was

nothing more than just a taxi driver, only there to transport me all around the south west of Scotland to fish in places that I didn't even know exactly where they were located, let alone how to get there (all before I myself could drive, of course). For his companionship at the river side during these early years.

In more recent years, my two sons for accompanying me to the water's edge at every opportunity as they themselves, learned to fish. I loved every minute of that period of my angling life. Both are now more than accomplished in the art of fishing, probably more so than their mentor.

My wife; there are not enough pages in this book to allow me to list every situation in which she has supported me. Enough said.

Thanks to the many friends and fellow anglers from all the clubs of which I have been a member. In particular, those members of my local angling club Dreghorn Angling Club.

To all those "strangers" I have met during my travels, all of whom having the patience and courtesy to spend some time with me. I thoroughly enjoyed their company and their "craick." It is these guys who undoubtedly contributed much to my life-long angling memory and recollections.

In more recent times, to one particular gentleman, an author in his own right, namely Mr Gerry Farrara, who, relatively recently, briefly viewed my fishing diaries and was amazed at the amount of historical notes I had compiled throughout my angling life. He encouraged me, and yes at times pushed me, to use these notes as a basis to write this book.

There is one acknowledgement I feel I must make above

all others but taking nothing away from those already mentioned. I, of course, refer to Mother Nature. She alone is the one who has provided me with all the ingredients, opportunity and privilege to experience these events. Throughout these years, Mother Nature has taught me to build and mature in my passion and overwhelming respect for my quarry - I obviously refer to – the fish.

# INTRODUCTION

Since the age of 10 years, I (Keith Lynch) locally known as Kipper, have had an unquestionable passion for angling, in particular angling for freshwater game fish. I do not profess to be one of the greatest anglers of all time, but class myself simply as an average Joe Bloggs angler, but a 'reasonably competent' Joe Bloggs angler. Throughout my lifetime I have lived, breathed, practised and dreamed of fishing, predominantly on my own two beloved local rivers, namely the River Irvine and Annick Water, both of which are located in Ayrshire, Scotland.

With close on 50 years angling experience I have learned and practised my skills on a range of small spate rivers, wild Scottish lochs and, in more recent times, (that is to say since the early to mid-nineties), rainbow trout fisheries, most of which are located throughout Scotland but, on occasion, venturing across the border into England to broaden and enhance my experience. There is no doubt each one of these venues has contributed to my experiences, successes and losses but most of all - my memories.

I have fished over one hundred different venues, some of which to most may be somewhat obscure in terms of national recognition, but still provided me with some special experiences. But from source to sea, from rivers to the depths and shores of lochs, lakes to small "put and take" fisheries, throughout the British Isles there are numerous seams of gold and silver to be found.

Gold and silver in angling terms I of course refer to:

Gold, in the form of lovely golden-flanked wild brown trout.

Silver, in the form of fresh run migratory Atlantic Salmon, the King of fish; but let us not forget its close relative, the enigmatic sea trout. It too can support the same glistening silvery flanks.

All of these species are to be found within the many waterways and river systems throughout the home countries. These lovely wild expanses of water and little spate rivers are just begging to be explored and searched just to see what treasures may be found.

I have diligently and meticulously kept a detailed record of my angling exploits in the form of a personal diary, maintained for over forty of these years.

I felt it was time to share some of my exploits, experiences, thoughts, feelings and memories in the form of a book and as the reader progresses through the different sections, I sincerely hope these writings will "trigger" the memory buds, not just of fellow anglers but those open to the wonders of the wide outdoors. Maybe they too can compare, recollect, reflect and remember their own similar, but just as special, events which they themselves have experienced, during their outdoor ventures.

The book highlights a mixture of seriousness, fun and sometimes downright worrying events. The contents are written based on events which really did occur and are factually true, as recorded within my diaries.

There are two venues which form the back-bone of my fishing life and most of the following recollections referred to within this book have taken place somewhere along the course of these two little rivers. However, a number of other venues do feature.

I have simply got to introduce these two rivers first. Two rivers with so many special memories, two rivers which I hold so dear to my heart and from which I know where I "learned my trade."

Please enjoy the following recollections.

# River Irvine

*Holmsford Bridge (Red Bridge)*

This little spate river rises as nothing more than a ditch behind a mass of ancient volcanic rock (or plug) known as Loudon Hill. Loudon Hill is located virtually right on the border between East Ayrshire and Lanarkshire. It flows due west for the best part of thirty miles of relatively slow gradient before entering into Irvine Bay on the Firth of Clyde. Subsequently, it is not considered to be one of the fastest flowing nor one of the most prolific of salmon rivers located in Scotland.

As with most rivers at their source, the river is nothing more than just a few feet wide with clear flowing water and as it flows through semi-moorland and farmland in its upper reaches, the main stream widens with a number of smaller streams and tributaries joining the river as it flows towards the sea. With the ever-changing landscape the river flows through a number of what were once considered to be large industrial towns with each town supporting its own range of industry. Industries from textile mills producing fabrics and lace, to heavy engineering manufacturing plants producing products ranging from agricultural tractors to friction bearings. In the early days these "textile" mills, and similar industries, relied heavily on water-power to assist their production needs. Hence, even today there is much evidence along the course of the river of its industrial past. A number of ruined and derelict mills and dams can be found throughout the river system. The whole characteristic of the river changes dramatically from section to section as it flows towards the sea.

Passing through the first two towns, the river is relatively narrow and begins to form many short, well-oxygenated, gravel-bottomed streams and many deep, dumpy pools, perfect spawning environment for the migrating salmon and fish of salmon-kind (salmonoid), a species which ascend the river with only one thing in mind - to reproduce. The river bed, at this point, does not really suffer from excessive sediment deposits which are so evident in the lower reaches. Reference to this will be mentioned later. These upper reaches also include a few vertical-faced dams which act as a hindrance or barrier to the migrating fish. However, fish are still able to progress upstream by swimming through the lade (millstream) of the disused mills thus by-passing the vertical face of the dams.

As the river leaves the town of Galston, heading through Hurlford, the streams are becoming longer and the pools and glides are also increasing in width, length and depth which has the effect of increasing the distance between these running streams. The river bed itself is also changing, proving to be more of a sandy, silt-type bed with an increase in aquatic flora (weed) covering; perfect habitat and volume to support good numbers of resident and migrating fish. The river now enters the major town of Kilmarnock. Here, the river's characteristics really change with much longer, deeper slower pools, or – in local angling terms - flats. Obviously, the gradient of the land has decreased which in effect means the river does not flow at the same "speed" as found in the upper reaches.

We are now in the middle reaches where the number of towns along its banks reduce and the river heads out into mainly low-lying farmland. Long, deep pools are now the main feature until we reach a hamlet known as Drybridge. At this point, the river returns to streams and long(ish) pools for the best part of two miles. This stretch of the river fishing is managed by Dreghorn Angling Club (my home club). Finally, we reach the Royal Burgh of Irvine where we find the confluence of the River Irvine's second largest tributary, Annick Water.

Just below the confluence with Annick Water there is a section of the river known to locals as "The Ripples." These ripples are the last "real" streams before the river continues to widen and flow through the centre of the town and down towards the estuary where the River Irvine's main tributary, the River Garnock, joins within the harbour area just before both enter the sea - technically flowing into the River Clyde estuary.

# ANNICK WATER

*Peirs Bridge – Annick Lodge*

This little river, at one time, could only be described as the perfect trout stream. There are many who would argue, possibly the best little trout stream in Ayrshire. Like its mother river, the Annick rises in nothing more than moorland well above the town of Stewarton. The river appears to have a totally different rain catchment area to the River Irvine even though the source of each river is not, in real terms, that far apart. So, the Annick Water can be carrying a high volume of water levels when the Irvine is virtually bare.

From its source to its confluence with the River Irvine, the Annick Water is constant streams and pools and you have to come right into the lower reaches before you find any long slow "flats" of any tangible distance.

On leaving Stewarton (again a former industrial town) the Annick enters open farmland with some excellent river features and fishing opportunities, predominately for brown trout. However, there are definite runs of migratory fish which run this little stream later in the year. Its path now reaches the boundary and extremities of the town of Irvine, that is to say Lawthorne and Bourtreehill, both heavily populated housing developments which have risen since the late seventies and early eighties as part of Irvine new town. Development to this day still continues along its course thus taking away much of the lovely, picturesque countryside bordering its course.

Since the formation of the Bourtreehill community during the 1970s, there is absolutely no doubt that the Annick Water has suffered a decline, both in feature and in productivity, downstream of this development. Those who can still remember and fished the Annick before Bourtreehill I'm sure would agree. Nevertheless, plenty of fish can still be caught throughout this stretch if you are willing to "suffer" interruption from the kids who may be playing alongside the river. I personally have a lot of tolerance for the youngsters of today, but I ceased to fish this area because of the environment and I miss it! The building of Bourtreehill was definitely the downfall of this stretch of the Annick Water.

# So Inexperienced

## SEASON 1972

*How many fish can one accept to lose in one day?*

*The Bogie Bridge*

What's the relevance of the question above? Well, the question relates to one particular day I encountered during my early attempts of fishing for the "King" of fish, the Atlantic Salmon (Salmo Salar), and not forgetting its cousin the enigmatic sea trout. Both of these species are generally viewed by many as the cream of freshwater fishing. Both species are migratory and are born in the clear running headwaters of our freshwater rivers and streams.

For approximately the first two years of their lives they live and feed on a parallel to their freshwater relatives, the brown trout, but after two years or so some form of metamorphosis to their genes and anatomy takes place. These small immature fish experience such an urge to migrate to saltwater, and migrate they must if they are to survive, that they make their way downstream towards the sea. On reaching the estuary of their river of birth, they enter the sea and strive to reach their food-rich feeding grounds of the North Atlantic. For the next year or two they feed ravenously, gaining weight at an enormous rate. Then, the second major change to their body takes place, the urge and need to breed overcomes them.

Once again these fish embark on one of the world's most fascinating migrations. These two species of fish can only reproduce in the very same headwaters of their river of origin. It is during this period of entering and ascending their river of birth the salmon angler ventures out to practice his skills. It has been scientifically proven salmon do not feed whilst in fresh water, so why should any angler be able to tempt this fish to take any of his baits into its mouth? This is why the capture of an Atlantic Salmon is so highly prized by the angler. He or she considers themselves to have conquered nature! Man against beast!

Fortunately, I have had the good fortune to have not one but two salmon rivers on my doorstep. Although these two rivers cannot be rated as classic salmon or sea trout rivers, they have provided me with a lifetime of opportunity to at least fish for these magnificent species at a more than acceptable cost.

The two rivers to which I refer are, of course, the River Irvine and its second most major tributary, the Annick Water, as previously mentioned. The River Irvine, bordering the south side of my home village, and the Annick Water bordering the North side. The local club who manage the fishing is Dreghorn Angling Club. Both rivers support a "reasonable" population of salmon and sea trout during the latter part of the season.

They will never be in the same league as some of Scotland's more renowned rivers such as the Tay or Tweed, totally different in character altogether.

During the late 1960s and early 1970s, I remember, at the appropriate time of year the River Irvine had some fantastic runs of migratory fish. Salmon and sea trout could be regularly seen leaping out of the water in many of the pools and streams. However, in recent times (the past twenty or so years) there is no doubt the number of salmon and sea trout returning to the river has notably declined, particularly sea trout. To be fair, there are still a few fish about and if you are really lucky, the odd sea trout or two can be enticed.

Like many fishing locations they all have their "resident" experienced riverside characters and the River Irvine is no exception. During my teenage years I remember Sammy Piper, Harry Downes and Johnnie Colquhoun and Auld Sanny Turner (The KING of sea trout fishing). Sanny would often be seen trotting a small worm down a stream or a pool, casting slightly upstream with the worm passing in front of him no more than five feet from the river bank, and by here he certainly caught his sea trout, it was a pleasure to watch and learn from him. In more recent times, Wilson Gillespie, John Sloan and John "Minty" Miller, all of whom virtually lived on the river bank and appeared to be always catching salmon. These are the anglers, particularly those guys from my teenage years, I (for the want of better words) idolised and wished to emulate in the years to come. These guys had a wealth of knowledge and an abundance of experience under their hats. I, however, during these early years, was at the other end of the scale, just embarking on my quest to catch - the King of fish.

I seem to have lost my way from the original question, I shall return to our tale.

Just a couple of weeks prior to this particular experience to which I now refer, saw the river produce its first real spate of the season and I had been lucky enough to catch my very first salmon (a grilse weighing 3 lbs). Certainly not the biggest salmon ever caught, but I was on a high, so pleased with myself and thinking, "it's not that hard to catch and land a salmon. What is all the fuss about?" I was just about to find out how wrong, naïve and inexperienced I really was. I was just about to learn the hard way.

It's 12 July 1972 and the River Irvine was in a relatively good condition supporting a clean running spate. The water could be described as tea colour and overhead conditions were favourable, clear and dry, a slight breeze, not cold, in fact a pleasure to be out fishing. I left home at around 11:00 a.m. to walk a mile or so downstream to one of my favourite locations, the Bogie Bridge. It was so called because this old bridge of wooden construction had once carried coal wagons (bogies) from Montgomeryfield coal pit to the mine entrance where the bogie line rail track disappeared underground just on the south side of the river. The original bridge was eventually replaced with a metal suspension bridge during the 1980s and now the bridge only facilitates foot passengers.

The Bogie Bridge pool and stream was one of the locally renowned locations where salmon and sea trout were regularly caught. Indeed, this is where I had recently caught my first salmon, mentioned earlier.

On arrival at the Bogie Bridge I decided the method of fishing would be "spinning", so Toby's Blue and Silver Devons or Mepps (brightly coloured pieces of shaped metal used by anglers to attract and hook fish) were the order of the day. After about 30 to 45 minutes of fishing, it was very clear and evident there was a fantastic head of fish moving through the stretch. Fish were being hooked by others, fish were leaping and showing themselves all over the pool.

Indeed, I seemed to be just in the right "taking" spot at the right time and apparently using the right method. It's a pity I didn't have the experience to match. Within a relatively short period of time I had hooked and lost FIVE fish. Other anglers on the river witnessed this including a gentleman I mentioned earlier, Mr Sammy Piper, an angler in whose company I had spent much time over recent weeks indeed, if the truth be told, actually over the past couple of seasons. He had demonstrated his tolerance and patience with this young pest, sorry budding angler! This young angler probably didn't really appreciate this gentleman's patience and time. I had spent many hours watching Sammy catching salmon and trying to learn from him.

After the fifth fish lost he said, "Right son, come and have a seat, we need to talk." We sat there and talked about what had just happened. He asked if I wanted to become a dentist.

Very puzzled by such a strange question, "I do not" was my reply.

"Well, why try and pull the poor fish's teeth out?" It took me a while to understand that comment.

We agreed two of these five fish were probably salmon and three were most likely to be sea trout of varying size. Being a lot more experienced than me I didn't disagree, but I was still absolutely gutted and no amount of sympathy was working, as I said I was STILL gutted!

By now, the bankside of the pool was beginning to look like Sauchiehall Street in Glasgow on a Saturday afternoon.

Considering I had been at this location for the past couple of hours I decided it was time for a move, so I moved downstream alone to fish the pool just above Shewalton Dam. It was formerly a dam which once serviced water to an old working mill sited on the south bank. The mill was no longer there, but the remnants and the ruins of the mill are still evident today. If my information and belief is correct, the dam was "blown-up" as a training exercise for the forces during World War Two. In reality, the dam is now nothing more than a big, long, rough section of fast-flowing water. On arrival at Shewalton Dam, I met another angler who was spinning directly above the lip of the dam (or stream). As usual when anglers meet on the bankside, the first greeting or question is, "anything doing?" Within seconds it became pretty evident this angler appeared to be just as gutted and disappointed as myself; apparently he too had hooked and lost a number of fish within the last three-quarters of an hour or so. However, this part of the story has a slightly better ending. As luck would have it as we were speaking, he hooked yet another fish and after a short but strong fight he allowed me to net his fish. A sea trout of around 2 lbs, its silvery flanks shining like a bar of silver in the sunlight. Finally, success for one angler!

Anyway, he was now a happy angler and his mood and body language changed immediately, but to my amazement he didn't really stay long after this. Maybe he isn't as tolerant as Sammy Piper!

I continued to fish the pool above the dam for a little while with no success, although I could still see a few fish showing as they successfully negotiated the lip of the dam and disappeared into the pool above. I decided to return to the Bogie Bridge.

By this time, a couple of fish had been caught from those anglers who had remained fishing the pool. The only space left for me was directly under the bridge at the top of the stream. I took up position and started to cast and, you've guessed it, after only four or five casts I hooked another fish, only for it to turn and head back down the stream as if to return to sea. Mistakenly, I think! I tried to stop the fish and held onto it and after the fish "pig rolled" for a few moments on the surface of the water it was gone. AGAIN! So much for me listening to Sammy's coaching!

It was late afternoon by now and hunger was getting the better of me so I returned home absolutely disappointed and disgusted with myself and wondering what do I have to do to land a fish? What do I tell folk if they ask if I've had any luck? Would they believe me? I don't think so, a right fisherman's tale from one so young.

Having been fed and watered again, it wasn't too long before I was desperate to return to the river. This time I had the company of my good friend, John McEwan. I told him of what I had experienced earlier in the day but as expected I don't think he really believed me!

Anyway, we made our way down to one of John's favourite spots, just above the stream flowing out of Milligan's Pool. This pool is about half a mile upstream of the Bogie Bridge. Milligan's Pool is another renowned pool in the local angling circles. Still using the same spinning methods and lures I began to fish, picking the prime casting spot and drawing my spinner across the top of the small weir. Guess what? Another fish hooked! John, however, had just disappeared around the bend into the next pool below. I shouted at the top of my voice thinking it might be a waste of time shouting as John may not hear me due the sound of the rushing waters flowing down over the small weirs.

Fortunately, and to my surprise, John did hear my shouts (or screams) and came running with a net. As John arrived it was pretty obvious the fish was virtually played out and exhausted. The salmon came towards the net on its side, its silver flanks glinting in the evening sunshine. John lowered the net into place, preparing to net the fish and I began to draw the fish over the net thinking to myself "at last you're mine!" A fish of approximately 5 or 6 lbs!

I don't believe what happened next - the fish had one final twist to the tail (get it? tale?) and just as it reached the lip of the net it gave one last kick, hit the banking and the hook became dislodged, my rod straightened and my line went slack. Another fish lost. I have never felt so disappointed. I was shaking all over and felt like crying – seven fish lost for the day. John could only stare in disbelief and after that I think he accepted what I had told him earlier was true. A few days later I once again met Mr Piper and once again we talked over what had happened. Mr Piper then gave me a piece of advice, advice which I clearly remember and still respect to this day. I have passed his words of wisdom on to many since. He said: "Remember, within reason, the longer you have got the fish in the water, playing the fish under control, the more chance you have of landing the fish."

What I think he meant, no, what I know he meant, was that I was far too hard and severe on these fish and I was in too big a hurry to get them into the net. As of that point, the dentist comment sunk in.

You live and learn!

# NOTEABLE BROWN

## SEASON 1975

1975, not one of my most prolific of seasons, for one reason or another I hardly managed to catch any fish during this year. However, one really notable catch which I do remember was caught one warm, bright and breezy autumn evening in September. Wednesday 15 September, to be precise.

After recent spates the river had dwindled to nothing more than a trickle, only some of the deeper pools were holding water (and the odd fish or two), but the condition of the water was very clean, weed free and the clarity was very good. I decided to fish from just after 6:00 p.m. until darkness fell *which - in reality - meant less than a few hours of daylight remained at this time of year. I also decided to fish from the north bank around the no.11 stream or bend area, which is unusual in itself, because it is better and much easier to fish from the south bank.*

Anyway, due to the water level and water conditions there was one major question pending. Do I take my spinning rod or my fly rod? I decided to cover all options and take both. On arrival at the waterside, fly fishing won first crack at catching fish. Fishing the stream below a deep slow pool around a bend of the river, I carefully and methodically fished down the stream which took me about half an hour.

No takes or offers were received which meant no success at this point.

I turned my head and glanced upstream and just at that moment, above the small weir and in the tail of the pool above, I saw a fish rise, a good fish by the looks of it, but I wasn't convinced it was a salmon. I was just too far away to be certain but it could possibly be a decent sea trout. So I thought to myself, I'll give it a go. Carefully and stealthily, I moved upstream to where I had seen the fish rise but once again I was undecided whether to cast a fly or give the spinner a chance.

Considering the extra depth of water in the tail of the pool, I thought I would give it a go with a small no.1 silver Mepp. I was still slightly downstream of the fish, therefore I cast upstream and brought the Mepp back towards me at speed to ensure the blade was spinning and on the third cast BANG! Fish on! Obviously a good fish by the feel of it, fighting like a demon but remaining deep. After a few minutes or so playing the fish, it headed downstream and swam right past me just under the surface of the water and in this clear water you can imagine my surprise when I could distinctly pick out red spot. Absolutely no doubt, I was fighting a large brown trout. What a size! Well it was for this water!

A few moments later this beautiful fish came to the net exhausted. What a fantastic brown trout for our river, considering a half pounder during this decade was considered a good fish. Historical records of the local club provide evidence that NO stock fish of this size had ever been stocked by Dreghorn. This fish, a cock fish measuring from nose to tail 20 inches, weighing in at 2 lb 9 oz, was in prime condition. There is no doubt this was truly wild and was undoubtedly the largest brown trout taken from our waters in recent history. I felt honoured to have caught such a quality fish. I continued to fish for a short time however no more success was experienced during the remaining daylight but I didn't care, I had my wonderful prize. I returned home a happy angler.

In fact, on the way home I met the club secretary's son and showed him my prize. Word of the capture didn't take long to progress through the village's angling fraternity and later that evening I was contacted by the secretary at the time, Mr Robert Mullen, to seek the opportunity to take a few photographs of this unusually large fish and maybe even insert a photograph into the local press. Too late, my father had already cleaned the fish and prepared it for the table.

Since that day I have been lucky enough to catch some trout of similar size, some even bigger, and all have been returned to the river, but this particular fish still remains paramount within the memory buds of the old grey matter. As I have aged and become more knowledgeable, experienced and in some ways wiser and more respectful towards my quarry, I sometimes wish I had not killed this fish but returned it to the river to continue its life. Who knows how many other "wee troot" it could have helped to bring into this world. But at that time I thought nobody would believe me, so I had to show my prize!

Season :- 1978

| Date | Species | Location | Length | Weight | Method | Conditions | Total on visit | Accum Total | Notes |
|------|---------|----------|--------|--------|--------|------------|----------------|-------------|-------|
| 01/04/1978 | Brown Trout | River Irvine | 10"<br>10" | 12 onz | Fly & worm | Raining & wet | 2 | 2 | Caught in the stream below Red Bridge. Both fish returned. |
| 04/04/1978 | Brown Trout | River Irvine | 10 1/2"<br>11" | 14 onz | Fly | Dry, windy & cold | 2 | 4 | March Brown in Gibson Pool |
| 09/04/1978 | Brown Trout | River Irvine | 10 1/2" | 6 onz | Fly | Nice day – water low | 1 | 5 | Caught behind SKF – lost 2 others |
| 06/05/1978 | Brown Trout | River Clyde | 12" | 10 onz | Fly | Water low,dry breezy day | 1 | 6 | River very busy but only a few fish caught |
| 16/08/1978 | Sea Trout | River Irvine | 20" | 2 lbs 10 onz | Spin – B&S Devon | Dry day & in small spate | 1 | 7 | Father caught two sea trout – 1 lbs 8 onz and Ian caught one the night before – 1 lbs |
| 29/08/1978 | Brown Trout & Sea Trout | River Irvine – Holmes | 9"<br>11" | 5 onz<br>9 onz | Worm | River very low, bright & sunny day | 2 | 9 | Returned the Brown Trout |
| 05/09/1978 | Sea Trout | River Irvine | 11" | 8 onz | Spin – No.1 Mepp | River at normal height after spate | 1 | 10 | |
| 23/09/1978 | Sea Trout | River Irvine No.11 stream | 12" | 10 onz | Worm | Water in spate – very pleasant day | 1 | 11 | Stream below Sandy Bend – No. 11 |
| 25/09/1978 | Brown Trout | River Irvine Wash – house pool | 9 1/2 | 6 onz | Worm | Water in spate – still raining | 1 | 12 | Returned the fish |
| 04/10/1978 | Salmon | River Irvine | 34" | 9 lbs 8 onz | Spin B&S Devon | Good flow on water but not in spate | 1 | 13 | Above stream at Sandy Bend – No. 11 |
| 07/10/1978 | Brown Trout | River Annan | 9 1/2 | 5 onz | Worm | Bright & sunny – water low | 1 | 14 | Also caught a 3 lbs 2 onz Chub |
| 27/10/1978 | Brown Trout & Sea Trout | River Irvine No. 11 stream & top side of Red Bridge | 10 1/2"<br>12" | 8 onz<br>10 onz | Worm & No. 2 Mepp | Dry & dull water running off from spate | 2 | 16 | Returned Brown Trout |

# Major Fish Kill

## SEASON 1977-78

Over the years there have been many incidents of pollution on the River Irvine system but beyond a shadow of a doubt, in angling terms, the worst, most devastating of all to date happened due to an industrial incident which occurred during the latter part of the nineteen seventies. This incident produced some of the most horrifying, upsetting, but hopefully never to be repeated, sights any angler would ever wish to see.

Following a long dry summer spell of weather, the river was fining down after a good spate. There was no doubt the river was experiencing one of the best early runs of migratory fish seen in recent years. Large numbers of salmon and sea trout combined with the resident brown trout occupied the pools and streams throughout the mid to lower reaches of the river; the pools were full of fish. An angler's dream which, unfortunately, was just about to turn into an angler's nightmare...

It was early one morning when our club secretary received a phone call from a member of the club reporting a major oil slick on the river. He also stated that there was a very strong odour in the air. As you approached the river the odour became stronger and appeared to follow the course of the river for miles. The odour was familiar to him but he couldn't identify the pungent smell.

Immediately the club secretary wasted no time in visiting the river to investigate the report. Sure enough, the river was "polluted" with something that totally discoloured the river and already there were signs of fish dying in the pools. No doubt the unknown substance was most definitely toxic to fish life, could it have the same effect on humans? The secretary immediately returned home and contacted the appropriate authority with a view to visiting the scene as a matter of urgency, which they duly did. By this time word had circulated to other members of the committee and members of other clubs, a team of "investigators" was assembled.

Tracing and locating the source of ingress of this pollutant is paramount. It was agreed by those present the only sensible way to trace the source was to systematically move upstream point by point (where access is easy) and try to locate the point of entry of this deadly pollutant, swiftly followed by locating the exact source of the offending contaminant. This had to be the priority as fish were dying in great numbers in front of our very eyes. Once the source had been located, then steps could be taken to stop the toxic material entering the river system. Subsequently, this action would greatly reduce or eliminate the obvious devastation to fish stocks.

Eventually, the source of this substance was indeed located and it was discovered the pollutant substance was entering the river via a storm water overflow drain exiting from a large industrial site five miles upstream from our beat. Access to the site was immediately sought to discover the real source. Finally, it was traced back to a large storage tank in which large quantities (thousands of gallons) of CREOSOTE was stored, that explained the strange odour. A drain tap had been left in the open position, which obviously meant the fluid contained within the vessel could run free. Where does the fluid run? Obviously, down to the lowest point in the ground - in this case, a storm drain - which subsequently drained directly into the river. By this time, a number of clubs had teams of volunteers removing dead fish from various sections, downstream of the ingress.

Over the next 48 hours hundreds, if not thousands, of fish were found dead and were recovered from the river. The club secretary volunteered to collect and store the dead fish from our stretch for a few days before disposal could be arranged. This is the sight to which I referred earlier at the beginning of this story. So sad, not just from an angler's point of view, but also from an environmental and general wildlife point of view. It was not just fish that suffered. Insects, birds and plant life all suffered too.

One thing was for certain, the fish stocks had been devastated and more than likely, totally wiped out below the point of discharge. The general consensus of opinion was that it would take a number of years to recover from this one, if indeed it ever would.

Most of the fish recovered from the Dreghorn AC beat of the river were duly taken to the secretary's home. At the rear of his house was a grass lawn with an area of approximately 40 square yards. The fish were laid out in rows, nose to tail, side by side, top to bottom. Salmon, along with the other two main species in our waters - sea trout and brown trout - we didn't bother laying out eels etc. There is no doubt this was one of the worst sights and memories I have of my angling life. It was devastating!

Salmon and grilse ranging from just a few pounds to weights reaching the mid-teens of pounds; sea trout (many herling), averaging just over the pound with the largest of around 7 lbs; and a few of the brown trout, the size of which you wouldn't believe were resident in our river, quite a number in the region of 3-4 lbs. Where had these been hiding? The largest brown trout reported being removed from the river was removed about three miles upstream of our stretch and this was a fish weighing-in at eight and a quarter pounds. Wow!

Obviously, fish of this size were there, but never to my knowledge had any been caught. Considering our club average brown trout caught by rod and line is usually about 9-10 oz, these fish were monsters, they're obviously there!

There were so many fish covering the grassed area they were overflowing onto the pathways; a terrible sight. Photographs were duly taken and slides were produced for future reference. I personally have seen these photographs and slides, once they had been developed, so I know they did exist. These were then placed into the club secretary's records for safe keeping. Many years have now passed with quite a number of club secretaries having held office since that time and on numerous occasions they have tried to relocate these slides but, sadly, to no avail. It is a pity, as these slides could have served as a reminder to following generations of the devastation uncontrolled pollution can cause.

As expected, as I remember this incident did indeed have a devastating effect on fish stocks for a number of years afterwards. One positive - if indeed there is one - the incident happened in the earlier part of the salmon season so once the river was cleared of the pollution with deployment of bunds and pumps and natural high waters we did manage to get some fresh salmon to enter the river system before the end of the season.

Over the next few years, much negotiation and legal investigation and correspondence took place involving the guilty company, local councils, lawyers and local clubs. The company, from where the source was identified, claimed thieves had been disturbed within their premises and they were unaware the tap had been left in the open position and therefore were not ultimately responsible. They put the blame firmly on the intruders.

Eventually, out of court compensation was agreed and if the clubs were to restock with trout, then the local councils would match pound for pound (in monetary terms), whatever the restocking cost to each club. It's a good job our club had reasonable funds to allow this to happen. However, this offer of compensation was duly accepted by the clubs and greater numbers of brown trout than usual were introduced into the river. It still took many years for the salmon to recover their numbers and some would argue they never did when compared to the numbers of salmon in the system during the 60s and early 70s. Maybe other influences also had an effect on this. Yet recover they did, but to what extent?

Pollution is and always will remain a major threat to our natural environment. Dozens of pollution incidents on our waterways are reported every year to the authorities. On the one hand, this is absolutely great because it allows possible action to be taken against the perpetrators and highlights what kind of actions need to be put into place to try and prevent, or at least reduce, the risk of such incidents happening again. However, incidents like the one described should never happen in the first place, people need to be educated and more respectful towards the world in which we live. I'm sure many conservationists would agree. If we don't look after and successfully help our natural environment and our wildlife there will not be any left to protect.

# First for Bert

SEASON 1982

This particular memory gives me as much pleasure as if it was myself who had actually experienced the root cause of my memories. My recollection of this event is one of joy for another person's joy. This pleasure still remains with me many years after his death and is still close to my heart. The person to whom I refer is my late father. I have mentioned my father on a number of occasions throughout this book and have stated my father, Bert, was not really a serious nor an experienced angler but he just loved to be out in the wild countryside with the peace and tranquillity that only a few sports provide. This tranquillity relieved a person of some of the pressures one might experience in everyday life.

I'm quite sure many anglers can relate to this. Maybe even other sportsmen and sportswomen who participate in other sports can relate to a similar peace, quiet and enjoyment as witnessed by anglers. For example, Golf; I'm sure many participants of this sport, whilst out on the golf course, forget about the everyday pressures and experience these feelings.

During my teenage years and into my early twenties, my father accompanied me to various rivers and lochs throughout Ayrshire and Dumfries and Galloway. However, when I think back, it was more a case of "Dad's taxi" rather than him becoming a serious angler. Serious angler? He didn't even dress like the normal everyday stereotypical angler. Collar and tie was his dress code no matter what location or what the occasion may be. Collar and tie was the dress and that was that! I'm quite sure the fish didn't mind. As long as one is comfortable and enjoys what one is doing, then does it matter what one wears? I certainly was not complaining because the freedom and range of opportunity he provided for me was fantastic, especially before I could drive myself. We spent many good days down and around the waters of Galloway in the south west of Scotland.

The following memory of my father is one of my favourites. This particular event actually happened on our own local river and, technically speaking, I wasn't even with him when he actually tasted sweet success.

It was mid-morning on Saturday 28 August 1982. The sun had now risen and was providing some heat in the morning air. There was still some cloud lingering about which provided the occasional dull periods of cover. The river had fined down from a small spate which had been present during the previous day and my own thoughts were definitely telling me I would rather be out fishing than doing what I was actually doing.

I'll explain; at an earlier committee meeting of the club I had volunteered to erect some poles onto which we would be attaching some notices informing the public that fishing on this stretch of river was by permit only. Today was the first opportunity I have had to fulfil my promise, but oh how I wanted to have a fishing rod in my hand instead of a spade, a bag of cement, bags of sand, chippings and a bucket, but I had promised, so notices it was.

My head was down and I was so engrossed in what I was doing, I was totally oblivious to the two figures approaching on the far bank when from that side of the river I heard a shout! A shout which was distinctly from a child. "Uncle Keith! Uncle Keith!" was the cry. I raised my head and stood, looked across the river and low and behold there was my nephew, Iain. He must have been only about five years of age at this time (I knew he was born on mid-summers day 21 June but don't ask me what year) and he was standing directly opposite on the far bank. He was trying to lift and show me a large fish but he could hardly lift it.

Draped across his arms in front of him was a salmon and he shouted, "look what we've caught!" There in the background stands my father, Bert, with the largest smile I had ever seen on his face. I'll never forget that smile. Immediately, the posts I was busy erecting seemed to disappear into the depths of insignificance and from this point on they definitely took second place for the next half hour.

The two of them could not cross the old sandstone bridge quickly enough to get to my side of the river to display their catch. Unsurprisingly, both were totally out of breath, basically put down to Iain carrying this heavy fish for such a distance and Bert due to age. By the time they reached me they could not wait to tell their story.

Excited? That was an understatement. My father was more excited than my nephew.

"Slow down, slow down," I said. "I can't make out a word you're saying." But as I said, what I remember most and will never forget is the look on their faces, beaming with pride!

Once they had finally calmed down and composed themselves, I eventually began to hear their story. Apparently, my father had decided to take my nephew fishing pretty early that morning (by the way, he never mentioned to me that he intended going fishing when I spoke to him the night before) and decided to fish in and around the location where I myself had been successful (lucky) on the night before, Friday. That location was about 400 yards upstream of where we were now standing.

I mentioned earlier Bert was not a very experienced angler and what I really meant was, in terms of methods and techniques, he never did master fishing with the fly rod, but always admired those who could. Therefore, I could not class him as an all-rounder. He was, however, reasonably proficient with the spinning rod and liked, on occasion, to trot a worm. The following account of what actually took place I relay second hand.

This particular morning I think fishing with worms was my nephew's duty. Father had set up Iain's tackle and got him started, leaving him to fish his chosen method of spinning a small no. 1 silver mepp. He started at the head of the pool, with his grandson close by his side, who was watching every move his Papa made and then questioning it: "Why are you throwing your line more than me? Why are you bringing your line in quicker than me? When will we catch a fish?" I'm sure you know what I mean.

They slowly worked their way down through the pool, eventually reaching the tail end where the river narrows and there is a well-known salmon lie. The lie is sited just behind a submerged "obstacle" positioned on the far side of midstream with the obstacle causing a disturbance to the surface of the water. My father cast his small silver Mepp just upstream of this sunken obstacle, his line swinging around in the current, passing very close to the disturbance. Apparently this is when "all hell" let loose.

Bert had hooked and was now playing his very first salmon. I wish I had been there! I can only imagine what fun, or panic more like. As it happens, I found out later the fish had been hooked EXACTLY where I had hooked and caught a fish on the previous evening.

With my nephew shouting in his Papa's ear, "Get it Papa, Get it Papa," and his Papa shouting, "Stay back son, watch yourself, don't go too close to the water's edge," which, roughly translated, probably meant: "Get oot ma bloody road," after a short but memorable fight in which the fish went skywards on a couple of occasions, Papa Bert managed to successfully land the fish in the net.

He told me later, he couldn't believe the feeling he had experienced deep inside as he realised he had just caught his very first salmon. He said, "I was shaking from head to foot, I couldn't get the hook out of the fish's mouth due to my hands shaking, my heart and adrenaline was pumping, what a feeling!"

If the truth be told, he was still shaking as he relayed the story to me. God knows what he might have been like if it had been a really big salmon. I don't mean to sound as if I am belittling his achievement, after all my first salmon wasn't as big as his and if I were to go through life catching salmon of this size (5 lb 2 oz grilse) I would be absolutely delighted. What he had just experienced is exactly what catching a salmon does to you, no matter how experienced you become. Yes, you may very well outwardly become much more composed and in control with experience, but the catching of a salmon always produces those inner feelings and those feelings will forever be present, no matter how many salmon you catch. I, for one, would not change those feelings for the world. Nothing compares. Or maybe it does? I'll leave that to your own imagination.

There are those other feelings associated with catching, or should I say not catching, a salmon such as when the salmon you have successfully fooled into taking your bait fights for a few minutes and then parts company. Your line goes slack and the rod straightens - ***yes you shake, yes your heart pumps hard,*** yes you try hard to refrain from inwardly swearing again. Feelings very similar but yet totally different. I would not wish those feelings on anyone. Expletives can't describe these feelings, but some people have a damn good try.

Remember those poles I mentioned at the beginning? I still had to finish bedding them in. One thing is for sure, no pole has ever been erected and bedded more quickly. We had to return home, photographs had to be taken - Auld Bert insisted assembly for photoshoot would be at 11:30 a.m. prompt on the back garden lawn.

The fish I had caught the previous evening was still lying in the sink; I had fully intended cleaning this fish on my return after erecting the signs. Retrieving the salmon I had caught less than 18hours before from the kitchen worktop, we both proceeded to the agreed meeting point in the back garden. Photographs of father and son with their respective prizes were duly taken. Who took the photographs? It could only be, and who else, my five year-old nephew. Unfortunately, we only managed to recover one relatively decent photograph of father and son but ten out of ten to the wee one for effort, well done!

# Right on Cue

## SEASON 1985

In 1985 I was an active and serving officer within that worldwide and well respected organisation known as the Boys Brigade (BB). The Brigade offers a wide range of activities, interests and programmes to gain the necessary life skills to enhance the future lives of these young men. The method of achieving this objective is promoted by the use of a badge achievement programme, a programme in which the boys are encouraged to participate and work hard towards reaching their goal within that particular subject. Once that standard had been achieved they were then awarded a badge to recognise their achievement. One of these Badge categories was - Interest and **Hobbies.**

Obviously, angling and the angler can be pigeon-holed into this category. Technically, it could also be included in the Sports Badge category. During 1985 there were two young boys from the village, namely Ian Shaw and John Thompson, who were both members of the 1$^{st}$ and 2$^{nd}$ Dreghorn Company of the Boys Brigade and both, at this time, were very, very keen on angling.

It doesn't take a genius to work out that I was the officer within the company who was volunteered to oversee and mentor these two boys in the gentle art of angling – not because I was the best angler, nor the most experienced angler, amongst the officers in the Company; I was the only angler in the company section. Some may ask, what qualified me to mentor these boys? I had been fishing since the age of 10 years, progressing through the skills of bait fishing, spinning and eventually progressing to the art of fly fishing for trout and salmon on my local river and, indeed, many rivers and lochs throughout Scotland. I could tie my own flies and I felt more than comfortable enough to be able to mentor these two youngsters in their quest to achieve their award, and possibly catch a fish or two along the way.

Throughout the BB session (winter months) I would run the angling class, instructing and teaching the boys on the skills they would require once the season opened in March. I instructed them in areas varying from the fishes' anatomy, their life cycle (particularly the Atlantic

Salmon, which holds so many mysteries), introducing them to a wide range of angling equipment and techniques, setting up and preparing to fish for their quarry and finishing off with demonstrating and getting them to tie and produce their own flies. ALL of which can be done indoors. Why indoors? Well, many of the country's rivers and lochs are closed during the winter months for game fishing, due to the fact it is the breeding season for the salmonids species. The BB session is a predominately winter activity, thus clashing with the period leading up to spawning time and closed season for fishing (November, December and January).

Many fish are so "out of condition" they are not worth eating, nor catching. Therefore, there is no opportunity for practical instruction on the river bank until the fishing season opens in the month of March. Even then, weather conditions are often so inclement, it is better to wait until further into the season before any practical riverside instruction could be undertaken. The BB session normally closes for the summer break sometime in late April therefore, contact with the boys (except those going to summer camp) can sometimes be lost until the start of the following BB session, which is normally late August. The reason for summer session closure? Holidays! During the summer months it can be difficult to keep in touch with the boys. Numbers attending Brigade evenings during the summer months decrease quite considerably, therefore disrupting the continuity and effectiveness of the Brigade.

To get over the problem of teaching and demonstrating "live" practical and water-craft skills, I promised I would take the boys fishing on a few occasions during the weeks and days leading up to the start of the new BB session which would be at some point during August, once most family summer holidays would be finished. These outings of instruction would also serve to whet the appetite of the boys for the new BB session ahead.

A special effort to contact the boys was made and a day, date, time and place were agreed for their first practical riverside instruction session to take place, allowing the boys to put into practice the skills previously acquired in the church hall during the previous winter session. It was time to find out if they had been listening!

Ensuring both boys had the appropriate club permit and parental permission to fish and were appropriately attired, we ventured onto the river. It had been a rather wet summer and regular rain showers had been prevalent for about six weeks prior to the agreed date of our "Fishing expedition." These rains had ensured water levels had risen and lowered like a yo-yo throughout the summer. This in turn had allowed runs of salmon to enter the river system at regular intervals over the past few weeks. The boys were full of excitement and anticipation. Their expectation of successfully catching fish was unnerving and seemed to put extra pressure on me. I did stress to them that the art of catching fish every time you venture out is, what one might say, not guaranteed. I think it was more to hide the undoubted embarrassment if I, or they, were not actually to catch a fish.

On this particular evening, the weather conditions were dull and warm but with a very slight drizzle of rain. Water conditions were absolutely perfect for fly fishing for salmon and sea trout, with a great possibility of catching a brown trout. The river was fining down after a spate, carried a decent flow and with just a hint of colour (weak tea), as I said perfect fly water - fantastic! So, as far as I was concerned, it was a "no brainer" - demonstrating fly fishing for salmon it would be. I would demonstrate and instruct the boys using their own single-handed fly rods first and maybe, once they were making progress, I would demonstrate using a double handed fly rod. At least that was my last-minute plan.

Unknown to the boys I had another reason and motive for demonstrating fly fishing for salmon that night. That very day I had bought myself a new 12 foot double-handed salmon fly rod and so, in casting terms, I wanted to "try" the rod and see how it, and I, performed. Selfish I know, but as they say, "never miss an opportunity" and "Kill two birds with one stone." I could provide instruction for the boys and satisfy my own objectives at the same time. Definitely a plan! However, catching fish for myself was not even in the equation and was not a prime objective.

We arrived on the river just before seven o'clock in the evening and, as I said, it was just perfect for fishing the fly. There was only going to be about an hour or possibly an hour and a half of daylight remaining at this time of year, but this would be long enough to achieve a decent period of instruction and allow the boys to put into practice the instruction they were about to receive.

We decided to fish a stream and pool just downstream of a little island which was sited in the middle of the river. In reality, the two streams straddling the island duly merged just downstream and actually formed the pool below. I began to talk the boys through some watercraft, trying to pin-point whereabouts a fish may be lying and, in the trout's case, feeding.

As we tackled-up our fishing rods, I continually described, explained and reminded them as to the function of each piece of tackle (just as I had discussed and demonstrated in the church hall during the previous session). The approach and mechanics of casting techniques were relayed and I suggested they just sat on the bank and observed me for a few moments taking cognisance of stance, rod positions, casting timings and hand to rod coordination before I would let them try on their own. So much for my plan, but I thought it would be beneficial for them to watch me for a few moments first.

I tied on a size ten single-hook home-tied Dunkeld (variant) and I started to feed out line and cast across the stream, leading into the head of the pool below. I had only completed about three, possibly four, demonstration casts when, "Right on Cue", but I would suggest more down to good luck rather than perfect skill, my line tightened and the water at the end of my line erupted; a fish was on!

The boys couldn't believe how easy salmon fishing was! Oh, to be young and naïve. Once I pointed out the error of their belief, they looked at each other and then still insisted it was down to the skill of the angler. I didn't enlighten them any further, but I knew the truth. Anyway, still in tuition mode I explained every move I made as the fish fought for its freedom. Rod up, firm but not too much pressure and try and keep below the fish if you can. This means the fish is not only fighting you but also fighting the current, rather than the fish using the current to its advantage.

After two long, deep, dogged runs the fish decided to introduce some excitement into the fight in the form of an aerobatic display. The fish rocketed skywards clear of the water on more than one occasion but finally it began to calm down. By this time, a well-known local angler had seen what was happening and decided to come and see if I required a "helping hand" to land the fish. Not a problem; I knew Wilson Gillespie very well and I knew he had not only caught but also netted many salmon over the years (and I for him I may add).

I was now beginning to make some headway. The fish was tiring fast and as it turned on its side, it was pretty well exhausted. I guided the fish towards where Wilson was standing with the net. He carefully slid the net under the fish and lifted it clear of the water, the fish lying neatly folded at the bottom of the net. My very next immediate memory was hearing the sound of the boys cheering. By this point, I must admit I had momentarily forgotten the boys, who were supposedly to be under instruction. Once I had calmed myself down, I realised this had now given me the perfect exhibit; a chance to explain more about the anatomy and the different stages of the fish's life cycle and to explain that the fish lying before them was, in fact, a grilse. A 4 lb bar of silver, straight from the sea complete with sea lice. No, I really did take time to explain to them what a grilse was which, if they had been listening in the church hall during the winter, they should have known anyway but there is nothing better than an actual exhibit, now they could really relate to it. Two hours ago this fish had probably been out in the salt waters of Irvine Bay!

The boys spent the next hour practicing fly casting and fly fishing. Unfortunately, they were not as lucky as me!

So - what's so special about catching one small grilse? Timing – "Right on Cue."

# Experience Counts

## SEASON 1986

There are many anecdotes and sayings which one comes across in life, one of the most popular I hear being used: "There's no substitute for experience." But one must question how much credibility and truth is behind this. There is one particular recollection I would like to share which may just answer this particular question.

It is 31 October, the last day of the salmon season. A friend and I decided to obtain the two complimentary tickets from our club secretary allowing us to fish a beat in the upper reaches of our local river. By complimentary tickets, I mean the exchange of club permits scheme. Two club permits were exchanged between each club as a gesture of good will. These complimentary tickets were for the use of the receiving club's members, if they wished to fish on a different beat of the river. Verbal agreement between each club stated that each member of any individual club could only use this facility on a maximum of two occasions to visit the chosen club waters. This scheme actually gave great scope, considering there were approximately ten clubs throughout the river system, all of which provided a wide range of diversity in river characteristic, methods and techniques used.

On this particular day, my fishing companion was actually one of my own parent club's characters, every club's got them. His name was Wilson Gillespie.

Everybody in the club knew Wilson. During the salmon season, Wilson was always a permanent feature on our stretch of the river spending most of the day, every day, trying to catch his salmon. To be honest, he was pretty successful in this area.

Wilson did not drive, transport to other areas was a bit of a problem for him, so occasionally I would invite him to accompany me if he so desired. It was agreed I would pick him up at his house, not too early though, remembering at this time of year the dark mornings were with us and it was more than likely to be very cold.

It was only a 20-25 minute drive to the stretch we had decided to fish, so we arrived at 10:00 a.m. The water was fining down after recent spates and it was a lovely clear autumn morning with the trees lining the course of the river looking absolutely fantastic in their autumn dress. The wild autumn and winter winds had not yet stripped these trees of their colourful leaves.

Reds, burnt ochre, bright yellow, bronze, browns, oranges, greens, a kaleidoscope of colour was on display and, as I said, in the morning sunlight they looked absolutely spectacular. By now, the sun had risen in the sky and heat was starting to take the numbness away from the tips of your fingers. On such a beautiful autumn morning where else would one rather be?

We had been fishing for approximately two hours and by this time Wilson and I had lost sight of each other as I had decided to walk right up to the top of the beat, whilst he remained fishing pools further downstream. I fished unsuccessfully but suddenly I became aware of an older gentleman standing on the bank directly behind me, dressed in a smart, light-grey suit looking more suitably attired to attend a Sunday morning church service, rather than trudging about in the long grass along a river bank. He was watching intently with every cast I made as I fished across and down through a fast water stream at the head of a long narrow pool.

However, after about ten minutes of watching me moving very slowly down the stream, still with no success, the silence was broken with the old gentleman shouting "whit hav ye goat on son?"

Rather than try to describe the fly I was using, I decided to reel in and duly show the fly to him. Looking at my fly and pulling a strange face he said, "Naw, naw son, ye'll no catch onythin' with that flee, no up here ye'll no. Have ye got a Yella Dug in yer box?"

To be honest I hadn't a clue and after searching through my fly boxes, guess what? I didn't! I did have a similar, but no true Yella Dugs.

What happened next was amazing. This nice old gentleman reached into the inside pocket of his suit jacket and removed a lovely little brown varnished fly box. On opening the lid, a plethora of salmon flies were exposed. A few moments of searching and he selected a lovely tied Garry Dog (Yella Dug) salmon fly tied on a size 10 hook.

"Here son, stick that on."

Without any hesitation I thought to myself, "I'm going to listen to this gentleman." I removed the existing fly from my cast and replaced it with the one he had chosen from his own box, I think it's called a no brainer!

Thinking I was now ready to recommence my fishing I thanked him - wrong!

As I turned towards the river again, he stopped me in my tracks. "Forget that bit son, come wi' me."

He then proceeded to march me downstream for approximately thirty yards with me following like a little dog. He stopped, turned to me and pointed out a sunken tree trunk which was just visible below the surface of the water and lay hard against the steep far bank. He then proceeded to instruct me exactly where to cast, mend my line and to where I should let my fly swing around.

I carefully approached the edge of the water. I released my fly from the holding ring on my rod and began to feed out my line. As I began to cast, and for some strange reason, I felt a little pressure hoping my fly would land exactly where he had suggested and did not get fouled up on the far bank. By luck, rather than skill, my fly landed perfectly.

"Well done son, now be ready for the pull." As true as I write this, on my third cast the line tightened and the colour drained from my face, a good fish was hooked. Not once during the short five minute fight did the old gentleman interfere, trying to tell me how to fight the fish, which often happens with "more capable" spectators, but he did kindly net our fish. A lovely little grilse of 3 lb 4 oz and although sporting a touch of autumn livery, the fish was nowhere near ready for spawning. Maybe it was a late runner? I was absolutely delighted and amazed in relation to what had just happened. I just stood in awe of this gentleman's contribution. I could not thank the gentleman enough for his guidance and coaching.

"We're no by yet son, come with me."

"You're kidding?" I thought. "Lightning can't strike twice?" But who was I to argue? Again, just like a little puppy dog following at the heels of its owner, I moved downstream missing out the next stream and pool, a pool which I would have never passed without fishing through, it certainly had a salmon look about it. So why were we walking on past? Don't argue Keith, just keep walking.

The gentleman stopped at the head of the very next stream. The deeper channel of the river was now flowing hard against the far side of the river, a bank in the form of a high vertical wall of sand which stood about two metres above the water line, the face of which was littered with evidence of nesting burrows where sand martins had nested earlier in the year.

He once again began to "guide me" to where I needed to cast my fly and how to mend my line to gain the best possible presentation. I duly did as instructed.

"That's fine son, now let it swing round," and once again those words echoed in my ears. "Be ready for the pull."

Sure as fate, a few casts later my line shot away, yet again a fish had taken my fly. I couldn't believe it! The only difference this time was I wasn't as lucky; I raised my rod but didn't manage to firmly sink the hook into the fish. After a couple of rumbles on the surface, the fish came off.

"Aye son, you'll live and learn, ye canni' win them a'," said he.

At this point, I reeled in my line and just sat my rod to the side. I sat down on the bank and spent the next twenty minutes or so, listening and learning from this wise old gentleman.

Eventually he said, "Well son, av' got tae go, other things to do, other people to see." I immediately lifted my rod to remove and return the fly which he had given me earlier. "Naw son you keep it, tie a few fir yersel' for the next time yer up this way." I then shook his hand, thanked him most sincerely for his company, his advice and his coaching and maybe someday we'll meet again.

"Yer welcome," he said, and at that he turned and walked away.

There is one thing I regret till this day; that I didn't ask the gentleman for his name and even though I have asked other anglers who fish this stretch of river and work colleagues who I know lived in and around this area, I have not been able to find out who he was. But there is no doubt, the gentleman obviously had a wealth of local knowledge and experience for which, in my mind, there is no substitute. I am fully indebted to that old gentleman for my success and enjoyment on that day.

Eventually, I once again caught up with Wilson, my companion for the day. I explained and described to him exactly what had just happened and to cap it all I had the fish and fly as evidence.

As for Wilson, he didn't have the guidance nor the coaching which I had just received so he caught nothing.

There's definitely no substitute for experience. "Experience counts!"

# ONE AND ONLY

## SEASON 1988

Saturday 2 April 1998 - first venture of the season to the river bank and I was competing in the local club's first competition of the season, The Dunlop Cup. I immediately stress, The Dunlop Cup is for club members only and is strictly for brown trout only.

Being this early in the season, it was the general belief, and an accepted fact within the local angling fraternity, that it is only brown trout which will be within the local river system at this time of the season. The chance of connecting into any other species of fish is very remote, with the exception of the odd rare salmon or sea trout kelt being hooked. Even the catching of kelts was very rare. However, locals will tell you that in recent years there has been the very odd spring salmon (and I do mean spring salmon, not kelt) caught during the early weeks of the season on the River Irvine, but again, these occasions are even fewer and far between.

My fishing companions for the day: my brother-in-law, Jim Hay, and a work colleague named Willie Stewart. It was Willie's first time fishing for about 10 years. He wanted to resurrect his interest in the sport. We registered our names for the competition in the Braehead carpark at the agreed time as printed within the permit, the car park being a handy place to register due to the fact it was situated just about equidistant from the two rivers to which the club holds fishing rights.

The first decision we were required to make was do we fish the River Irvine or do we fish the Annick Water? Considering the historical knowledge of this particular competition, the cup had been won on numerous occasions by members who have fished the smaller Annick Water so with this in mind, I suggested the Annick Water was where we should start. It was agreed.

We clambered into the car to travel the three miles or so towards the upper reaches of our beat. We arrived on the river at about 10 a.m. at the Piers Bridge, an old single arch hump-back bridge which spans the river within the Estate of Annick Lodge. This stretch of water is particularly picturesque, the river itself comprising of a selection of streams and a regular scattering of pools, each with its own characteristics, the beat's water varying in width, depth and length. Tree-lined banks with the trees and bushes still supporting their winter condition showed a few signs of pending foliage which had still to bloom, clearly evidenced by the amount of buds occupying the branches of the trees. A few days of warm weather and sunshine would undoubtedly bring these branches to life, such a pleasant area to fish.

We decided to head upstream from the bridge for about half a mile before we started to cast a line. The fishing conditions of the river were absolutely perfect, supporting a good flow and a really good colour, considering the amount of big spates during the previous few weeks. It was a beautiful, bright, crisp and clear spring morning with the overnight dew sparkling like diamonds on the grassy fields. Woodland birds such as Chaffinches, Blue Tits, Robins and numerous others were fleeting from tree to tree and branch to branch. A great morning to be out along the river.

Within fifteen minutes of starting to fish, Jim had managed to hook and land two nice brown trout caught with the natural minnow. As we progressed downstream, fishing towards the Piers Bridge, both Jim and myself continued to receive a number of offers from trout but failing to hook or land them. However, I eventually did manage to land one good trout in the pool above an old railway viaduct so I continued to fish down the pool.

On reaching the viaduct, I decided to change tack and change from fishing with the natural minnow to trotting a worm. I attached a small stewart-type tackle which comprised of three size 16 hooks to my 5 lb BS line. I threaded a single worm straddling three small size 16 hooks attached "Stewart" style. I was once again ready for action.

Switching techniques turned out to be a great decision, within a few casts I brought a second nice trout to the net but unfortunately this fish didn't quite make keeping size, so the fish was carefully unhooked and safely returned to the water. Going well I thought, continue like this and we should end up with a good bag of fish before the end of the day. However, with no further offers from that particular pool, I decided to go back up to a pool in which I had missed a fish earlier and try it with a worm.

With my very first cast I received a brief but very definite bite from a fish, but the fish appeared to only show interest as the worm passed by. So with my next cast I dropped the worm in exactly the same place hoping for my bait to "carry" downstream following much the same path. This time the bite was a much more positive, "knock-knock-knock." I took a few steps downstream pausing for a while before I felt the fish again. Now convinced the fish had taken the bait I "struck." At this point, and to my surprise and delight, my rod all of a sudden became severely bent and I knew right away this was no ordinary half pound trout. Just as this happened, David Cronie, another angler and club member, just happened to be passing on the opposite bank. I shouted to David that I thought I was into a really "good fish." Of course, I had no way of knowing exactly how good but past experience told me it definitely wasn't a half pound trout.

Unfortunately, by this time my two companions, Jim and Willie, were out of sight fishing different pools further downstream. Davy was on the other bank, so he couldn't help me. I was on my own. The fish fought deep and hard and as the early fight continued my thoughts reminded me of the very small hook and light line I was using. Take your time Keithy boy! The fish still hadn't surfaced and I knew within myself it was not a brown trout, but it might be a late kelt trying to return to sea.

A further ten minutes of playing the fish and once again I had to adjust my thoughts. It can't be a kelt, a kelt would be exhausted by now. It was fighting too deep, too hard, too long for it to be a kelt. It was more like a better quality fish which was obviously in good health. I still had not seen the fish and when the fish did finally surface, what a sight! A fish about a yard long, bar of silver, slate- blue back. I immediately realised to my delight I was actually fighting my very first fresh-run spring salmon. The fish had obviously made its way upriver during the recent spates. Not even the Annick's mother river, the River Irvine, is renowned for spring salmon, let alone this little water of Annick. My first ever spring salmon, wow! But I hadn't landed it yet, which then made me realise how easily the fish could be lost and once again my thoughts turned towards the very light tackle I was using.

I now began to shake, legs like jelly and sweat pouring from every part of my forehead but after 20-25 minutes of patient and careful playing the fish, my patience was rewarded. The fish came to hand clearly exhausted and on its side. I gently tailed the fish and lifted it clear of the water. It wouldn't have fitted in the small trout landing net I had with me anyway. I had to tail it! I like the sound of that, too big for the net!

A hen fish and, as I mentioned earlier, a bar of silver with a beautiful slate-blue back which, in the morning sunlight, gleamed like crystal and dazzled like a mirror. But how lucky was I with the fish being hooked right in the corner of the scissors but with just one single hook of the Stewart tackle! Earlier, during the fight, but not before watching me play the fish for a little while, Davie Cronie had moved downstream to see if he could catch up with Willie and Jim to inform them what was happening upstream and for them to maybe assist in the landing of the fish. By now, I had humanely dispatched the fish and as I stood admiring my prize, I glanced downstream only to see both Jim and Willie hastily making their way back upstream to see me. Or, more likely, to see the fish, rather than me. Whichever, their faces were a picture. They couldn't believe a fish of this size could be in a small stream like this.

Eventually, I got around to asking, "how are you two doing?" Apparently, as I was engaged with my own battle,

Willie had managed to catch another trout and had missed a few others. Not bad for someone who had not fished for the past ten years.

The morning's total of "competition counting" fish caught to us so far:

Willie - 2 trout Jim - 2 trout

Keith - 1 trout plus 1 salmon *(non-counting for competition)*

Over and above the fish caught, all of us had experienced hooking and losing a number of other fish throughout the morning.

At this point, but against my better judgement, Willie and Jim wanted to change location and fish the River Irvine. In my opinion, why change? When fish are being caught like this, I thought it could be the wrong decision, but to be honest, trout and the competition were the last thing on my mind now. I had caught my prize and I couldn't care less if I could not weigh-in the fish for this brown trout only cup. But, majority rules, and we returned to the car and moved across to the River Irvine.

What followed was, in my opinion, two and a half hours of good fishing time wasted; none of us had managed any success at this new site. Another session of discussion took place and eventually it was decided to return to the Annick Water, but by now it was late afternoon and time was drawing close to weigh-in time. There was no time to return to the Annick Lodge area, but we could relocate down to the Station Brae in Dreghorn and fish just behind the old graveyard, the graveyard being the nearest point to the Braehead car park - the location where the weigh-in would shortly be taking place. During this short time we had left

I was lucky enough to land another trout and so did Willie. Time had now beaten us, we had to return to the Braehead if we were to meet the time of the weigh-in.

All the competitors' fish were systematically weighed as per norm, but, to be fair, the salmon appeared to be attracting more attention and interest than the weigh-in.

The salmon statistics were - 31 inches long with a 15 inch girth. The fish wasn't weighed for quite a few hours after capture but officially weighed in at 8 lb 15.5 oz (9 lbs).

Official placings for the competition: Willie was placed second, Jim was fourth and I was fifth. As I previously stated, The Dunlop Cup is for brown trout only and my "One and Only" lovely spring salmon did not count. The eventual winner of The Dunlop Cup was, guess who? Davie Cronie with 4 fish! He had fished the River Annick all day, up and around Annick Lodge. When we left David at 1:15 p.m. he had only managed one fish. I honestly and truly believe if we had remained on the River Annick, any one of the three of us may have won this competition as the Annick Water was fishing great. At the end of the day it didn't really matter, we all had a great and enjoyable day and I had caught my very first spring salmon. Fantastic! This fish was officially registered for the club's Irvine District Council Cup which is a cup for the heaviest salmon caught on club waters throughout the season.

This salmon stood as the heaviest fish caught on club waters throughout the remainder of the season until 5.30 p.m. on the 31 October (the last day of the season), when Wilson Gillespie arrived at my door in darkness, with a 9 lb 9 oz cock salmon caught on the River Irvine in Gibsons' Pool, displacing my salmon into second position.

*Photograph a little blurred – but authentic*

Due to the rarity of the capture on such a small river, I entered this fish into a national newspaper, "Fish of the Week" competition, following the date of capture. I took great pains within the supporting letter to stress this little stream was not renowned for salmon, let alone a spring salmon, but I didn't win their prize either. The following week the newspaper printed their winning entry, a brown trout of over 8 lbs caught at some other location in Scotland so my beautiful springer wasn't featured, but what a fish to be beaten by. Did I really care? The memory of my first, my one and only springer to date, will always be a winner in my eyes.

# CHASING SALMON

## SEASON 1989

Do salmon ever "chase" flies or lures? Or do they just wait until the angler's bait is virtually placed right in front of their noses before taking?

I have often heard it said that you will not catch a "running" salmon. It will not be interested in chasing or taking your lure or fly whilst it is on the move. I am quite sure every angler will have his or her own thoughts on this. What this statement implies, if it is true, is that one must assume a salmon will only "take" once it has either stopped to rest or has taken up residency in a particular lie within a stream or pool. It is well known that once a salmon has settled into a lie of its choice, a lie which usually incorporates some form of protection for the fish such as a submerged boulder or sunken tree trunk, a lie with some depth and a good flow of oxygenated water, it will stay in this place where it can conserve its energy for the next part of its journey. Why should a salmon be interested in, or indeed want to chase, a fly or lure?

Once again, I have heard it said on more than one occasion that salmon will not chase a lure at all, even when it is in a lie. One has to put the fly or lure right in front of its nose before it will take. I don't agree. We do know that a salmon will leave its lie and come from a depth of eight or nine feet to take a fly or a lure and if it refuses the take at the last moment, the fish immediately returns to the original lie from whence it came. So, if a salmon does come from these near vertical depths to take a bait, why do some people believe they will not chase a bait over the same distance, or an even greater distance on a horizontal plain? As long as this fish can see the bait, I personally believe, occasionally, it will do so.

The following experiences may shed some light to answer this question.

It was one September day in 1989; a beautiful clear autumn morning, just perfect for fishing at this time of year. I was casting a fly directly above an old sandstone bridge consisting of three wide arches. The remnants of a much larger spate from the previous day was still evident in relation to water level, the clarity of the water could be described as tea colour, perfect fly water and still just about high enough to entice salmon to leave the deep pool on the downstream side of the sandstone bridge to continue their upstream journey.

On leaving the pool, the fish have to pass through the archways and run approximately 30 yards or so of shallowish water on the upstream side of the bridge, before the river bed quickly disappears into deeper water. This shallow water has never been renowned as a "holding" lie for the salmon, they just appear to pass right through this section. I know from experience many anglers just walk past this area thinking it is not worth fishing, believing the pool below the bridge is the better option and the place to be. How wrong they are! Those of us who know better never pass it without casting a line or two in front of these arches. Believe it or not, many salmon over the years have been taken in this shallowish water directly upstream of the bridge.

However, once a fish is hooked it can be quite daunting and quite a challenge preventing (or hoping) the fish from turning and running back downstream through the arches, particularly the far away arch or the middle arch. If it goes back downstream through any of these arches the fish will undoubtedly be lost. If, however, the fish decides to run down through the nearest arch, there is a chance of following and even landing the fish in the pool below the bridge. It all adds to the excitement!

On this particular occasion, I cast my fly towards the far archway, mending my line to compensate for the flow of the river, thus allowing my fly to sweep across in front of the middle arch at the preferred depth and speed. My line was now nearing the end of the sweep and it began to straighten due to the current taking hold of the fly line. It was at this point, just under the surface of the water, I witnessed the flash of a fish slightly downstream of where the end of my actual fly line was attached to the leader. Was this a fish showing interest in my fly? What was more interesting, the flash literally appeared to totally change direction and all of a sudden a large bow-wave was clearly visible on the surface of the water just behind my fly line.

By now, my fly line was approaching the end of its true swim, reaching a point whereby it would start to skate across the surface and also nearing a point of no return when I would be forced to recast. The fish followed my fly right across the middle arch towards the nearside pillar section of the bridge. I have seen rainbow trout follow like this many times in lochs and still waters, but I had never seen a salmon react in this manner.

For some reason right at this moment, from the depths of the old grey matter, I recalled a conversation which had taken place some years before with a much more experienced angler than myself. It was a conversation on this very subject of following or chasing fish and what action to take if you realise what is happening. He said "If you ever see a salmon bow-wave following your lure don't panic, just bide your time, let the fish take, let it turn and then just calmly lift into the fish." Easier said than done! Nerves are playing a part by this time and there is a rush of blood; remember, all this is happening within seconds.

After what seemed like an eternity waiting in anticipation, watching this fish "chase" my fly, the fish finally decided to take. Surprisingly I didn't panic, I did let it turn and I did lift slowly into the fish. I had put into practice as I was told, fish on - text book! What is it they say? Satisfaction comes to those that wait.

As I hooked the fish, other anglers, namely Hector Wark and his companion, were just about to climb over a fence stile onto the footpath which crossed over the old sandstone bridge. Hugh Skeoch was just approaching on the high bank behind me after walking down from fishing the pools upstream. They all bore witness to this. Needless to say, all began to spectate and unlike the old gentleman I mentioned in "Experience Counts" who remained totally silent as I played the fish before bringing it safely to the net, at least one of the spectators offered so much advice on how the fish should be played, one would have thought it was him who was at the thick end of the rod.

During the early stages of the fight, the fish was very lively and gave a very good account of itself, going airborne on at least three separate occasions showing us quite clearly it was a fresh run bar of silver. After the fish had calmed down and, thankfully I may add, had never considered running downstream through the arches, the fish started to swim upstream and fight deep and dogged. I thought to myself, well, you've been out of the water three times and you have not come off, I am now in control and all I need to do is take my time and the fish will be mine.

If I were to successfully land this one it would be salmon number five caught in the past couple of weeks. The fish came close to our bank wallowing virtually under the rod tip. The fish was really tiring now, we all thought it wouldn't be long now before it was in the net. The fish obviously had other ideas. It slowly turned away, took line and headed back out into the middle of the river. Honestly, I didn't apply any excessive force, I just applied steady pressure to try and turn the fish back towards me, but you've guessed it, the line went slack and the fish was lost. I couldn't believe it! I thought I had done the hard work. It just goes to show, even with text book hooking you shouldn't count your chickens or, in this case, salmon. Mental and verbal post-mortems were duly performed - you can imagine some of the comments from the side-lines!

My verdict? It happens, that's fishing!

However, even though the fish was lost, I believe my opening question has been answered. Do salmon ever "chase" flies or lures? Considering the experience and memories described, there is only one answer! But I'll let you decide!

I refer to a similar "chasing" salmon story later in the book.

# SHALLOW RUNNING

## SEASON 1989

During the early part of the season, the weather conditions ensured that the River Irvine experienced excellent water levels throughout March and into mid-April.

Many members of the local club produced some good catches of brown trout. However, by the third quarter of April very low water levels were recorded. In actual fact, with the exception of a very small rise in water during the last week of July, these levels remained throughout the summer months. May, June, July and even into August levels remained very low. Due to these extremely low water levels, many features of the river bed which normally would not be seen were exposed. Certainly, this drought produced the lowest water levels I could ever remember.

By the time mid-August arrived, large numbers of salmon and sea trout were congregating in the estuary and lower reaches of the river, behind Ayrshire Metal Products and adjacent to the old shipyard, which was once located slightly upstream of the main harbour area. These fish were desperately awaiting some badly needed rain. In truth, the spectacle of witnessing hundreds, if not thousands, of salmon and sea trout constantly leaping and splashing around on every tide, became something of a tourist attraction down at the harbour. Many people would stand on the harbour-side walk or park up in their vehicles in the car parking area which overlooked the estuary and spend hours watching in disbelief at the sight of so many fish producing such an aerobatic display. Anglers from towns located well into the upper reaches of the river valley would come and view what they were missing. Or was it these people were just eagerly waiting in anticipation for things to come?

Then it happened! On 11 August anglers' prayers were answered. Major rain clouds were building in the sky above the moors of East Ayrshire and this alone appeared to spark off a strange phenomenon and reaction from the fish. Even before the major rains had made any significant effect on the river's water level (rains which undoubtedly would produce higher water levels and entice these salmon and sea trout to run the river), the fish became very agitated and appeared impatient and began to run the river in low water. In my mind, I have no doubt these fish must have sensed major rains were imminent and guaranteed to follow. Nature at work! An amazing number of these migratory fish were running shallow streams, some streams only a few inches deep. Every few minutes, two, or sometimes three or four, fish at a time were heading upstream, many with their backs fully exposed and clear of the water, bellies scraping the river bed, their tails powering them up through these decimated streams.

High up the valley, the upper reaches were now experiencing some serious rainfall and over the next twenty-four hours with water levels slowly rising due to this persistent rain, I witnessed the unprecedented sight of these fish running the river as described above. On this occasion, the viewing took place approximately three miles upstream of the estuary where stands an old bridge constructed of red sandstone. Immediately downstream of the bridge is a deep wide pool and as the water exits this pool, the depth changes dramatically and quickly shallows as it flows through the tail end of the pool.

The river now splits into two main channels circumventing an island. One channel was virtually impassable due to the amount of weed growth which had appeared throughout the past few months. This forced the fish to run upstream close to the south bank where there was indeed a little more water flowing, and I mean a little more! Fish were running the head of the shallow stream with sounds of thrashing tails as they powered their way through and over the river bed, water spraying outwardly from their heads and bodies as it passed over them. They were like silvery torpedoes as they negotiated this shallow water before finally reaching the safety and sanctuary of the deeper water of the bridge pool.

There were so many fish one could have literally walked out and picked up a fish by hand, if one was so inclined. I had never seen so many salmon behaving like this, especially in such a short period of time. Fish of all sizes; sea trout ranging from half a pound to between 2-3 lbs; grilse and salmon, some of which, in terms of weight, estimated to be in double figures - ten pounds plus!

Just like the "tourists" down at the harbour, to whom I referred earlier, word quickly spread around the village. "Come and see what is happening down at the Red Bridge!" Before long, a crowd had gathered at the water's edge to witness this rare sight.

I actually spent hours watching this spectacle, but

unfortunately time was getting on and I had to leave for another appointment. In other words, I was hungry.

However, when I returned to the river some time later suitably fed and watered, I crossed the bridge. At this point I noticed the river level had increased and the clarity of the water was getting dirtier. I also noticed there was an older gentleman fishing (legally) on the north bank at the tail of the Red Bridge Pool.

On the south bank some of the crowd of earlier still remained. Dare I suggest undesirables? Poaching throughout the river system in these recent years had been on the increase and was currently at a very high level. The people who were now in attendance were all known to me and, indeed, I was known to them. I would not have classed them as serious poachers at this point in their lives, nor would I have classed them as a major threat to stocks, but potentially they were. I stress they were known to me and were known to be "dabbling" in these poaching activities. As I mentioned, the water level of the river had risen somewhat but the salmon could still be observed running the stream, albeit not in the same numbers as witnessed a few hours earlier. Was it because the water level had risen and the fish were not as visible due to the fact they were running deeper? Or was it that the main surge of fish was now past?

A short period of time elapsed when suddenly I was left alone with all the other "observers" leaving the waterside. In fact, after another short period of time, the gentleman who had been fishing on the far bank crossed over the bridge and came to talk to me.

Initial greetings exchanged, after which his first words were, "I don't know who you are, but as soon as you appeared the suspicious activity came to an abrupt end."

I then proceeded to inform him I was a past President of the Club and I was also a warranted bailiff for the Crown.

"Oh, that will explain it," he replied.

The gentleman and I then spent some time chatting about what had just happened over the past 12-24 hours. It was absolutely amazing! By now, the heavens had really opened up and it was raining very hard. The water had risen dramatically and was quite coloured. Time for home to leave the fish in peace.

From that day until this, I have never witnessed anything like the spectacle of 11 August 1989 from the banks of the River Irvine. It is a memory which I treasure and it will live with me forever. Probably, a sight which will never be repeated.

Needless to say, salmon catches during the latter part of the season on the River Irvine system saw a dramatic increase, as did my own individual tally during August, including a beautiful, bright, fresh-run bar of silver of ten pounds, caught just a few nights after that spectacle.

## Record of Fish - Diary 1989

| Date | Species | Location | Length | Weight | Method | Conditions | Total on visit | Accum Total | Notes |
|------|---------|----------|--------|--------|--------|------------|----------------|-------------|-------|
| 20/03/1989 | Brown Trout | River Annick Behind Doctors | 14.25"<br>11.5"<br>11.25"<br>10.25" | 15 onz<br>11 onz<br>10 onz<br>7 onz | N/Minnow x 3 No.1 Silver mepps | Water in small spate, bright crisp morning, one small shower | 4 | 4 | Off night shift – fished between 10am till 12.15pm. 2 fish wild, 2 stockies. Missed another 5 fish. |
| 08/04/1989 | Brown Trout | River Irvine – Flat below Bogie Bridge | 10.5" | 8 onz | Fly | Water running well – slightly coloured. Warm bur breezy | 1 | 5 | Kevin & Brian also caught one each Brian now with 5 fish. |
| 18/04/1989 | Brown Trout | River Irvine – below Island, Red Bridge | 9.5"<br>10.5" | App. 5.5 onz<br>6.5 onz | Fly – Black PTN | Water running very clear, warm sunny evening | 2 | 7 | 3rd. Time out |
| 06/05/1989 | Brown Trout | River Irvine below Shewalton Dam | 12" | 10 onz | Fly | Water very low, bright sunny difficult conditions | 1 | 8 | Lynch Memorial Cup – unplaced – lost another two fish- wild fish |
| 30/05/1989 | Brown Trout | River Clyde Crawford | 12.5"<br>10.5"<br>9.5" | 12 onz<br>app 6 onz<br>app 5 onz | Fly | Water very low, sunny bright day, fish caught just before nightfall. Excellent stretch of water to fish. | 3 | 11 | Returned the two smaller fish. Must have hit at least another 20 fish throughout the afternoon/evening – just couldn't seem to hook them properly. Most of these fish appeared to be relatively small but lost other good fish. Also caught 4 small fish, also returned. Lovely wild yellow flanked trout. 5th outing. |
| 03/06/1989 | Brown Trout | River Clyde Gordon Streams | 13"<br>10.75"<br>9.5" x2 | 13.5 onz<br>7 onz<br>app. 5 onz each | Fly – Iron Blue Dun | Water low, very weedy, morning dull & dry, afternoon – warm, sunny, breezy | 4 | 15 | First outing with Cal-air AC. Returned the two smaller fish. All fish caugh before 11am. Also lost another 5 or 6 fish including one breakout. After losing the only Iron blue dun fly I had in my box I only raised another 3/4 small fish throughout the afternoon – 2nd in competition. 6th outing |

| Date | Species | Location | Length | Weight | Fly/Lure | Conditions | No. | Outing | Notes |
|---|---|---|---|---|---|---|---|---|---|
| 14/06/1989 | Brown Trout | River Annick Above Station Brae Bridge River Irvine Shewalton Dam | 9" 9.25" | App. 5 onz each | Fly | Water in small spate after long drought – bright & breezy | 2 | 17 | Lost one other fish of approx. 9-10" Returned one smaller fish. 7th outing. |
| 22/06/1989 | Brown Trout | River Annick above Piers Bridge | 10.25" | App. 6 onz | Fly – Black Spider | Water very low – bright & breezy evening – caught after 9:00 pm | 1 | 18 | Caught one smaller fish, both fish returned. Good fighting fish – 9th outing. |
| 06/07/1989 | Brown Trout | River Irvine Shewalton Dam | 9.75" | App. 5 onz | Fly – Teal & Black | Water very low – caught after 9:30pm | 1 | 19 | 12th outing |
| 11/08/1989 Friday | Sea Trout | River Irvine – Top side of Red Bridge | 12.5" | 9.5 onz | No. 1 Silver Mepps | Small Spate – first main spate since April – Dry between showers | 1 | 20 | Salmon & Sea Trout running in six inches of water. Unbelieable sight – literally hundreds of fish coming through the shallow streams at the Island below the Red Bridge. This run continued right into and throughout Sat 12th. By time Monday 13th water was in an unfishable spate. 13th outing. |
| 17/08/1989 Thursday | Salmon Cock fish | River Irvine Fordside pool | 24" | 3 lbs 12 onz | Fly – Size 10 Thunder & Lightning. | Dry breezy evening just before dark. Running off after spates. | 1 | 21 | Colin Bismor also lost a fish on the fly. More Salmon & Sea Trout in the river this year than I can ever remember. Lost a fish the night before. |
| 18/08/1989 Friday | Sea Trout | River Irvine Top side of Red Bridge | 13.5" 12" | 13 onz app. 10 onz | Fly – Size 10 Shrimp fly | Water was nearly back to normal height. Caught just before dark | 2 | 23 | Brian also caught a Sea Trout of 13.5" (13 onz) on the worm. I returned the smaller Sea Trout to the river. 20th outing. |
| 19/08/1989 Saturday | Sea Trout | River Irvine – No. 11 stream | 11" | 7.5 onz | Fly – Size 10 Black Pennal | Water low but rising due to torrential rain. Very difficult fishing conditions. | 1 | 24 | Caught just before dark. |

| Date | Fish | Location | Length | Weight | Fly/Method | Water Conditions | No. | Outing | Notes |
|---|---|---|---|---|---|---|---|---|---|
| 26/08/1989 Saturday | Salmon Hen fish | River Irvine No. 11 Stream | 27.25" | 6 lbs 12 onz | Fly – Size 10 Peter Ross | Water in spate and rising slightly. Mostly dry, windy with a little drizzle. | 1 | 25 | Tailed a 3.5 lbs Grilse for another chap. Still plenty of Salmon moving up. A number of Salmon are being taken daily. |
| 28/08/1989 Monday | Sea Trout Salmon Cock fish | River Irvine below No. 11 stream River Irvine – No. 11 Stream | 12" 30.5" – 16.25" girth short deep fish | App. 9 onz 10 lbs 0 onz | Fly – both on Size 10 Thunder & Lightning | Time now 9:00pm – darkness fallen – breeze subsided. | 2 | 27 | Also lost another fish, slightly bigger? Evening was dry, breezy caught and returned the Sea Trout at 7:00pm. The Salmon was a lovely fresh run fish with sea lice. Gordon Dailly netted the fish. Fish entered for the IDC Cup and officially weighed on the chip shop scales at 11:00pm (9lbs 14.5 onz) |
| 18/09/1989 | Salmon Hen Fish | River Cree Picture house pool | 25.5" 12.5" girth | 5lbs 0 onz | Fly – Size 8 Thunder & Lightning 10:15am | Water low but rising due to torrential rain during the morning. Afternoon virtually impossible to fish due to rubbish being swept down. | 1 | 28 | Jim Hay also lost a Salmon on the Thunder & Lightning just after I had caught mine. Also seen a chap catch two Salmon on the worm during the afternoon. 30th outing |
| 20/10/1989 | Sea Trout. | River Irvine above Drybridge Dam | 11.75" | 8 onz | Silver Toby | Water in small spate. Caught just before tea time. Cold, dull but dry. | 1 | 29 | Didn't see any fish running Drybridge Dam |
| 25/10/1989 | Brown Trout | River Irvine | 11" | App. 7 onz | Worm | Water rising and dirty | 1 | 30 | Also caught two other smaller fish – all fish returned – after season |

# GARDEN OF EDEN

## SEASON 1993

During 1991, I had been invited to join a small band of angling friends to fish for brown trout in another country far, far away. Somewhere different, somewhere away from the normal haunts of my local rivers, somewhere I will undoubtedly love, catch fish and a place I will not forget. With my appetite well and truly whetted, I duly agreed and waited for this experience to begin. This country far, far away turned out to be 140 miles from home, just across the border into England to be precise. "Hook line and sinker," comes to mind.

But as the years passed, I wasn't to be disappointed, fishing a Cumbrian trout stream in the vicinity of the small town of Appleby. Appleby is a beautiful little historical town with the river running through its centre, where trout and grayling could be viewed from the parapet of the town's bridge. Fish holding station in the crystal clear water and constantly feeding on the local fly life which was being washed towards them by the flow of the river. However, the beat we had been fishing in recent years was actually just upstream of the town, a private beat owned and managed by our contact, Mr John Pape. He was the local tackle shop owner within the town and a professional fly fishing and fly tying instructor, not that we ever used John's services as an instructor, but we certainly fished for his local knowledge and recommendations on what flies to use. Just to put a new angle on our skills and techniques - you understand.

His shop, located within the bounds of the town's main square, could only be described as compact, and likened to nothing less than Aladdin's cave. You name it, he had it - it was just a matter of finding it. His shop was actually located just around the corner from his home, a little mid-terraced cottage aptly named Last Cast Cottage.

It is Saturday 12 June 1993 and John Lindsay, Sandy Tweedie and myself left Dreghorn at 7.00 a.m. and arrived in Appleby at 9.00 a.m. As usual, we purchased our permits from Mr John Pape (£12.00 per day) and spent some time with John discussing the quality of fishing in recent times and what flies he would recommend.

Then John said, "I think you will be in for an exceptional day today," but he wouldn't elaborate on his comment when questioned at this point.

"You'll see what I mean by the end of the day, but could I request one thing? You boys limit yourself to retaining no more than two fish each."

Not a problem, we were not here to kill fish, we were here for sport. By this time, Sandy was lost and not really part of the conversation. Sandy, his head buried and rifling through box upon box of John's beautifully tied trout flies, was trying to find the "Killer" fly. Eventually, he surfaced and bought his customary dozen or so flies which invariably turned out to be exactly the same flies as he had bought the previous year - Waterhen Bloa, Partridge and Orange, Snipe and Purple and various Olives with the odd Sedge thrown in. We took our leave with John wishing us "tight lines" and we once again thanked him for giving us the opportunity to fish his beat. We bid him farewell, promising to return next year even if we did not catch anything. Creatures of habit, we will return.

We left John's little cottage and proceeded to purchase our rod licence from the local Post Office (£6.50 weekly only). We had breakfast in the Copper Kettle café and then booked into Wild Rose campsite, pitched our tent and organised things for the overnight stay which, loosely translated, means we threw our sleeping bags into the tent. There was no great hurry, we would be fishing right into the night. Plenty of time!

After pitching the tent, our thoughts changed from away-day mode to fishing mode; that is to say, the important thing from this point onwards was the actual day's fishing which lay ahead. On leaving the campsite, our access to the river was by driving along a narrow Cumbrian country road for approximately one mile which located us just about in the middle of the beat - this was really handy.

We parked the car under a lovely big, old English oak tree where the base of the tree was encircled by a series of stone steps built in the style of an old stone dyke. These steps would serve as seats for us to use when we returned to the car for lunch. By now, the atmosphere was changing and we couldn't get our rods out of the boot and out of their covers quickly enough. Our minds were being transported further away from that original away-day thinking into the deeper depths of catching fish.

However, there was still one final and very important tradition to perform before we "thrash the water to a foam."

Out came the hip flasks and measures carefully filled to the brim with a quality Single Malt Whisky, and with the three of us positioned like standing stones at the points of a triangle, we toasted the day ahead and, of course, hoping we all experienced "tight lines" throughout the day. Ahh lovely! Warms the cockles of the heart! Tradition and ceremony over we could now proceed to the river to do what we came do, we were actually going fishing.

Time-check – 11:00 a.m. I mentioned earlier we were creatures of habit and as usual, even the hours of the day were going to be split into three equal sessions of fishing as follows:

### Session One: Pre-lunch (11:00 a.m. till 2:00 p.m.)

Overhead conditions were perfect. The river had a reasonable flow for this time of year and its clarity was very good. It was immediately apparent there were plenty of fish in the river; many trout could be seen breaking the surface of the water, gorging themselves on an abundance of summer fly-life.

Within five minutes of starting, both John and myself had hooked and landed fish. Sandy was still deciding where to start - upstream or downstream. Within the first 30 minutes the experience was posing a number of questions. There was something not quite right here. Why were we already catching fish so regularly? Sometimes two fish at a time and occasionally hooking three fish on one leader comprising of a top dropper, middle dropper and a point fly. This was just not normal! We all knew the river was capable of producing good catches, but not to this extent. A scattering of small Olives, Waterhen Bloa, Partridge and orange or black Spiders - all these flies were taking and catching fish, no wonder Sandy kept buying these recommended flies. What's going on? We're not used to this! Normally, we have to fish so hard for our sport, but this was so much fun. I'll say one thing, when you hook two or three fish at a time it plays havoc with your mind. Once you have gently played them out (without breaking your leader) which fish do you net or land first? Needless to say, quite a few were dropped at this stage.

The majority of these fish weighed anywhere between half a pound to one pound and were definitely in prime condition. Great sport, great fun - but not really posing any real challenge. This session saw many fish caught and all, I may add, were released unharmed.

**Tally for session one:**

John had estimated 30 plus fish to hand.

I had 27 fish to hand (I actually counted, for my personal diary records you understand).

Sandy had estimated 20 plus fish to hand.

We returned to the car for lunch very, very well satisfied, but confused.

**Lunch:**

Back to the big, old English oak tree, pork pies, sandwiches, chocolate biscuits, crisps and the obligatory beer was all on the menu, and if you didn't really fancy what was in your own lunch box you could always scrounge something from someone else, share and share alike with this team. What was the conversation during lunch? Guess! Football? NO! Don't be silly. It wasn't even how well the

Single Malt was going down, the same Single Malt we had earlier sampled and enjoyed as our toast to a successful day, it appeared to have worked. Every single one of these fish caught during the first session were once again hooked and caught over lunch. We certainly could talk a good fish. So what did we do before we returned to the river for the next session? You've guessed it – WHISKY! Well, it appeared to work very well in the first session so why change tack? Another toast to the mid-session.

**Session Two: Afternoon (3:00 p.m. till 6:00 p.m.)**

Once again the fishing was unbelievable. It started the way it had finished the previous session. What followed was three hours of constantly hooking and playing fish. No matter which stream, under which tree, which glide or pool we fished, we all caught and lost many more fish. If the truth be told, we were catching so many fish I actually reduced myself to fishing a single fly just to stop multiple hooking. Again, a mixture of dry flies and wet flies respectively were all catching fish.

**Tally for the afternoon session:**

John landed 25

Keith landed 29

Sandy landed 25

John and Sandy were by now taking a leaf out of my book and were actually recording and counting their success during this session.

By now it was 6:00 p.m. - time for dinner. No pork pies this time, it was into Dexters country pub for a bar lunch; the obligatory Cumberland sausage, beef and ale pie or a fish and chips, washed-down with a very welcome pint (or two) of local ale. During this break we always took part in a friendly pool competition. It's worth noting at this point, Sandy "the shark" always achieved top place in this field. I suspect signs of misspent time in the local bowling club practicing. Whatever! But he really was very competent at the game of *p*ool.

By this time our bags could have been full, our stomachs were definitely full, and our satisfaction was even fuller, but we wanted more. On to the evening session.

### Session Three: Evening (8:00 p.m. till "dark o'clock" approximately 11:15 p.m.).

This was always my favourite session, fishing through the gloaming and well into the darkness. There is no doubt this is when the River Eden's larger resident fish appear to leave their day time hidey-holes and come out to play. In fact, in the past we have, on occasion, hooked but unfortunately lost some of these legendary fish. Anticipation was running high in the hope of connecting with one of these beauties. Surely this night was not going to be any different, not after the day we had just experienced.

Even though our tiny flies had worked so well for us during the day, we decided to change tack and use a different style and type of fly. Off came the tiny flies we had been using and on went much larger sedges to fish just before darkness fell. Needless to say, "tight lines" during this final session were once again experienced by all. Two fish in particular, which I myself hooked, stick in my mind.

We fished well into the darkness and from under the overhanging trees just below the railway viaduct my line tightened. There is no doubt in my mind this was a fish of substance, but I couldn't see a thing! It was pitch black, but what a fight I was getting! True screaming reels on a few occasions and eventually I began to make some headway, bringing the fish towards the net. What size was the fish? I hadn't a clue! With just a few feet to go before it was safely landed, it gave what must have been its last bit of strength, kicked and the bloody thing was lost. One thing was for sure, I have no doubt it was definitely one of the Eden's big boys.

Once I had recovered and gathered my senses, I carried on. No more than two or three minutes had passed when the line tightened again. My god, another good fish hooked and another fantastic fight ensued. Fighting fish in the dark adds another dimension to playing a fish. Fortunately on this occasion, I managed to safely bring this fish to the net. A brown trout in prime condition of around the 2 lb mark. Fantastic, but till this day I still believe this fish was nowhere near the size of the fish I had lost just a few moments before. By now, tiredness was beginning to take its toll. A joint decision was made - let's bring the day to a close.

We left the waterside and returned to the car to dismantle the rods, using the car headlights to tackle down.

**Tally for the evening session:**

John - 30 fish

Keith - 25 fish

Sandy - 20 fish

We returned to the tent thoroughly satisfied and exhausted.

As Mr Pape had requested earlier that morning, a bag limit of two fish per angler was being imposed, a limit to which we had no objection and honestly we endeavoured to comply.

However, the odd fish had been rather greedy and taken the fly rather deep inside their throat than normal, hence making safe release of the hook very difficult. They were too severely hooked and these fish were very unlikely to survive if returned to the water. Hence, the slight discrepancy in the total number returned shown below. The average weight of fish caught throughout the day was approximately 14-16 oz.

It wasn't until sometime later we discovered the river had recently suffered a major pollution incident just prior to our visit and the river had obviously been very well stocked with sizeable and excellent quality brown trout. Just as obvious, these fish were still not "river-wise." A total of 236 fish were caught but 225 were returned to the water unharmed to fight another day.

Shown below are some statistics of my own personal and individual catch.

Fish weighing between 4 oz to 8 oz - 5

Fish weighing between 8 oz to 12 oz - 10

Fish weighing between 12 oz to 1 lb 4 oz – 60 (average weight 16 oz)

Fish weighing between 1 lb 4 oz to 2 lb - 6

What a day! I was quite sure I will never experience this amount of sport and fun ever again. It will be very interesting to see what next year's visit will bring.

As a group, we fished the River Eden for fifteen consecutive years before we called it a day. If on the rare occasion, one of our group was unable to attend through illness, we always invited a reserve, namely in the shape of Hugh Skeoch or Willie Watters, both of whom are more than proficient at catching the odd brown trout. In actual fact, some years later Hugh earned the honour of gaining international honours by representing his country in his beloved angling. Both these gentlemen thought the River Eden was right at the top of the ladder when it came to dream venues and quality of fish. Many fish were caught throughout these years and I feel I must mention, along with the year mentioned above, a number of fish between 2-3 lbs were regularly landed, but one fish stands out more than any other and it fell to John Lindsay.

Yet again we had just experienced and enjoyed another superb day's fishing and by now the sun had disappeared and we were only fishing by a glimmer of moonlight. Both Sandy and myself had packed-up and were sitting on the bank side patiently waiting for John to finish his final casts of the day. We thought we would "allow" him to finish fishing the tail of the pool. As he approached the tail of the final pool, the water depth reduces to not any deeper than six inches (150 mm).

As John reached the final few feet of the pool he stated, "Right lads, last cast." His big, ugly sedge fly (and I really do mean ugly) swung around and just as his line straightened in the current, his line really straightened and tightened, the water erupted. A fish was on it and it didn't take long for him to realise what a fish, a big heavy weight!

Fortunately, the fish did not turn and take him downstream into the faster water below, but unexpectedly ran upstream into the deeper water of the pool above. Due to the limited light, we couldn't get a good look at the fish but it was obviously a fish of substance, producing one long strong run after another, the reel screaming as it did so. Eventually, the exhausted fish had tired and it came towards the net on its side. Oh my God! Suspicion of a good fish confirmed!

John guided the fish towards the net and the fish was expertly (maybe a bit of bias here) netted and folded into the net, as I lifted the fish clear of the water. Wow! What a fish - a beautiful wild brown trout of over five pounds in weight. What colour, what a shape, what condition - and that was just John's face! No seriously, the fish was in prime condition and what a fight it had just given John. This was a fish of a lifetime! A fish of this size from nothing more than a Cumbrian stream. The next few moments were spent taking some appropriate photographs for posterity. Well done John Lindsay!

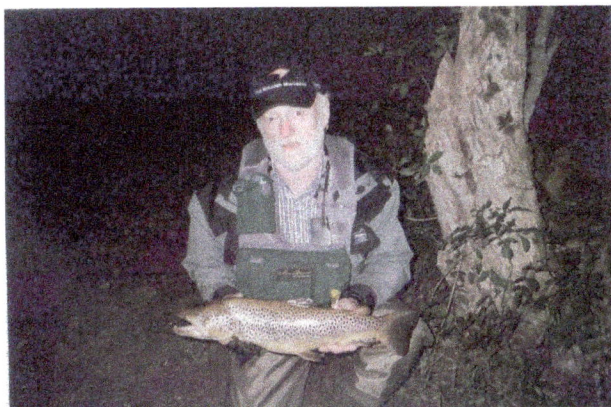

*John with his magnificent Brownie*

I have numerous memories of our visits to the Garden of Eden but there is one other memory I wish to share with you.

There was one year we arrived in Appleby, only to find this little clear-water stream of the Eden in a full blown bank to bank spate and the colour of mud. A plethora of debris, including full trees, was being washed downstream and through the arches of the bridge which, as previously stated, was located in the middle of the town. It was pretty obvious the previous few days had seen major rainfall across the upper fells and this spate was the result.

Our hearts sank, what are we going to do now? This was normally a grade one fly water. It certainly wasn't a grade one fly water today, nor for any other method for that matter, the river was totally unfishable.

We arrived at Last Cast Cottage to seek John Pape's sympathy with a view to securing the possibility of rescheduling our visit.

"All is not lost today," he claimed. "If you so desire, I can offer you a day fishing for rainbow trout on my small, private, well-secluded lake, which is very rarely fished and has an excellent head of fish."

He had never offered us this facility before, he had never even told us about it before. Considering we had travelled the best part of 140 miles to fish, this would be a definite change to what we were accustomed to. Maybe worth a cast?

It appeared really appealing and it did not take much time to decide - we'll go for it!

John P quickly changed his attire, jumped into his car and duly guided us well into the fells, somewhere above Appleby. We arrived at a little secluded three-acre trout lake surrounded by trees, with only a few openings where normal standard casting would not be hampered. We're here now let's go for it!

Fish could be seen rising freely all over the lake, which certainly whetted the appetite. One slight problem, we were not really kitted out for Rainbow fishing in terms of recognised Rainbow itinerary. Although I'm sure I had a few somewhere in the darkest corner of my bag. Mr Pape assured us we would not need these ugly lure-type flies. So what do we use? Mr Pape suggested for us to offer small, traditional top-of-the-water trout dry flies as an alternative.

Taking his advice on board, using tiny traditional flies coupled with the obvious casting difficulties it was at least going to be interesting, if not a challenge!

At this point Mr Pape bid us farewell telling us to enjoy the day, wished us "tight lines" and said he would return at some point in the afternoon to see how we were getting on.

We tackled up, constantly watching for rising fish and where the most activity was. On went a small pearly winged Wickhams and first cast BANG - fish on! After a brief encounter the fish parted company with my Wickhams and the line went slack, it must have caught me cold. Fault probably at the thick end of the rod, but all bodes well. This was only a sample of what was in store and what we were about to experience.

Along the far shoreline stood a row of trees virtually touching the water's edge with no room behind to facilitate a back-cast but, as life would have it, this is where most of the rising fish appeared to be located - typical! The most difficult place to cast a line, however was there a possibility of wading along the shoreline in front of these trees. We would investigate! I took to my heels and walked the short distance around the perimeter of the lake and I was in luck! I could wade along in front of the trees but not too far out into the water as the bed of the lake fell away quite steeply. If we wished to fish this area some casting improvisation would have to be the order of the day.

Over the past few years I had been practicing and perfecting (don't think so) roll casting, spey casting and double-spey casting during the salmon season on my own river back in Ayrshire. Would these techniques be appropriate or modified here? Only one way to find out!

I entered the lake very gingerly, found a comfortable wading depth and began to fish and cast in the manner just described and guess what? Success was followed by more success, great! John Lindsay was still sited in one of the easier locations but being very observant, and never one for missing a trick, it wasn't too long before he took the opportunity to join me along the tree line and quickly mastered the improvised casting techniques which he had been watching. Within a short period of time, John was also sampling regular success and sport with small top-of-the-water trout flies.

Meanwhile, Sandy was determined to fish the "easier" option where more traditional casting techniques could be practiced and, it must be said, Sandy was also experiencing occasional success, but not on the same scale as John and myself. However this really didn't matter, Sandy was still attracting sport and enjoying the experience.

Being creatures of habit, we still decided to stick to the three sessions for the day and true to his word, John Pape revisited during the late afternoon session. He couldn't believe what he was witnessing, he was totally amazed and so impressed with the improvised casting technique which we were demonstrating. He had never witnessed anything like this on this small lake before AND producing such success. These comments from a qualified and renowned fly fishing and fly tying instructor was praise indeed.

Between us, over sixty fish ranging from one pound to one and a half pounds were caught and released throughout the day with quite a number also being missed or lost. It didn't quite reach the totals of one of the previous visit to the river mentioned earlier, but one thing was quite different: the lake had not been stocked (or fished) in recent times. Considering this venue was totally new to us, coupled with the experience being totally unexpected and unprepared for, not to mention the limited choice of flies, then arguably this may have been a more satisfying experience than fishing our beloved Cumbrian stream. I just think it was a fantastic alternative. Oh, by the way, every fish was returned to fight another day. Great sport!

Once again, we had just participated in yet another exceptional pilgrimage across the border to the northern edge of the Pennines.

One not so very good recollection of our visits to Appleby could be classed as, "want to forget." It was on one of the earlier annual visits, our weekend away just happened to clash with the Annual Romany (Gypsy) Appleby Fair. As we arrived and headed into Appleby, we could see many of the fields which surrounded the little market town brimming over with Gypsy caravans. Caravans of all ages, all types, all shapes, all sizes and the town was absolutely heaving with people, even at

8:30 a.m. in the morning. There was a definite buzz about the place and it may have been interesting to wait and see what all the fuss was about.

I had never seen anything like this and I would have loved to observe, but we were here to fish so we didn't hang around. We just went through our normal routine of acquiring our daily rod licence, visiting John Pape for our permit and set off to the campsite to erect our accommodation for that evening. We had used my spacious ridge tent on a few occasions by now and found it perfectly adequate for the four of us. So it was not a problem.

However, we never, ever left anything of value inside the tent due to the fact we knew we would not return until "dark o'clock" that evening. Therefore, the tent would be unattended for the full day and evening, but as I said it served the purpose - somewhere dry, somewhere to get the head down after a hard and long day fishing and we had never experienced any problems before.

At this point it must be noted that as the day progressed the weather deteriorated and turned out to be very inclement. Torrential rain, thunder and lightning and cold, accompanied by strong(ish) winds but nowhere near gale-force or anything like that. Anyway, at approximately 10:00 p.m. that evening (slightly earlier than we normally stop fishing) we decided enough was enough. No more thrashing the water to a foam, let's get back to the tent dry off and get something warm inside us.

Turning into the campsite and into the area where the tent was pitched, the beam from the car headlights shone directly onto the tent. What a sight met our eyes - the tent was lying in a heap. Guy ropes loosened, pegs pulled from the ground and what little was left in the tent, exposed to the elements. It's a wonder the tent was still in one piece. What the hell had happened? I personally have camped on many, many occasions, man and boy, in similar conditions for a period of over 30 years as part of a youth organisation. I refuse to accept that this tent had fallen down by natural causes and I still believe to this day that the tent had been tampered with at some point during the day. Whether it be as part of a practical joke or something more sinister, I'll never know! What I did know was it was going to be a very uncomfortable night for all of us.

To be fair, none of the company went into meltdown, we just accepted this was the situation in which we found ourselves and it needed to be rectified by best means possible. Remember, it was dark with very unpleasant overhead conditions. We all mucked in and re-erected the tent the best we could but we couldn't use the sleeping bags because they were soaking wet and, by this time, any thoughts of just lying back and enjoying a brew had disappeared. Two (John and Sandy) ended up spending the night in the car and two, Willie and yours truly, slept inside the tent still wearing our chest waders to keep us warm. It wasn't one of the most comfortable evenings I have ever experienced.

Over and above all this, earlier in the day our fishing had been disrupted and spoiled by a substantial number of horses being led down to, and through, the river to be watered - what can one do? We laugh about it now but I can assure you it wasn't funny at the time. Needless to say, we never again attended on the same weekend as the fair. We always checked the date of the Romany fair first before booking. It was trout we were after, not horses.

We still used the tent on a few more occasions before going "up-market" and using a static caravan which one of the party purchased a couple of years later and it just happened to be located in the very same campsite, Wild Rose.

I personally continued to camp for many years afterwards, taking part in hiking events, some of which were in storm-type conditions, but to this day, I have never had a tent collapse in the manner in which that one did on that occasion.

We continued to fish the "Garden of Eden" for many years following this and there are many more memorable moments. I could write about 99.9 per cent of those fantastic memories but this one, however, was obviously the extreme on the darker side. Overall, the experience, memories and recollections of the "Garden of Eden" are ones I will forever treasure.

# BUTTER FINGERS

## SEASON 1995

The time of year was autumn, early September 1995 to be precise. In some respects, there are some specific incidents referred to in the following recollections I would rather forget, or at least wish they had never happened in the way they did. These unfortunate incidents to which I refer still haunt me till this day. I'll leave you to decide if you can recognise them.

It is the first few days of September and after a very long, dry summer the rains finally arrived and as a result of this the first reasonable spate of the season was underway. Salmon and sea trout were now entering the river system in decent numbers, running the gauntlet of numerous anglers as the fish made their way upstream towards their spawning grounds.

By the sixth day of September, the river conditions were absolutely perfect - perfect height, perfect flow, perfect colour, and, with regards to the overhead weather conditions, dare I say perfect? This, coupled to the fact we were actually on the river fishing, made it all the more perfect.

Brian, my son, was now at the ripe old age of fourteen, but Brian had been accompanying me fishing since he was the age of six. Therefore, his angling ability and capability in the art of fishing was not in doubt. For one so young he really was quite comfortable not only fishing with bait or spinning, but was also more than comfortable casting and fishing with a fly rod. He had caught plenty of trout using all of these methods during these early years.

On the morning in question, we decided to fish a stretch of the river we didn't normally fish, but occasionally we did take the notion so this particular morning was going to be one of those occasional visits to this area. There was no particular reason why we didn't fish this section on a regular basis. It certainly was not down to the fact this stretch was not very productive, quite the contrary, over the years it has actually been quite a productive stretch for myself. The truth of the matter is down to the fact it was a nightmare trying to fight your way into the water's edge through the wild, untendered and overgrown foliage on the approach bordering the water's edge. A one-hundred yard stretch of vertical sandy bank stood towering directly behind our intended fishing positions which, in itself, added other challenges. For example, room to cast a fly in the traditional way was obviously not an option. It was definitely not an easy place to fish.

Roll casting, Single Spey or improvised casting techniques would have to be adopted. However, on a brighter note these sandy banks on the south side of the river did provide a perfect nesting environment for the summer visiting sand martins. It was fun dodging these birds as they entered and left their burrows, amazingly, never to hit, nor be hit by one.

Undeterred we took to the challenge, fought our way through the undergrowth, some of which was as high as six feet, carefully negotiating all the obstacles in our way and finally arriving at the top of the steep sandy bank. Sweating profusely due to the combination of outdoor clothing, the amount of fishing equipment we were carrying and the fact we had just completed what can only be described as a natural "assault course," we dropped our bags and heavy outer clothing and began to assemble our rods. With appropriate reel and line assembled, we attached to the leader what we thought would be the "killer fly," selected for the conditions.

We began our descent and scaled our way down the steep bank onto the water's edge but due to the difficult underfoot bank conditions, we actually had to safely enter the water and carefully wade down the fast flowing narrow stream. Experience told me that we had to ensure we "hugged" close to the bank and in doing so it would be perfectly safe to wade - we would not disappear into the deeper, faster water.

After giving Brian some guidance on how to follow this known wading path, Brian set off first and after allowing him to gain a few yards between us, I would follow. However, even before I had time to enter the water and unhook my fly from the eyelet on my rod to cast a line, Brian shouted, "Dad, I've hooked a fish." Lucky wee *b*****r.

I lay my rod back down onto some overhanging reeds and turned to watch him play his fish. It very quickly became apparent he had hooked a good fish.

I shouted to him, "don't panic, take your time." I moved downstream towards him until I was standing beside him.

He stated, "Dad, I think I have hooked a big Brownie."

After a few minutes of coaching him through playing the

fish I realised this is no normal brown trout, it's fighting too long and hard. Could it be possible Brian has hooked his first ever salmon? The fish still had not come to the surface and was fighting strong and deep. I suggested he carefully applied a little more pressure to the fish, which he duly did and up the fish came to break the surface - salmon confirmed.

For such an inexperienced salmon angler, he was playing this fish as if he had been doing it for years. No panic, not a case of, "let's just get it in" as quickly as he could, where I believe many young lad would. Maybe me at that age! Sheer concentration was etched all over his face, letting the fish take line when required, applying just the right amount of pressure on the rod at the appropriate times, thus ensuring the fish was under control and hence tiring the fish more quickly. Then, retrieving just the right amount of line as the fish came closer after a long run, thus enhancing his chance of landing his fish. Landing the fish? Then it struck me - oh no! I've left the net 30 yards away, along with the other equipment we had brought with us sited at the top of this very high bank, including a priest, an instrument used by anglers to administer the last rights to the fish (kill in a quick and humane manner). This priest was probably buried somewhere in the deepest darkest corner of my bag. Where else would one keep it - just in case we needed it - 30 yards away?

I now had to consider the extra pressure of where and how do I land this fish for him. I began to look around. With water just above our knees, virtual cliff face towering above us, overhanging reeds into the water and no shingle or sandy bed to beach the fish there was not one suitable easy option. However, about 30 yards upstream (just below the net and bags) there was a very small stepping out platform where we had set up our rods and entered into the water. I thought, "That's where we'll get out."

*The scene of the crime*

An angler with much experience may have been able to "lead" the fish to this platform, but I couldn't risk Brian dragging (for the want of a better word) the fish 30 yards. Not with him having no experience of playing salmon, plus dragging the fish against the strong current. My conclusion, tailing the fish by hand in "deepish" water appeared to be the only option, but the fish would have to be totally played out.

Taking into account the predicament in which we now found ourselves, surprisingly Brian appeared to be holding himself together and remained calm, cool and very much in control. One would never guess he was playing his first ever salmon.

Another few minutes elapsed and the fish was now tiring rapidly and with the fish now on the surface and on its side, we could clearly see it was a hen fish with a slight loss of its silvery fresh run livery, but just as obvious it was still a nice clean fish. Brian was now able to carefully guide the fish towards me. I placed my hand firmly around the wrist of the fish's tail, lifted the fish clear out of the water and the fish was ours, no problem.

"YES!" shouted Brian.

I have got to admit I really felt a sense of pride at this point. My young son had just caught his first salmon and I was there to not just witness it, but actually assist in the landing of the fish.

All we had to do now was to wade back upstream to the small platform 30 yards away, then take the fish onto the high bank, quickly despatch the fish with the priest and we had dinner – easy!

We carefully waded upstream towards the point at which we had originally entered the water earlier. On reaching the small platform, I was still holding the fish with a firm grip with the hook still firmly in its mouth. Brian was following close behind. I stepped out of the water onto the platform and at this point I looked at the steep bank behind us and started to plan my route back up to where my bag lay. Then disaster! As I took my first step to climb the slippery bank, I lost my footing. The fish wriggled and I lost my grip on it - Brian's salmon landed squarely on the top of some reeds back down beside him. Brian, by the way, was still up to his thighs in the water.

For a few seconds, which seemed like an eternity, the salmon just lay motionless on top of these reeds, just long enough for me to grab the fish and clamp it to the ground, or so I thought. Then disaster number two! I quickly dropped down onto the fish, hoping to clamp it to the ground for just enough time to secure another good grip, but as I clamped the fish, the reeds on which the fish lay parted and with my full fourteen stone weight being applied I had actually pushed the fish back into the depths of the river. Little did I realise, the reeds on which the fish was actually lying were, in effect, floating on the surface of the water - there was no terra-firma beneath.

Well, I'll give you a guess what happened next. You're right - the line broke, the fish recovered very quickly (within seconds), even though it had been out of the water for quite a time, and within a flash and a kick of its tail it disappeared back into the deep water as if it hadn't just taken part in such an exhausting fight.

I lifted my head and stared right into Brian's eyes. There was a moment of deafening silence, only for that silence to be broken by me begging Brian for his forgiveness and apologising most, most sincerely. I will never be able to replace the moment of Brian's first salmon and the opportunity for him to show his prize to his family and possibly a few friends, with him taking their admiration and congratulations - you know what families are like! The one and only saving grace about the whole incident is the fact that we, Brian and myself, know he did indeed, fairly and squarely, hook, play and successfully land his first salmon and nobody has the right to dispute the fact.

Although totally stunned and disappointed, amazingly Brian did not immediately hold this against me. In truth, and undoubtedly to his credit, I was absolutely blown away when he uttered his first words.

"Well, I hope the poachers don't get that fish." What a thing to even think about, let alone say, at a time like this

- fantastic attitude! Especially after his old "experienced" father had just let him down so badly.

For the record, I mentioned earlier the fish was obviously fresh-run but was not quite a bar of gleaming silver. Nevertheless, it was still a very clean, fresh-run hen fish hooked on a size 12 Dunkeld. But I didn't mention the weight; an estimated weight in the region of approximately 5 lb.

Dreghorn Angling Club present a trophy to any of its junior members who catches the heaviest salmon or sea trout on club waters throughout the season. At the following committee meeting of the said club, the club's committee kindly accepted Brian's entry on the proviso that if no other junior member caught and weighed in a salmon or sea trout (even if it was smaller in weight) his entry would be accepted and this fish would qualify him to win the trophy, and win the Trophy he did. Credit must be given to the club's committee for applying some degree of common sense which can only encourage the young junior members.

No other salmon or sea trout was weighed in during the remainder of the season, therefore the committee presented Brian with the cup for the 1995 fishing season. Unknown to his old dad, the club committee also asked Brian to present his dad with a special prize during the prize giving, this prize being in the form of the "Butter Fingers" trophy which, by the way, his father still has in possession till this day. The trophy sits on display, taking "pride and place" in his private fishing "howf."

*Butter fingers trophy, lest we forget – a net.*

Ever since that day, I always carry a priest in the pocket of my waistcoat rather than in my bag - just in case.

# Chalk Stream Magic

It's early July and we are about to embark on a family holiday visiting friends living in the small Wiltshire village of Wylye, a village not too many miles away from one of the areas main tourist attractions in the form of historic Stonehenge. The village also stands on the banks of a small Wiltshire chalk stream, the River Wylye, a tributary of the nationally renowned and famous Wiltshire chalk stream, River Avon. It has always been one of my self-imposed rules that I never take my fishing equipment on a family holiday. However, this occasion turned out to be the one and only exception.

My host, John, who happens to be a self-employed plumber, had just recently completed a bathroom conversion for one of the local land owners and it just so happened that the River Wylye flowed through his land and he had the "fishing" of a small stretch just upstream of the village.

On many previous holiday visits, John and I had often taken an evening walk along the river bank with his two Airedales, Tigger and Rosie, as company. Unknown to John, my main objective was not to walk or exercise the dogs to the point of exhaustion, or to exercise ourselves, but was to spot as many trout or grayling as I could in the crystal clear chalk stream water. Once you mastered the technique of spotting their preferred haunt amongst the patches of long flowing weed, with their strands dancing and fluttering in the flowing current of the river, there was definitely plenty of fish to be seen.

Although not an angler himself, John did have the knowledge that I was an avid angler with a dream of one day fishing an English chalk stream. I had hinted often enough in the past. Armed with this previous knowledge, John had an unexpected and very nice surprise for me up his sleeve. Just a few weeks prior to our visit, he phoned to inform me he had pre-arranged and agreed with one particular local land owner for me to experience my dream, an evening's fishing session, and to have a few casts on this privately-owned stretch of the River Wylye, free of charge. Brilliant!

The next few weeks waiting for the holiday to arrive seemed like an eternity, the holiday couldn't come quickly enough. The sense of anticipation and thoughts of achieving one of my life-long ambitions was immense.

A few weeks later, the holiday visit in question arrived and after the customary welcome from Stella, John and the two dogs, it wasn't too long before John and I were yet again going fish spotting. Throughout the next few days leading up to my big evening, every time we walked along the river I ensured I was taking plenty of mental notes where the fish were to be found and possibly caught.

The day finally arrived and John introduced me to the gentleman who had kindly agreed to let me fish this lovely little chalk stream. Mr W Collins was his name, and he met us with a firm handshake and appeared very much in favour of letting an angler from north of the border sample the excellent dry fly fishing on this delightful little stream.

It was no more than twenty or thirty feet wide with many overhanging trees lining both banks and long untended grasses which, in places, could be seen growing right up to the water's edge and even then, the grasses were overhanging across the water.

All of these factors culminated in a scenario which was a little more testing and challenging than what I was accustomed too on my two local rivers. Although, in slight contradiction, some parts of the River Annick could be likened to this stretch. The beat of the River Wylye, which I was now about to fish, was located slightly upstream of our normal route for walking the dogs. However, on occasion whilst walking the dogs, we had indeed ventured onto this land following the river to spot fish. The point being, it was pretty evident there were still plenty of fish to be seen along this beat. The characteristics of the stretch were very similar to the beat below, still supporting lovely clear water with good flowing, well-oxygenated water. The beat also supported the same weed cover for the fish, with the tentacles of the sunken weed still fluttering and dancing in the stream's current. This cover was obviously well-used, judging by the number of fish which hugged close to these weeded areas.

After spending some time digging into Mr Collin's knowledge and experience of how to catch fish from his stretch of river, it was time to bid him farewell, but not before presenting him with a small token of my unquestionable appreciation and thanks in the form of a gift. A bottle of the world famous Johnnie Walker Black Label whisky was duly handed over. I thought this was rather appropriate, considering I was about to sample his product, he could now sample some of mine.

At this time of my working career I was actually employed in the engineering department of the company who produced the world famous whisky, the Johnnie Walker plant in the founder's home town of Kilmarnock, Ayrshire. It's quite strange, but a whole host of world-renowned famous people appear to have originated from Ayrshire. The poet Robert Burns from Alloway; inventor of the first pneumatic tyre, John Boyd Dunlop of Dreghorn; John McAdam, inventor of road surfacing material, from Irvine. Sorry I digress…

Back to the fishing and back to John's house to get ready for the experience. It was a typical Wiltshire evening; fine, dry and warm with very little breeze, absolutely no need for waterproofs. In fact, the very opposite! Sunscreen had been the order of the day earlier, but now the sun was going down and the temperature was a little more comfortable and acceptable but, as can be seen with the photograph below, my dress sense for angling was not as one might say as per norm!

Finally, we set off for the river which consisted of a short two minute walk, the route taking us through the middle of the village, past the village pub, where some patrons were sitting outside enjoying a summer cider or two. I couldn't work out why they were all staring. A few did acknowledge our presence with a nod of the head and said, "Good evening, good luck!" before we crossed the little narrow road bridge to gain access to the river.

We started making our way upstream towards the beat where I was to fish. At this stage, John was being gainfully employed purely as an observer (a fish spotter maybe). To be fair, by now the water clarity appeared to be slightly discoloured for some reason, compared to what it had been earlier in the day, or was it just because of the fading light? It might have even been the effects of the special juice we had sampled after tea! However, in reality the water was still pretty clear.

We didn't have to venture far before eagle-eyed John stopped, pointed and shouted: "There's a fish!" Sure enough, Mr Trout was lying just off one of the clumps of weed. We watched for a few moments as more than one fish was spotted, each one lying in wait to ambush a poor unsuspecting insect and gently pluck it as nice as nine-pence from the surface of the water. Going by the rate in which these insects were being plucked, there was no doubt these fish were definitely gorging themselves but on what were they actually feeding? Even with a new pair of glasses I couldn't really make out what natural fly the fish were taking.

Undeterred, I tied the "killer flies" onto my leader and proceeded to gently cast my line out across the water. I was now approaching the fish on the downstream side, casting towards the fish in classic dry fly fishing style and technique, upstream fishing and casting just a few yards above the feeding fish, trying desperately not to disturb the fish with a bad cast. Watching intently and following my dry deer hair winged olive floating back towards me, I witnessed, on numerous occasions, fish coming from the depths to take the fly only to turn away at the last moment. Why were the fish not taking my fly? They were obviously interested, but just would not take the final decision to attack my fly.

It was at this point of the evening I learned, or stumbled across, one of the most valuable lessons of my angling life, one which still stands me in good stead today as it did then.

As I mentioned, the fish were at least interested in what I had on the end of my cast, they were definitely coming regularly to take the fly. I thought to myself, I have to change something but what do I change?

I must have uttered these words louder than I thought because John quickly replied, "take up bowling?"

Haha. Do I change the fly? Do I change tactics and fish just below the surface? No! Governed by the powers of common sense I thought well, that particular fly is bringing them up but none are taking, something is just not quite right. I delved deep into my fly box with a blank and confused expression on my face, then it struck me - same fly dressing, different size. I'll change the size of the fly. Off came the big fly and on went a size 16 tying of the same fly.

First cast - BANG, fish on, you beauty! John was amazed and, dare I say, impressed. He thought, "this guy certainly knows what he is doing, pure skill." So why enlighten him? I knew better, I'm sure it was more down to lady luck.

Well, whichever way, it worked and after a short but exciting fight this excellent mid-summer condition trout came to hand. A lovely wild brown trout of approximately three quarters of a pound, which I carefully released sliding my hand down the cast and unhooking the fish without lifting it out of the water, watching her swim away and return to her home environment.

Fish number one! Big smile, great! "What's next?" I thought. Change the size of the other flies on the cast - so I did. And John said, "Try again," so I did.

Fish number two and three followed shortly afterwards, each fish increasing in size as the evening progressed (and that's the truth). Fish number two was just over a pound and fish number three was a beauty, a fish of just under 2 lb, again in prime summer condition. Obviously the natural fly life around these parts had certainly fed this fish well. It's worth noting at this point that all fish were hooked on the same size of fly since changing.

The following one and a half hour period provided me with the following sport. Caught three, hooked and lost two, with at least another three raised or missed. Watching, understanding and fishing for these fish throughout this session was fantastic, great fun. Dropping the size of fly appeared to have been the key to success and undoubtedly worked.

Moral of the story? If fish are coming short or turning away just at the last moment, change something.

We returned home just before dark very satisfied and with me being a much more knowledgeable angler. The dream and experience of fishing a small English chalk stream had been satisfied and so very much enjoyed.

I am forever indebted to John and Mr Collins - thanks for the memory.

*The author ready for action*

***Stella's comments – "Can you believe he walked through the village like this?"***

# STRANGERS IN THE SKY

## SEASON 1996

The reservoir to which I now refer lies close to the northern edge of the central belt in Scotland. Over a number of years, this venue has provided many fantastic memories for me, not just in terms of catching fish but observing and appreciating the diverse wildlife which resides in and around the surrounding countryside. The countryside at this location is absolutely beautiful and fishing this venue offers such an impression of total seclusion, peace, quiet and contentment with only the sounds of the countryside filtering through the air. Spectacular scenery which is second to none and an aura of historical presence, any angler would probably give an arm and a leg to experience such. In actual fact, this venue lies just over the hill and only a few miles from one of Scotland's most ancient and busiest historical cities. Many a battle has been experienced in and around this area, and I don't just mean fishing battles. I, of course, refer to the city of Stirling.

I have no intention of mentioning every occasion and memory I have experienced during my visits to this beautiful secluded place, but I would like to mention one or two, maybe three. By far the most memorable recollection I have I call "Strangers in the Sky." It seems strange to pick a title such as this when talking about fishing recollections, but there is more to fishing than catching fish.

On my original visit to the reservoir, I recall approaching the reservoir from the south via the motorway approaching Stirling. On leaving the motorway, we travelled along a single track road for a number of miles driving through open countryside and skirting forestry plantations, a tight squeeze in places if one met another vehicle travelling in the opposite direction. Eventually, as I turned the corner over the brow of the hill, the whole reservoir and its stunning surroundings opened up into full view. I stopped the car there and then, just for a few moments, to savour the view.

*The Grags – Northird Reservoir near Stirling*

My travelling companion immediately made one of the most appropriate comparisons I have ever heard. He unreservedly described the view before us as, "Canada in miniature." Never having visited Canada I could only accept what he had to say. The only connection I could relate to, with regards to Canada, was images relayed second hand via pictures in magazines or TV films which featured large areas of countryside. With reference to these pictures and images stored within the old grey matter, coupled with the actual view standing in front of me, I could totally understand and appreciate where his comments were coming from. The view was absolutely breath-taking. The morning sun beat down on the cliffs on the far side of the reservoir with rays which were accentuating every face, every crevice or void of these rocky crags. Pine trees were standing like soldiers along the ridge face. I immediately fell in love with the place, and that's before I had sampled the fishing.

On this basis I thought to myself, one day I will bring my own two sons to fish this venue, if not to fish then just to witness and experience what I had just experienced on my first visit. True to my thoughts at that time, that day arrived.

It was about two thirds through the season when that opportunity became available. My two young teenage sons, Kevin and Brian, were now about to experience Northird Reservoir, undoubtedly one of my favourite venues. As I mentioned earlier, Northird Reservoir lies just on the outskirts of Stirling and I'm sure many anglers from all over the central belt are well aware exactly where Northird is situated. It is a very popular venue and no wonder.

The day began as a day's fishing usually begins by assessing the weather conditions and considering what tactics should be deployed for the forthcoming battle. The battle of Stirling. This day was a typical autumn day - warm and dry with some scattered cloud cover and the occasional sunny spell breaking through the cloud with a moderate breeze producing a good ripple on the surface of the water. Fish could be seen regularly feeding all over the reservoir.

Certainly experience tells me we could possibly be in for a good day with conditions like this. Kiss of death!

After obtaining our permits and tackling up, we headed for an area known as Reedy Bay sited at the shallow end of the reservoir where a couple of small streams can be found entering the reservoir. Northird caters for both boat and bank fishing, but today we were going to be fishing from the bank. We elected to fish close to where we hoped the trout would be congregating, somewhere around the mouths of the two streams. As we approached our selected area we were encouraged by the sighting of quite a number of fish regularly feeding close to the bank and well within the casting capabilities of the two boys.

We had been fishing for about two hours and, it's got to be said, with a degree of success, all of us catching a fish or two. All of a sudden from high over the crags, crags which raised vertically from the right-hand shoreline of the reservoir towering hundreds of feet into the air, came the unmistakable sound and sight of not one, not two, but three Ospreys, obviously looking for a fish lunch.

Ospreys are one of our most majestic birds of prey which migrate from West Africa to Scotland every year during the spring and summer months to breed. The birds circled for some time directly above our heads, occasionally flying off to the side to scan the bay. It was as if they were performing a risk assessment on us to ascertain if we posed a threat to them. In reality, they were probably just fish spotting. After the initial scouting it became clear one of the bird's behaviour was totally different to the others but just as quickly it became apparent this was undoubtedly one of the parent birds and possibly two off-spring. What happened over the following 45 minutes can only be described as a training session for the youngsters, a lesson on how to catch lunch if they are to survive, and an honour for us to bear witness to this lesson.

What I assumed to be the mother bird proceeded to continuously dive into the water and, on a couple of occasions, actually lifted a fish (perhaps a rainbow trout) clear off the water, only to drop it again from a height so that one of the other birds could then dive to retrieve the stunned fish. I don't know if this is normal behaviour for Ospreys but it was an absolutely amazing sight to witness. At this point, we decided to take a break from our own fishing exploits just to watch these birds. We watched in sheer amazement for quite a period of time. Was this a training session or were they really fishing for lunch? I thought this was the perfect opportunity for us to dive into our bags and retrieve our own morsels of lunch. We sat, we ate, we watched and we learned - not only the Osprey chicks were receiving training - so were we. Fantastic!

Then, just as quickly as they arrived, all of a sudden they were gone. A few moments passed when there came an even more amazing sight. Away in the distance, approaching from the direction of the dam at the north end of the reservoir, another large bird appeared to be flying directly towards us. A bird which appeared to be of much bigger proportions than the ospreys we had just been observing for the past forty minutes or so, it was indeed flying directly towards us. At this point I deduced that there's only one bird of prey of this size and proportion in Britain - could it be a Golden Eagle? (Remember this was before the reintroduction to our shores of the Fish Eagle from Norway).

Confused thoughts were going through my mind and I found myself questioning that there were two different species of large birds of prey in the one territory. Unusual! But of course, one is predominantly fish eating and the other feeds predominantly on carrion, so it's quite possible. So why should the Ospreys have vacated the area so quickly?

The large bird flew nearer and nearer and, indeed, flew directly above us (well slightly to the side if the truth be told), probably only about forty feet, and we got a great view of the magnificent bird. It was massive. However, it was too big to be a Golden Eagle. No wonder the Ospreys disappeared so quickly! But what was it? I had no idea! I thought I was pretty well-up on wildlife in Britain and in particular birds, considering I used to be a member of the Young Ornithologist Club whilst at school, but I had no idea what species of bird this was. Nevertheless, a fantastic sight to see at such close quarters. To see it effortlessly glide past us before veering sharply to the left and disappearing over the tree tops, skirting over the high crags. We just stood for a moment in disbelief, trying to compute and make sense of what had just happened.

Unfortunately, neither the Ospreys nor the strange-looking bird made another appearance for the rest of the day. I was left searching the memory buds and digging deep into my extensive encyclopaedia of wildlife knowledge, but I was still left wondering, what the hell was it?

Only one thing remained to be done to take our mind away from these birds. With lunch well and truly devoured, it was time to carry on fishing. The fishing during the afternoon appeared to slow somewhat, but we did manage another couple of fish late into the day.

Travelling home in the car, I think every part of that day was relived. There is no doubt the day had been a total success and the boys appeared to have thoroughly enjoyed their trip to Northird.

That evening as we sat on the sofa having supper and watching the late national news, we were astonished to find a feature reporting earlier sightings of a strange, large bird which had been seen flying in the skies around the Stirling area. This feature was also followed by a report in the national press the following morning. The reports confirmed that a large bird had escaped from a bird sanctuary located near to the city of Stirling. A number of columns were dedicated to sightings of a large, strange-looking bird having been spotted in the area of the Northird Reservoir.

Till this day I firmly believe this is the bird which we had experienced during our visit, a close encounter indeed. What was the species of bird? I was finally put out of my misery of not being able to identify that bird, as the bird reported missing was actually confirmed as a Red Vulture, definitely alien to our shores. No wonder I didn't recognise it, but what a memory! Undoubtedly, Kevin, Brian and myself must be some of the few people in Britain who have seen a "British" Red Vulture in the wild. It wasn't a case of that well-known song, "Strangers in the Night" but, "Strangers in the Sky" - and they don't come much stranger!

For the record, the two boys and I actually had a reasonably successful days fishing, catching six Rainbows and one good brown trout between us, with quite a few other fish missed or lost. This, coupled with the very good weather conditions and the birds, culminated in a very enjoyable and memorable day.

*Kevin and Brian working as a team*

**There's more to fishing, than catching fish!**

Another most memorable recollection of Northird I wish to share I call, "Row, Row, Tow the Boat."

It was the height of summer, 27 June to be precise. A lovely warm, but not too warm, day. A most welcome moderate breeze was present which as it skimmed across the surface of the water produced a slight ripple. The reservoir water levels were not as high as they usually are, probably being reduced due to the local region experiencing a long spell of dry weather throughout recent weeks. These unusually low water levels were exposing some very rocky islands and outcrops located nearer the shallower end of the reservoir.

On this particular occasion I was fishing with colleagues and members of the Johnnie Walker's Angling Club. Yes, that world famous whisky producer from Kilmarnock! I use the term "angling club" very loosely, as for the majority of the members these outings usually consisted of a regular flow of liquid refreshment throughout the day (except, of course, for the poor old driver, guess who?) with everyone being very sociable towards each other. It was more of a party atmosphere, rather than a competitive angling competition atmosphere. With these guys there was certainly no overwhelming desire or competitiveness to ensure one didn't catch more fish than your neighbour, but to catch a fish or two was a bonus. I think the word "angling" was just an excuse to get away from "her indoors!"

Anyway, we arrived at the carpark and completed the customary greeting which always consisted of everyone offering handshakes all round and partaking in a nip of Red Label, just to set the tone for the day. We all paid for a permit to fish and began to set up for the battle ahead. Standard angling dress code of course being of the utmost importance. Aye right! The sun, as one would say, was splitting the trees and there was no doubt what the weather was going to be like for the rest of the day. So I dressed accordingly. I donned a pair of green wellies, pair of matching green shorts and a pair of sun glasses with a bag over my shoulder. If I wasn't to catch fish I was determined I was going to catch a good sun tan. It really matters what you wear to catch fish, doesn't it?

Some of the party decided to fish from boats and some preferred to fish from the bank. I ended up on a boat with wee Hugh (Shug) Cummings. We embarked on the boat, got ourselves organised and set sail under paddle power, no outboards allowed on Northird Reservoir at this time. What I want to know is why was I always the engine? We set a course for the top end where the two small streams, which I mentioned earlier, entered the reservoir. This could be a place where the fish were hanging about? Fresh, oxygenated water and the possibility of good feeding from the stream being washed down into the reservoir itself. Feeding which may just be to the liking of the fish.

Off-shore from these inlet streams lies the largest of the reservoir's islands, with deeper water lashing its rocky shores just where on a previous visit I had experienced a very productive day. As time passed, it was clear we had made the right choice with me raising, losing and catching a number of fish on a regular basis. Then it happened wee Shug hooked a beauty - no doubt it was the biggest fish he had ever hooked.

I forgot to mention, Hugh was not a serious angler, nor an experienced one, but when he did occasionally hook a fish one would hear him using his famous catch phrase, "COME TO DADDY," usually directed and for the benefit of Big Reg (another member of the drinking, oh sorry, angling club). Hugh didn't really care whether he landed a lot of fish or not, he just loved being out with the Johnnie Walker boys (I wonder why?).

Once he realised that the fish he was now fighting felt much bigger than anything he had ever hooked before, panic set in. The colour drained from his face and all he could say was, "Keith what do I do, what do I do?"

After a period whereby the boat was towed about the reservoir and with him milking and making a meal of the situation he began to get very confident and cocky, continually shouting and tormenting Big Reg who, by this time, was stationed on the shoreline adjacent to the boat. Hugh continued to inform Reg just how good "Wee Shug" was in hooking such a fish and that Big Reg was rubbish and did he want some coaching lessons?

All of a sudden, Hugh burst into song. He started singing to the fish that well known children's nursery rhyme, "1-2-3-4-5, once I caught a fish alive" and once finished, followed up with his own familiar catch phrase, "COME TO DADDY!" I'll not repeat Reg's reply.

With a big, broad smile stretching from ear to ear, Hugh eventually pulled himself together and took control of the fish. All I can say, is it's a good job the fish was well hooked. Eventually, he brought the gigantic fish to the net which, I feel obliged to add, was expertly netted by his boat partner. Was it a gigantic fish? Certainly a fish worth catching - a lovely rainbow trout of 5.04 lbs, fully finned and a slab of sheer muscle.

"Well done wee Shug, let's have a drink from the hip flask to celebrate your new personal best." I think this was Hugh's cue to just forget the rest of the day's fishing.

"Let's just celebrate," he replied which, to be fair, he duly did and by the end of the day it was pretty obvious he certainly had not held back on his celebration.

This event didn't really finish here. The club always organises an "end of the season" dance and presentation of prizes night. These presentation dances were always held in the Barcastle Social Club in Galston and were always well attended by club members, their wives and invited friends.

The presentation of prizes duly took place with all the season's winners receiving their trophies, but there was one special achievement award to be presented.

Considering it was such a rare event for Hugh to actually catch a fish, let alone one of such quality and size as the one he had caught at Northird, the club decided to make a special presentation to Hugh just to remind him of this fantastic achievement. This memorabilia took the form of a framed picture and poem which encapsulates the essence of the battle with this gigantic fish.

# SHUG'S NORTHIRD RAINBOW

'Twas on that grey mid-summers day
When Kip, Big Reg and Shug did play
When oor wee Shug let oot a cry
I've caught a fish upon my fly.

Roond and roond the boat did burl
Saw the fish, his hair did curl.
"Holy shit" was the call, I really
thought he was going tae fall.
With bending rod and screamin' reel
Nae chance o' bein' a slippery eel.
"Naw, naw" says Shug, it is a fish.
But a' still thought he wiz talkin' pish?

The wind and rain, it did blaw
and oor wee Shug began tae craw
Closer to the net it came,
It's too easy this fishin' game.

Into the net the fish did drap
He really wisni' talkin' crap
"Naw naw" says Shug, it is a fish
A' really wizni' talkin' pish.

In a panic he really shook
For his hip flask he did look
Couldni' find it, so lit a fag
'cause oor wee Kip had it in his bag.

At least this time oor wee laddie
Didni' shout "Come tae Daddy"
"Naw, naw" says Shug, by Christ some fish
It makes a change fae Talking Pish!

August 1996 - Thanks for the memory Hugh!

# Two Personal Bests

## SEASON 1998

### Loch Dornal and Drumlamford

It was 18 July and it was pretty obvious that the lovely, fine mid-summer weather which we all expected, as per recent weather forecasts, must have been hiding elsewhere in Scotland. On the day in question I was fishing with one of my other local clubs, namely the Crown Fly Fishers.

The Crown Fly Fishers was a small club which had been established only a few years prior to 1998. The number of members within this club was positively limited to 11-12 at the time and was by invitation only. The club secretary of the time had arranged for club members to fish two lovely little Lochs sited within the Drumlamford House Estate. The estate stands on the border of South Ayrshire and Dumfries and Galloway, just about 12 miles north of the town of Newton Stewart.

As we approached the entrance to the estate, standing like a sentry on duty was the estate manager. The customary initial formalities and pleasantries of introduction were duly exchanged. This done, he promptly ushered us to what could only described as a "Fishing Barn" and, just like a tour guide, immediately started to feed us with information regarding the history of the estate and, more importantly from our point of view, the characteristics of the two lochs available for fishing. He covered the rules of the day's fishing to be observed, costs of permits, bag limits, the methods, techniques and flies to use on each of the two lochs, as well as much more.

Drumlamford Loch was the smaller of the two lochs containing brown trout only. The estate fishing log verifies some excellent "Brownies" have been caught on a regular basis in recent times, but fish of around three quarters of a pound was about the average. However, the larger loch, Loch Dornal, had been experimentally stocked with rainbow trout some two seasons previous with fish of around ten to twelve ounces, but records and evidence over the past two years show these fish have grown on enormously. Facts such as these were certainly whetting the appetite and fuelling the anticipation of what may be achieved later in the day. He then went on to explain how the timetable and format for the day's fishing would progress.

The group would be split into two parties; one party would fish Drumlamford for the morning session and one party would fish Loch Dornal. The two parties would then return to the barn for a buffet lunch, after which, both parties would then swap around and fish the other venue, returning to the main house for the weigh-in at the agreed time around tea time. Sounded like a fair plan to me!

These two little lochs were totally different in character. The larger of the two lochs, Loch Dornal, was a lovely looking hill loch with a scattering of small islands across the loch. Its shoreline also provided much character, many bays, promontories, deeps, shallows, incoming streams and short stretches of shingle beaches with heather, bracken and gorse sweeping up the hillside away from the shoreline of the loch. It had a total sense of being a "wild" place, lovely!

The other loch, Loch Drumlamford, as I remember was still very scenic with undoubted natural beauty, but the lochan was much smaller with more inaccessible sections of shoreline and with much of the lochan being arguably "unfishable" from the shoreline, unless you were prepared to dangerously wade deep into a strange water just to position yourself out beyond the many patches of lily pads. In many places, these floating patches of lilies radiated well out into the central depths of the lochan. However, there was the odd section of clearings along the shoreline, but these were few and far between.

**The Fishing**

The morning was dull and overcast with frequent heavy and squally showers of rain, accompanied by a strong westerly wind. The wind was causing quite a disturbance to the surface of both lochs, thus producing quite a swell, particularly on Loch Dornal, but on the plus side, it was not cold.

For the morning session myself, along with a few others, had been teamed up and allocated to fish Loch Dornal but I had a problem. Never having fished this venue before, I totally misunderstood the nature of the outing. I thought I was going to a "modern day" fishery, where the fishing would consist of casting to fish in nothing more than a featureless hole in the ground where access is very easy and often there was no need for waders and, in some cases, not even wellingtons. Don't get me wrong, there is a place for this type of fishery, it's really down to one's own personal needs. Needless to say, I had only brought wellington boots instead of waders. As soon as I set eyes on the lochs it was abundantly obvious I had made a BIG MISTAKE! Not so much for Dornal, but certainly for Drumlamford. Nothing else for it, I would just have to make the best of the situation, I thought to myself. I wasn't going to let it spoil my day. Who needs to wade anyway, says he tongue in cheek!

It was now a case of what do I do to fish in these conditions? I concluded I would fish along the east bank, which meant I would be casting directly into the wind. I thought I would be better to fish with a slow, intermediate line as it would cut through the wind easier than a floating line. What fly do I use? In conditions like these, with waves like this, I was quite sure there would be many insects being blown onto the water and subsequently drowned by the waves. Hence, the reason I decided upon a slow-sinking line, fishing a team of flies which would fish just below the surface. A team of three flies went on Bibio on the top dropper, Kate McLarren on the middle and a traditional Dunkeld on the point. It wasn't long before I "touched" a fish – encouraging, I thought!

On reaching a peaty section of the bank with about a 2-3 feet vertical drop into some deeper water the line tightened, fish on and a good fish by the feel of it. After a fight in which the fish gave two incredible runs which really tested my skills, and I have got to say the fish really gave a good account of itself, eventually a beautiful grown on Rainbow of 3 lb 8 oz came towards the net.

*3 lb 8 oz - The smaller of two personal bests*

Stevie McKendrick expertly slipped the net under the fish and the fish was mine. It was not the largest ever Rainbow to have been caught, but considering I was still in my infant years with respect to fishing for rainbow trout, this fish was a personal best for me and let me tell you this, I was feeling quite pleased with myself. Great!

At this point, I decided to dig into the depths of my fishing bag, hunt out my hip flask and drink a toast, just to steady the nerves you understand. Both Stevie and myself enjoyed toasting the fish. Ah - good! Little did I realise, at this point things were only to get even better.

Later that morning, continuing to persevere with the same cast of flies, it wasn't long before I hooked into another fish. This time the fight appeared to be somewhat different. It wasn't as severe, it seemed like just a dead weight but definitely a fish. As the fish came closer I could see the reason why. It was a small Jack-pike which, once duly netted, was unhooked and returned to the water, fish released unharmed.

About three quarters of an hour passed before I received another offer, but what an offer! The fish took hard and fast, turned and ran as if it was in a great hurry to reach the other side of the loch, stripping line off my reel at a fair old rate of knots and well into the backing I may add. I dare not stop it, I couldn't stop it! Well, not too severely anyway, in the fear of breaking the leader. By now, the fish was quite far out towards the centre of the loch when all of a sudden the fish leapt well clear of the water. It was like a salmon!

By sheer good fortune this fish decided this was as far as it wanted to run and just as quickly turned back on itself. It started to run back towards me, unable to stay in touch with the fish by reeling in as fast as I could. I had to change to hand stripping like mad and I struggled to keep in touch with the fish but eventually, I managed to get the fish under control and started to apply some form of steady pressure. Concentrate Keith! The line by now had landed in a heap around my feet. I couldn't risk the line getting entangled into the grass and heather if the fish decided to yet again turn and run.

Clamping the fly line between my index finger and the handle of the rod, I began to retrieve the slack line back onto the reel. Finally, I managed to retrieve all the slack line. Yet again, up and out of the water but this time much closer to us, what a fish! Don't come off, don't come off, were my thoughts. Just as expected the fish did turn and run, but this time I felt more in control, playing the fish from the reel. Oh come on! It seemed like an eternity playing this fish, but eventually the fish began to tire. I felt I was now winning. By now I was definitely in control, although that still doesn't mean it can't be lost! The fish continued to tire and it came to the surface on its side. Keep its head up, keep the pressure constant and slowly draw the fish over the waiting net, which was being held by acting Ghillie, Douglas Hek. As Douglas carefully slipped the net under the magnificent trout and lifted the net clear of the water, the fish folded and sank into the depths of the landing net mesh. Success – brilliant!

I thought the fish which I caught earlier was good, but this fish was much bigger and caught on the very same fly, a size 12 Dunkeld, I seem to recall. This called for the hip flask to make its second appearance, which led the way for another celebratory drink, ably supported by Douglas.

By now it was now nearing lunch time. I didn't want to leave, I was having a great time. However, a plan's a plan, you have to think of others.

We returned to the fishing barn only to be presented with what can only be described as a fantastic lunch. A buffet spread which had been prepared by the gamekeeper and his good lady. Us plain and simple guys were not accustomed to this kind of treatment. Many, many thanks were undoubtedly due to the estate's staff – fantastic!

You can imagine the conversations which took place over lunch and it appears I was not the only one catching fish. It was quite evident a few of our party were also sampling the sweet taste of success. A very good number of fish had been caught.

Lunch over, it was now time for the two parties to swap locations and fish a different venue. The weather conditions by this time had now changed. The rain had disappeared, the cloud was breaking up and there were some spells of warm sunshine, but there's always something - the wind had actually increased making it even more difficult to cast. Both parties set off bidding each other "tight lines."

Our party arrived at the smaller Drumlamford Loch. It was evident right from the word go I was going to struggle to fish this lochan - lily pads were everywhere. Those with chest waders might be able to get past the lilies but I certainly had no chance with just a pair of wellies. There appeared to be only one clearing which was lily pad free, a 40-50 yard stretch of bank away to our right. The only problem, the wind was blowing literally directly onto this shoreline. This was the only option open to me so at least I had to give it a try and try I did, but it was no use, I couldn't even fish along the margins casting parallel to the bank, the wind was making it totally impossible. When I tried to wade out just a short distance the waves constantly splashed over my wellingtons giving me wet feet. This was no fun! Certainly different from the morning session. The only consolation - the sun was now out and the wind had some heat in it.

So what did I do? Only one thing for it! I found a nice, flat comfortable section of bank side, lay down and fell asleep, dreaming of the morning's fishing. Fortunately, Douglas awakened me about 4:00 p.m. just in case I missed the bus. On awakening, I didn't start to fish again. I just sat there watching the other guys thrashing the water for the remaining three quarters of an hour of the session. Which, to be honest, I quite enjoyed.

We all reassembled and returned to the estate barn at the time agreed for the weigh-in. It would not be unreasonable for one to assume that any angler with two fish of nine and a quarter pounds would be in with an excellent chance of winning the outing, especially considering the type of day it was. WRONG! It wasn't to be.

Even though I had the heaviest bag for the day with two quality Rainbows, I still didn't win the overall competition. This competition was for quantity, not quality. Quite a few of our party had managed to catch more than two fish. Who cares? Good luck to them. I had a great day, even considering the welly situation. If the truth be told, all the fish caught were quality

Fish, even the brown trout caught from the smaller lochan.

With regard to the Rainbows of Dornal, my personal thoughts to these fish were that if these were only stocked at 12-16 oz two years ago, and considering the size and the rate of growth they appear to have achieved, there must be one hell of a good feeding in that loch. God knows what size these fish could grow to.

I thoroughly enjoyed my visit to Drumlamford, I hope to repeat the experience at some time in the future. Oh, I forgot to say, if you have not already realised, my second fish weighed in at 5 lb 12 oz - as I said Salmon (grilse) size.

Two personal bests in one morning - brilliant!

Post note: in terms of personal bests, by the end of the season the fish of 3 lb 8 oz was relegated into fourth position.

Fairlie Moor – 4 lb 0 oz Steelhead

Kirkchrist Fishery – 3 lb 10 oz Rainbow

Not bad for a novice and great memories!

Record of Fish

| Date | Species | Location | Length | Weight | Method | Conditions | Total on visit | Accum Total | Notes |
|---|---|---|---|---|---|---|---|---|---|
| 29/03/2002 | Brown Trout | River Irvine | 265mm | App. 6onz | Fly | | 1 | 1 | With Ian & Jack |
| 01/04/2002 | Brown Trout | River Irvine – Holmes Streams | 285mm | App. 10onz | Fly– Snipe & purple | | 1 | 2 | |
| 13/04/2002 | Rainbow Trout | Dalvennan | | 2lbs 14onz 3lbs 12onz 4lbs 0onz | Fly – Green Pea | | 3 | 5 | JWAC – Heaviest bag & Heaviest fish. |
| 22/05/2002 | Rainbow Trout | Howwood | | 1lbs.10onz | Fly | Wild | 1 | 6 | J Lindsay – nil, Brian 2 fish (3lbs 14onz & 1lbs 10onz) |
| 31/05/2002 | Brown Trout | River Irvine – Red Bridge to Silver pipe | | App. 8onz, 10onz, 12onz 11lbs | Fly – Black spider | | 4 | 10 | 14 smaller fish all returned – Lost one other larger fish |
| 15/06/2002 | Rainbow Trout | River Eden?- J.Pape's Lochan | | All between 1lbs to 1lbs 8onz | Fly – Wickhams | Clear summer day | 27 | 37 | Another fantastic day – River totally unfishable therefore we fished a small Lochan.Morning session – 10 fish. Afternoon session – 12 fish & evening session 5 fish. Raised & missed many others. J. Lindsay about the same total over the day. Sandy Tweedie – 5 fish. |
| 06/07/2002 | Rainbow Trout | Sprigwater | | 7lbs 13onz 2lbs 0onz 2lbs 9onz total weight 12lbs 6onz | Fly – Hares ear, PTN & Cats Whisker | | 3 | 40 | CFF Invitational competition – Won heaviest bag & Heaviest fish. |
| 01/08/2002 | Brown Trout | River Irvine – No. 11 Streams | | App. 12onz & 2lbs | Toby | Good Spate for spinning | 2 | 42 | Both quality fish & both returned. |

| Date | Species | Location | Length | Weight | Fly/Method | Water conditions | No. | Ref | Notes |
|---|---|---|---|---|---|---|---|---|---|
| 02/08/2002 | Brown Trout | River Irvine – No. 11 Streams & pool | | App. 2 x 10onz 2lbs 9onz | Fly – Doobry | Good run after spate – excellent fly water. | 3 | 45 | Best ever Brown Trout from River Irvine beating my old record by 2onz caught back in 1975. Also returned 3 smaller fish. Great night's fishing. |
| 13/08/2002 | Salmon Sea Trout | River Alness | 23" | 4lbs. 0onz. App. 12 onz | Fly – Dunkeld & Ally's shrimp | Good falling spate | 2 | 47 | Bill Gibson also caught a grilse of 3lbs 8onz. – Sea Trout returned.Both very fresh run. |
| 16/08/2002 | Brown Trout | River Irvine | | 2 x App. 6onz | Fly | | 2 | 49 | Four smaller fish returned. |
| 20/08/2002 | Salmon | River Irvine No.11 pool | 22.5" | 3lbs 4onz | Fly – Dunkeld | Good flow | 1 | 50 | Been in the river a little while. |
| 22/08/2002 | Sea Trout | River Cree | | App. 8onz & 12onz | Fly – Alexandria | Very low water this evening. | 2 | 52 | |
| 31/08/2002 | Brown Trout Sea Trout | River Irvine No.11 Carmel Mouth. | | App. 6onz, 10onz & 12onz | Worm | Water high & dirty but starting to clear. | 3 | 55 | |
| 07/09/2002 | Brown Trout | River Irvine Silver Pipe | 11" | App. 2 x 8onz | Fly | Good flow after spate | 2 | 57 | |
| 14/09/2002 | Brown Trout | River Eden | 10"–12" | App. 8onz, 6onz & 12onz | Fly | Water the lowest we've seen it – Bright day | 3 | 60 | Also caught a number of small trout and a few lovely small Grayling. |
| 15/09/2002 | Rainbow Trout | Regal Fishery – Drumclog | | 2lbs 0onz 1lbs 12onz | Fly – Damsel Nymph | Dull & overcast with slight breeze | 2 | 62 | New fishery just open. |
| 16/10/2002 | Salmon | River Irvine – No. 11 pool | 25.5" | 5lbs 4onz | Fly – Size 12 Ally's Shrimp. | Good flow after spates, very cold, caught at 6:00pm. Dark at 7:00pm. | 1 | 63 | Excellent fight. 25 outings this season |

| Species | Qty | Total Weight | Heaviest Fish | Average Weight |
|---|---|---|---|---|
| Salmon | 3 | 12lbs 8onz | 5lbs 4onz | 4lbs 3onz |
| Sea Trout | 4 | 2lbs 8onz | 12onz | 10onz |
| Brown Trout | 20 | 9lbs 9onz | 2lbs 9onz | 8onz |
| Rainbow Trout | 36 | 62lbs 6onz | 7lbs 13onz | 1 lbs 12onz |

| | |
|---|---|
| River Eden / Lochan | 30 |
| River Irvine | 20 |
| Dalvennan | 3 |
| Springwater | 3 |
| River Alness | 2 |
| River Cree | 2 |
| Regal Fishery | 2 |
| Howwood | 1 |
| Total | 63 |

Blanked — Burns Fishery whilst fishing with JWAC. Although I did hook and lose one.

**Highlights 2002**

Heaviest ever Brown Trout (2lbs 9onz) from the River Irvine.

Heaviest ever Rainbow Trout (7lbs 13onz) caught at Springwater.

**River Irvine:-**

At the start of this season I resigned from the CFF to allow me to concentrate fishing my own river again this year, as I felt I had neglected the river over the past few seasons. This season saw the river hold regular and constant spates throughout the summer months right into the first week in September where a spell of dry weather sent water levels very low indeed. However, by this time there had been an excellent run of Salmon in the river system - Best for a few years. The number of Grilse in the river between 3-4lbs. were the main feature, could this have been influenced and the result of the good work being carried out in the hatchery at Galston in recent years? I thoroughly enjoyed fishing the river this season with some good catches and excellent sport.

**River Eden :-**

This year seen us pay two visits to Appleby. On our first visit in June, we arrived to find the water levels "Bank to Bank" in spate due to recent heavy rainfall in the previous days. The river was dirty and the amount of rubbish being washed downstream meant the river was totally unfishable. However John Pape offered us fishings on his own small private Lochan which was stocked with Rainbow Trout. — That'll do for me! Even though we were tackled up with light tackle for the Brownies" in the river, although I was sure I had a few Rainbow Lures in some dark corner in the back of my bag? John assured us we wouldn't need them as he advised us to fish small Top of the Water flies.

Sure enough on arrival at the Lochan a few fish could be seen rising to natural flies on the surface. On went a small pearly Wickhams and Bang! I was into a fish with my first cast, only to lose the fish after a brief fight. This was only a sample of what was in store for us for the rest of the day. (Refer to the table notes for the catch results for the day. What another excellent fishing experience this was in the Pennine hills. Maybe it was just because it had been totally unexpected? Maybe someday I will be fortunate enough to fish this little Lochan again? But only if the river is unfishable.

Our second visit was in September and the river conditions were the very opposite to those , earlier in the year, really low water, bare bones stuff. The day proved to be very difficult and challenging fishing and with the darkness in the evenings at this time of year drawing in, it was getting dark pretty early ie. — NO evening rise? Talking of which there wasn't much evidence of free rising fish at all, even during the day — This is maybe why the fish were hard to entice and proved difficult to catch? — Still I did manage a few reasonable fish with some lovely smaller fish including small Grayling, all returned of course. We still enjoyed our days fishing but we will return to our mid-summer visit in preference.

# Netting Nightmare

## SEASON 2004

### River South Esk

Over ten years have elapsed since my previous nightmare memory. I of course refer to Butter Fingers 1995, as previously described and recorded in this book. Unwelcome memory number two I encountered during season 2004. It took place when two friends and myself decided to spend a week salmon fishing somewhere totally new, somewhere totally different and somewhere the experience presented new challenges. We wanted to fish a river with a reputation, but not one of the internationally recognised salmon rivers such as the Tay, Tweed or Spey, but one which was renowned for producing a reasonable return of salmon but lesser known.

A number of weeks were spent deliberating and investigating as to where that venue would be. Eventually, we all agreed that place would be the River South Esk, a lovely little spate river which rises at the head of the beautiful and truly spectacular Scottish Glen, Glen Clova. From these head waters the river runs due east with much of the upper reaches being managed by Kirriemuir AC, passing by Finavon and down through Marcus Estates before reaching the town of Brechin, eventually feeding into Montrose basin and subsequently into the North Sea on the east coast of Scotland.

Decision made, one week's salmon fishing was duly booked for the following August on the waters of Marcus Estates just north of Forfar, near Finavon. Our investigations suggested this would be an excellent time of year to fish the river on this particular estate. As historical records indicated, this beat should be holding a good head of salmon and sea trout during this period. We would base ourselves at a campsite in the centre of the town of Forfar utilising one of our party's motor- home as accommodation.

For three consecutive years this arrangement was to be satisfied. Throughout those three visits I can honestly say, as I look back, I thoroughly enjoyed every minute of the experience as a whole. However, in terms of actual fishing success from the river, it cannot be translated in the same way. I think we spent most of the time sight-seeing or trying to arrange alternative fishing or some other form of recreation, for example fishing for rainbow trout on Roscobie Loch or Loch Heath in Glen Clova, playing pool in the Glen Clova Hotel and visiting (not fishing) the famous Morphie Dykes beat of the North Esk. We even allocated and spent time visiting local towns Brechin and Montrose, and as if to rub salt into the wounds, we spent much time hanging over the parapet of Bridge of Dunn watching salmon assembled in great numbers in the lower reaches of our river, South Esk, Bridge of Dunn acting as the boundary beat to where tidal waters ebb and flow on every tide. It's got to be said, we must have been the most unlucky group of anglers ever to have experienced total unfavourable water conditions for three consecutive years.

First year - long, dry, sunny period leading up to and during our visit but NO water.

Second year - torrential rain during most of our week and too much water. We would have been as well fishing in the fields, water levels being so high that the river was inconspicuous by its absence. Just great expanses of flood plain. In many places the course of the river could not be distinguished from the fields.

Third year - returning to NO water.

During all of these visits, our week's fishing the River South Esk was somewhat, shall we say, restricted, but when we did manage to fish the river, there was a little (and I mean little) success for us.

It has been said there's always the odd daft one about and I think this may have been the case, for our combined total across all three weeks on Marcus Estate water was two salmon, three sea trout and a scattering of brown trout. There's challenging and there's challenging, but this was just not fair. However, as a consolation the days we fished for "Pet Trout", rainbow trout in the fisheries, we all experienced a reasonable degree of success. However we were not there for Rainbows! It was salmon we wanted.

So to our story. It was nearing the end of the week (Thursday), during our second visit to Marcus Estates Fishing. The first four days of the week saw water levels reach unseasonably high conditions, obviously due to the amount of recent rainfall but fortunately, by early Thursday morning the rain ceased and maybe, just maybe the river would fine down and we would get a chance to fish during the last couple of days of our week. Obviously, this would depend solely upon the chances of no more rainfall and water levels to fall and run off very quickly. According to the local Ghillie, water levels of the River South Esk do have a tendency and reputation to "run off" pretty quickly. Here's hoping…

By the time Thursday evening approached it was clearly apparent that fishing would be possible the next day. We had checked water levels often enough throughout Thursday for us to make an educated decision. Thursday evening consisted of sipping our way through a few nightcaps and the mood was definitely changing from one of doom, gloom and despair to one of excitement, expectation and great anticipation, especially when we knew fish were lying in some abundance down in the tidal stretches. We knew these fish would make good use of the high waters. It's funny, that evening many fish were caught and we hadn't even wet a line, we were in a motor home for Pete's sake!

Eventually, we had one for the road and we all turned in for the night stinking of fish, or whisky, more like! We thought we had better set the alarms to rise very, very early next morning.

With the alarms doing their job we surprisingly awoke with no hangovers, fully able to prepare and demolish in seconds, a decent breakfast. Packed lunches were just as quickly knocked up. We were going salmon fishing and were still tingling with anticipation and expectation.

Leaving the motor home parked up in the campsite, we climbed into one of the other vehicles and set off for the river. It was still dark when we arrived at the estate's fishing barn. We began to organise ourselves for the day ahead and as I was tackling up, I was aware of some strange noises emanating from behind me; huffs, puffs, and blowing coupled with a few quiet expletives and grunts. What was going on? I turned around. It was Ron, one our party, trying to slip into his chest waders at break-neck speed. He was obviously so desperate to get to the water, pick a prime location and try his luck before the rest of us reached the river.

Unsurprisingly, within no time he was ready. He bid us "tight lines" and said, "I'll get you down there." I've never seen him move so fast! Fifteen or twenty minutes had elapsed since Ron had left the barn before the other members of our party were ready, John and myself. We locked the barn behind us and set off down the short track to walk to the water's edge. By now, the morning light was beginning to break through and, believe it or not, considering the amount of rain that had fallen in recent times, it was actually a very nice, mild and clear morning. We could even pick out the moon and stars in the dawning light. As we approached the river bank I could see a big bend in a fishing rod. John and I looked at each other, surely not!

Low and behold, Ron had hooked into and was playing a fish. Ron sported a great big smile on his face as he realised we were approaching, a smile with just a hint of serious concentration. We stood and watched for a few moments as he expertly played the fish on the fly rod.

What's that saying? It's the early bird (Ron) that catches the worm!

Ron informed us the fish had already broken the surface on a couple of occasions and it became immediately apparent to him he was fighting a very clean, fresh-run fish, a definite bar of silver and obviously a fish straight in from the sea. John and I watched for a while, offering no fragments of advice or guidance on how to play this fish, after all, Ron was an experienced and most competent salmon angler. A further short period of time elapsed when I decided to confidently unhitch the net and ask Ron if he would like me to net the fish. Some people prefer to net their own fish but I felt it was only polite to at least offer. After all, I too was experienced in netting fish for others on many occasions (and occasionally for myself), so confidence was not a problem. His response was favourable. He asked me to enter the water and get ready which I promptly did, but at this point, deep down in my heart, I personally didn't think the fish was ready for netting. However, I did as I was asked. I was now standing in a depth of water which reached to just above my knees, standing with the net at the ready, totally confident I would net the fish no problem when the time was right. Ron started to apply some extra pressure on the fish bringing the salmon towards me, still really confident we would get this fish into the net.

Ron said, "right, take it now!" or words to that effect, but the fish was still deep in the water and still perfectly upright. I could scarcely see the fish under the surface and the fish didn't appear to be totally played out. Do I try to net the fish as instructed? Then it happened, the salmon appeared to take a lunge even closer towards me and seemingly wanted to swim between my legs! In a split second, I quickly plunged the net into the water just in front of my legs, hoping the fish would take fright and turn, which I must say appeared to work. The fish turned broadside right in front of my feet where at this point, I was lucky enough to get an excellent view of the fish, but it was still in "deepish" water. Nevertheless, this view allowed me to confirm it was indeed a lovely fresh-looking fish.

The fish turned as if to head back towards the centre of the river. I was now totally aware that the mesh of my net was beginning to flow downstream in the current and could possibly foul the hook or line or whatever. I raised the net high, clear of the water, to avert these possible snagging problems, or at least that was my honest intention. By this time Ron was located slightly upstream of me and on the high bank behind me. I was totally unaware the fly line was so close to my right shoulder and as I raised the net, Ron was in the process of shouting "WATCH THE…" Too late! It was at this point the actual scenario I was truly trying to avoid happened. My net caught the dropper fly which was hanging from the leader. No prizes for guessing what happened next. Two words - FISH GONE! What a nightmare!

To this day, Ron still believes when I dropped the net into the water I was actually trying to net the fish and just made a right mess of it but hand on heart, I can honestly state I believed the fish was nowhere near ready for netting at that particular moment. All I was trying to do was to prevent the fish from swimming between my legs. One might say just shut your legs, but remember, this all happened within a split second and I obviously was not in total logical thinking mode when the fish made that dash for my legs. At the end of the day, I alone lost that fish for Ron by raising the net far too high over my right shoulder, thus allowing the hook-up. Obviously, I didn't mean to!

There was an immediate difficult and awkward silence as we looked at each other, a silence eventually broken by myself grovelling and apologising most sincerely to Ron. I felt absolutely terrible. We had worked so hard and waited so patiently to get such an opportunity during that week, only to have his chance squandered by an idiot.

*I don't think this net is big enough!*

Hours passed and eventually Ron lost it. He said, "Keith, you're doing my nut in. If you don't stop apologising, I won't be held responsible for my actions."

It's alright for him to accept it but I was the idiot. Fortunately, Ron still speaks to me till this day and when our paths occasionally cross, even if we are in the company of others, these memories are resurrected and we have a laugh about it, but I can assure you, it definitely wasn't funny at the time. It was my netting nightmare. Hopefully, a nightmare never to be repeated.

# Loss of Memory

## SEASON 2006

**How long do fish remember?**

Have you ever heard of a fish being well-ighooked, landed or lost and then within a short period of time being hooked again?

Without doubt the one personal recollection I have of this actually taking place was when I was fishing with Johnnie Walker Angling Club. Once again I refer to the world's most famous brand of Scotch whisky, whisky often referred to as "The water of Life." Blended, bottled and packaged in John Walker's home town of Kilmarnock. The JWAC was part of the very same.

During this part of my angling life, I was employed within the engineering department and was so proud to work with such a world-renowned and prestigious company, so within weeks of starting with JW I had joined this small, but long standing, angling club. In actual fact, the club had been formed not too long after the company started production in its new facility, which had been built in the centre of Kilmarnock during the late 1950s. The angling club was founded in 1960.

Unfortunately, as the years have progressed, the number of members within the club diminished and subsequently left just a small band of friends to continue the club.

Some of these people were founding members. The camaraderie, enthusiasm and commitment of those remaining was as strong as ever, even after some members had retired and left the company, they continued to meet as a group and looked forward to their fishing outings and fishing with old friends from Johnnie Walker's Angling Club.

For many years the club had visited and spent many a good day on rivers such as the Clyde and Tweed fishing for wild brown trout, but venues of this type had to be increasingly reconsidered as some of our more senior members were finding it much more difficult to scramble about the river banks of these waters. Hence, the need and reasoning for a change of direction. Thoughts and times were changing and turning towards fishing for rainbow trout in small still waters and fisheries.

Many small, still-water fisheries stocked with rainbow trout had emerged since the early nineties. These new venues provided a much easier option for the angler in terms of ease of access, better conditions underfoot, the fisheries being well-maintained with no treacherous river banks to negotiate, new methods and techniques to consider, good lodge facilities, very few trees in which to get your flies entangled and, dare I say, better returns, to name a few. Therefore, club members had decided fisheries would be the better option for the club to continue.

From this day forward the Club Secretary, John Hall, would organise a number of fishing outings to such venues during each fishing season. It was May 2006 and club members had decided during the previous AGM that the May outing would be to Regal Fishery, just on the Ayrshire and Lanarkshire border near to the Hamlet of Drumclog, once again being within easy travelling distance from Kilmarnock. Regal was a man-made fishery consisting of a number of ponds, each covering an area of approximately 2-3 acres. Both main ponds housed a small island in the centre or just off-shore. These islands provided some form of feature on both ponds. Fishing on the ponds was strictly fly only. There was also one smaller pond, solely for bait fishing.

On the outing in question the overhead conditions could only be described as changeable with varying strengths of breeze and a little cold, but this did not seem to be detrimental to the quality of fishing throughout the day. Plenty of fish were being caught all over the fishery by most of the anglers in attendance, including members of Johnnie Walker AC. I, personally, had decided to fish at the bottom end of the lower lochan, fishing just in front of a small fishing hut of wooden construction located on the far bank, opposite the main lodge. I have got to say, I had previously experienced a fair amount of success on previous visits to Regal at this location. Fortunately, the morning session had seen me land a good few rainbows, not to mention those which I had raised and missed.

It was now lunch time so back to the cabin for a warm-up and a very welcome pie and beans, washed down with? No prizes for guessing the liquid refreshment. Obviously the lunch time conversation revolved around, "How are ye getting on?" "What are ye getting them on?" "Tartan Nymph." It's amazing what some folk will believe. No, seriously, most of the guys were just as forthcoming with that kind of information. It is the one club about which I can honestly say, even though an individual trophy was available to be won at every outing, nobody took it too seriously and all would help each other to try and land a fish or two. After all, there's more to fishing than catching fish!

Anyway, refreshment and conversation over and it was back to the water and to the task in hand. I returned to fish where I had left off. It was now early afternoon and there was one fish on this day which brings back memories more than any other.

Even though the water clarity at this fishery was always murky, small dry flies, buzzers and surface film flies could be just as effective as stripping a large lure. I assembled a new leader comprising of a combination of three small, surface film flies onto a long leader.

Satisfied these were the "killer" flies, I duly began to cast my flies towards an area where due to the slight breeze, a surface lane ripple was being produced, just off the point of the island. After only a few casts my flies had just settled on the surface when, as nice as nine-pence, a fish broke the surface to take the top dropper and as it disappeared, I gently lifted the rod. Fish on! Within a few seconds "ping" and the fish was off. I don't believe it, I was broken out? "B****r!" what a size of fish! Fortunately, this does not happen to me very often but when it does! I don't mind losing the odd fish or two, but I seriously and absolutely detest (for the fish's sake) losing a fish when it goes away with a hook stuck firmly in its mouth. Unfortunately, sometimes these things do happen.

I gathered myself together and constructed a new cast, attached a series of similar flies, and continued fishing.

Three quarters of an hour passed with no further offer of success, as I worked my way up to the top end of the small lochan. It wasn't long before I caught up with one of our other members, David Beattie, the company chef. We took a few moments out where we once again exchanged and discussed pleasantries with each other, telling stories of successes and failures including my "Break-out." We moved on to talking about well - David moved on to talking about, in great detail - his new set up, new rod, new reel and new line.

Eventually, and after a few well-dropped hints, he got the message and he asked, "would you like a try with my newly purchased equipment?" I immediately took up the invitation, passing comment to him how good the set up was performing and how comfortable it felt in the hand, when all of a sudden, line tightened and a fish was on. Did I hand the rod back to him? Did I let David land this fish on his new set up? What do you think? No way, tough! If it had been a youngster or an angler new to the sport, no problem. The fish fought hard and gave a very good account of itself and by the time it was played out and nearing a point of netting, David was armed with his net and was standing in the shallows like a kingfisher, ready to plunge into the depths onto its unsuspecting little victim. With net extended and poised as described, David was ready.

I drew the fish nearer and nearer to the net when all of a sudden David stood upright with a puzzled look on his face, turned to face me and said. "There's another cast of flies hanging from the mouth of this fish!"

"David, concentrate. Don't worry about that, just net the bloody fish," I said.

Now, as true as I write this story, and before he netted the fish, I had named the flies of which I suspected were attached to this fish and actually (with tongue in cheek) I said, "How weird would that be if they were my flies?" and I named the flies which would be attached to the trailing leader.

David, to his credit, successfully netted and lifted both net and fish well up onto the bank away from the water's edge. The inspection started. There was no doubt, every fly tier recognises their own unique style of tying flies. These alien flies, which were attached alongside David's flies, were indeed the ones I had lost when I was broken-out just an hour or so earlier. The other strange feature about this capture was that, in fact, the fish had obviously moved from one end of the lochan to the other. But the main question has got to be asked, why? Why did this fish take another set of flies after such a short period of time? Especially after getting such a fright earlier? Does it not have a memory? Is it stupid? It's maybe just suffered a temporary loss of memory. However, anglers do say, there's always one stupid one. I leave you to make up your own mind on how long a fish can remember.

I can hear everybody asking, "What was the size of the fish?" Well, it most definitely falls into the class of just about average. I must check my knots in future. It must have been an un-noticed wind knot in my leader which was the cause of the break-out? AYE RIGHT!

# No Divine Intervention

## SEASON 2008

2008 proved to be one of my most frustrating and disappointing, but by God one of the most exciting, seasons of my angling experience. I talk about the amount of fish hooked, the amount of fish lost and the amount of missed opportunities. Even the amount of rainbow trout I was losing was causing concern. For example, I recall one visit to Swanswater, near Stirling, where I actually hooked and lost six fish before finally managing to successfully net my bag limit. However, I do not consider losing Rainbows as being the end of the world. There's always more to be had. I didn't realise at this point of the season that this trend would continue in to the salmon season. What follows is notes directly extracted from that personal diary I have previously mentioned in this book.

Friday 29 August: Fishing one of my favourite salmon venues, the River Cree at Newton Stewart, along with John Lindsay as company. We had previously decided to arrive on the water mid-afternoon and fish into darkness. We know there is always plenty of salmon in the river by this time of year and, for a change, the evening session sounded a good option. Consequently, we arrived on the water at 3:15 p.m. to find the water in excellent condition. With expectation high, we decided to head up towards the top boundary of the town water and fish the stretch just above the weir and suspension bridge, but below the Ghille pool. One or two grilse were showing on the top side of the weir but these fish appeared to be few and far between, we have definitely seen more fish moving in previous visits than what was actually showing today.

Having no success at this location, we decide to cross the river onto the far bank and having the suspension close at hand to cross was a bonus. We fished down through the Brewery Pool and right down past water meetings (Penkiln Burn). No fish showing here at all! We could see down the full length of the pool before the river disappeared under the town's main bridge. Something not right, there is always fish jumping, splashing or showing themselves in this pool.

Relocation needed again.

We decided to move below the bridge past the waterfall down to the Picture House, Doctor's and Gas Works Pools. Unfortunately, fishing through these pools was, to all intent purposes, impossible. There were anglers everywhere. It was like Sauchiehall Street on a Saturday afternoon, overcrowded with shoppers. As we passed we asked these anglers how their day had been. On speaking to a number of these guys they informed us that not one fish had been taken from the river that day. Why? Right time of year, great water and overhead conditions, there seemed to be no apparent reason for the lack of fish.

However, across on the far bank opposite the town's main street, much industrial bankside work was being carried out adjacent to the Picture House and Doctors Pools. Could this be affecting the fish passage? Needless to say, John nor

I added to the fish caught tally on this visit. In the years I have been visiting the River Cree, I have never witnessed so few fish, even in low water. The River Cree has always been one of my favourite venues to occasionally visit during any one season, really disappointing to see the river in this state. Highlight of day; as we fished through the Gasworks Pool, and just as darkness was falling, a family of three otters passed by within feet of me - you don't expect to see otters in the middle of a town!

We fished for approximately five and half hours with no success, so we decided to pack up and head for home very deflated, bemused and disappointed by the lack of fish. Weeks later an article was published in a very well-known fishing magazine offering some sort of possible explanation. Apparently, the quantity and incorrect positioning of estuary nets near the mouth of the river had been severely detrimental to the run of migratory fish during this period, which raises the question, "What effect would this have on the salmon and sea trout stocks in the years to come?" Over and above this, there are suspicions that the effects of acid rain in the head waters of the river and spawning grounds was also causing the fall in salmon runs.

Tuesday 2 September: Fishing the River Irvine, Willow Flat – great water again but never touched a fish, never even saw a fish. Highlight of visit, again! Just before dark, a pair of otters, which I heard approaching long before I saw them, came swimming up river towards me, passing literally within touching distance and passed on by as if I wasn't there. Second time within a few days I have had an encounter with otters - it's great. Maybe not for the fish stocks in the river, but it's nature at work.

Friday 12 September: Not even divine intervention could help. (This is the main subject as the title suggests. Remember these are direct extracts as recorded and written in my diaries.)

Finished work at 12:30 p.m. and visited Red Bridge to assess water conditions on the River Irvine. As it had been raining during the previous couple of days, the water was a little too high for the fly, but it was an excellent spinning water and, surprisingly, relatively clear. Although on many occasions before I have fished the fly in such conditions, today I opted to spin for the first time in a few years. So, returning home to grab a quick snack, let the dog out and grab my spinning gear, I armed myself with a couple of Toby spoons, a no. 2 Mepps and a Blue and Silver Devon. Now deeming myself suitably kitted out, I headed back out for the river.

On arrival at the Red Bridge I immediately met up with John Sloan and the Rev. Ian Cameron (this was the moment I thought my luck was about to change.

Intervention from a senior member of the church must change my luck!). They didn't even see me approaching until I arrived at their backs. The Reverend Ian's nose sunk deep inside John Sloan's fly box. A feat, I have yet to manage. Ha!

After the usual jovial greetings about the size of the one that got away and "those flies will not work!", John informed me a good head of fish had entered the stretch this morning and he assured me fish were definitely there. So much so, in fact, he had caught two small grilse, both of which he had returned. Ian, being predominantly a brown trout angler who fishes regularly on the River Annick, appeared to be a little unsure of where to fish and with what method he should employ on the larger River Irvine. We all agreed Ian should accompany me along the river and I would point out some of the better fishing areas and taking points. John was so surprised at me standing with a spinning rod rather than a fly rod, he insisted he gave me a "special" Blue and Silver Devon from his own box and said, "if that doesn't catch you a fish, nothing will!"

We parted, wishing each other "tight lines," and as Ian and I walked upstream, I duly highlighted a number of salmon lies which had, over the years, proven to be good "holding and taking" points. Ian watched and listened intently, as I proceeded to start fishing just upstream of one of these lies which I had just pointed out to him. Slowly, I approached the first of them and low and behold, did a fish not take just behind a lie over against the far bank, great, right again! I lift the rod to sink the hook, keep the fish under control and adjust the tension if and when required, play fish the out, not a problem, maybe this divine intervention from above really does work! Then, the fish came off! After a few carefully chosen words of my own, and a lot of sympathetic groans coming from Ian, who at this point was standing directly behind me, I gathered myself together and recast my (John's) Blue and Silver Devon. Still squirming from what had just happened, once again the Devon neared the final feet of the retrieve which, by now, was slightly downstream of us and close to the bank on which we were standing.

I prepared to lift the Devon clear of the water, when all of a sudden from the depths a salmon decided he wanted this lure right below the tip of my rod. The water erupted, spraying everywhere, the rod bent hard and the fish came off. Another barrage of well-chosen words of dismay and certainly another bunch of excitable but carefully chosen sympathetic words expelled from Ian's lips. Both of us had been given an excellent side-on view of this fish as it turned close to the bankside. Ian's influence was not working. NO divine intervention was forthcoming.

Next cast, half way across the stream, yet another big swirl and a thump on my Devon. Guess what, the fish came off! NOW NOT FUNNY! Three fish missed in four casts - unbelievable.

By this time, I was convinced Ian's words with "the great man upstairs" were definitely not working. Still undeterred, and determined not to be beaten, I continued to fish. Eventually, Ian decided to leave me to my own devices, thanking me for the information and excitement he had just received and witnessed. He bid me farewell and said he was going to try his luck at some of the other places I had just shown him. For the remainder of the fishing that day, I received no further takes or offers. I returned home, not a happy chap. Divine intervention - HUH!

Saturday 13 September: Arrived on the water at 10:15 a.m. Water a little lower than yesterday but still holding well due to some "top-up" rain during the night. Now it's a fly water, just that beautiful tea colour. Back to where I started yesterday. I started working my way downstream towards the lies, only to see a good fish "head and tail." Great, I thought. It wasn't long before I came within casting distance of where I had seen the fish break the surface. The fly swung around in the current, BANG! A take like a ton of bricks. Guess what? I missed it. THIS IS KAK! I was now beginning to believe the fault definitely lies at the thick end of rod. I was really starting to beat myself up by now, inquisitions and post mortems going through my mind as I fished. What was I doing wrong?

I continued to fish downstream. It was now just after midday, 12:15 p.m. to be precise, and I had reached the stream at the head of Willow Flat. Rain had started to pour by now when all of a sudden, pull, pull, take, take. Fish on - guess what – no you're wrong, not this time. Finally managed to play and land, not the biggest salmon ever caught, but nevertheless, a very welcome and very lovely little bar of silver, a grilse of 3 lb 8 oz, sea lice in abundance. A hen fish which fell for a gold bodied black and yellow tosh. What is the saying? Satisfaction comes to those who wait. I just wish I hadn't had to wait as long! Success might have come earlier, like, yesterday!

For the last hour I decided to move location quite a distance upstream to another pool, Gibson's Pool. This is a pool in which I have never had great success, apart from a few sea trout over the years, but it always holds salmon and is always worth a try. Yet again failing to entice a salmon from Gibson's, I worked my way downstream fishing the stream just above an old farm bridge known as the Holmes Bridge. The original bridge had been washed away due to severe floods a few years previous, but a new strong metal Bailey Bridge was now in its place.

For the record, I actually managed to catch another two fish, not the salmon I was after but two lovely conditioned brown trout, one from each location, fish of 8 oz and 12 oz respectively and both fish returned unharmed to the river. By this time the weather had deteriorated so much and the river was once again starting to rise, so I decide to return home at 2:45 p.m. a little better satisfied than the day before.

Monday 6 October: I remember this day well.

Once again, as I returned home from work I stopped at Red Bridge to assess the water conditions and to see if it would be worth venturing out. Over the weekend water levels had been very high and, in reality, the river had been unfishable but today, it was great spinning water – the water even had good clarity. I decided spinning would be the order of the afternoon and once again I would be using the old faithful Blue and Silver Devon. I walked up to no. 11 pool (Carmel Mouth).

Within half a dozen casts, I hooked and landed a salmon, a hen fish of 26 inches long and weighing-in at 5 lbs 12 oz. Not a fresh bar of silver by any means, but certainly fresh enough to keep for the table. I continued to fish around the bend and through the pool until I reached a willow tree at the tail of the pool. In truth, and in this height of water, the tree blocks your passage to effectively fish the full length of the no. 11 pool, that is the tail of the pool.

I walked around the tree to the downstream side and cast over towards the rock on the far side. 5:40 p.m. by now - I hooked into another salmon. Playing the fish and well under control, or at least so I thought, for no apparent reason, the fish came off. What is going on? On inspection of the Devon trace, it became apparent the treble hook had virtually straightened. Maybe the recent amount of fish hooked and played had taken its toll on the hooks. There is only one remedy for this, change the trace. Second cast with replacement and I hooked and landed a brown trout of approximately 10oz (fish returned), little consolation! I continued to fish downstream, through the stream and into the flats below, fishing down to the willow tree where no further wading can be attempted.

I had to leave the water. I had only received one other offer which I believe was just another Brownie, I missed it anyway! By now, I had reached the top side of Red Bridge. First cast over to far side of the river, fish took. It was a sea trout (approximately 1 lb) up and out of the water a few times - fish came off mid-stream, half way across the centre arch of the bridge.

Now 6:45 p.m. and with the light fading fast, and as my Devon was approaching the near bank, I saw a flash under the surface. I actually saw the take, yet another salmon or grilse hooked, played and landed. YAHOO! A cock fish of approximately 4 lb and after the obligatory photograph, this well-coloured fish was carefully returned unharmed to the river. This was a first for me, having never landed two salmon in the one outing, although on a number of occasions I have come close. Recently the condition of the river had been great, I just wish my percentage of fish landed was as great – I have only managed to land three salmon from a possible eight takes. I eventually left the River at 7:00 p.m. in near darkness. Well satisfied, even though I had lost another fish or two.

What a fantastic two hours of fishing in respect of sport, rather than fish brought to hand.

Friday 17 October: Arrived at the Bogie Bridge at 1:45 p.m. to find the water level at a good spin and fly level and condition. Fished twice through the stream below the bridge with the fly, catching two nice Brownies of approximately 10 oz and 8 oz respectively. Returned to the head of the stream and fished through with a Toby. No success, with no signs of any salmon.

I decided to move the one and a half miles upstream to the no.11, armed this time with only the fly rod. Time was now 2:45 p.m. I tied on a size 12 Dunkeld double and within half a dozen casts I hooked a salmon, a really nice clean hen fish of approximately 7-8 lbs. Playing the fish well with no issues, up and out of the water and giving a good account of itself, but finally tiring and turning on its side. Time to net the fish. Unclipped the net and prepared to land, sunk the net into the water, gently and carefully guiding the fish towards the net. Just a few inches from the net the fish had other ideas. It turned and once again gently headed out towards the middle of the river. No problem, don't panic, the fish was tired, just keep a gentle constant pressure and the fish will come back. Disaster! For no apparent reason the fish came off. Why me? It is many years since I have had so many salmon hooked with so many opportunities for success only to fail, especially with this particular fish the hard work had been done, so disappointing!

Tuesday 28 October: Yet another chapter in the case of missed fish. Arrived at the number 11 approximately 9:00 a.m.

Cold, bright and crisp morning with water levels still on the high side after fining down from recent major floods on Sunday and Monday, but the water was in a condition to allow spinning methods. I decided to use a 3 inch red and yellow Devon and within ten minutes, fish on. Obviously a salmon, going by the weight on the end of my line, but I never really got a chance to see the fish as it remained deep and fought hard. Yet again the fish came off and parted company after a short fight. Fault at the thick end of the rod – AGAIN!

In relation to salmon opportunity this season, as follows:

Three offers - as in pulls or takes - but failing to hook-up properly.

Three fish hooked, played for a good period of time, but lost.

Three fish actually hooked and landed.

Three fish from a possible nine – 33 per cent success rate - rubbish! Could it be those stupid doubles again? I've not much faith in double hooks. No, I think as I said, fault must lie at the thick end of the rod.

My feelings for this year - absolutely sick! Definitely NO divine intervention from my maker.

*Rev. Ian Cameron with his salmon – I think it was favouritism*

# "Ottermania"

## PANIC OVER

Over the years, I have been fortunate enough to have encountered quite a spectrum of wildlife species whilst trudging along the riverbank or fishing from a boat in the middle of some beautiful Scottish loch. I make no apology to indulge in sharing with you just a few of these experiences and memories which relate to one of the most fascinating riverside mammals our country has been blessed with. In my opinion, the first memory I share with you is definitely one of the funniest I can recollect.

It took place one mid-autumn evening as I was fishing for salmon on the River Irvine, along with my son Brian. Considering it was autumn, the evening could have been more likened to that of a true summer's evening. Overhead conditions were clear with the sun shining brightly as it progressively lowered to set in the western sky. The breeze was slight, but aired with a very pleasant, comfortable and enjoyable temperature. The water level of the river was absolutely perfect, no doubt salmon and sea trout would be running following the higher waters which had been present throughout the preceding few days.

We had been fishing for a few hours without success and by the time we had fished through the upper pools of the river we had been joined by one of the real characters of the local club, a man I have known since we were kids. I'll not divulge his actual name, but suffice to say, for a number of years he was known locally amongst the local fishing fraternity as "Tombstone."

Why tombstone? The fact he had lost virtually all of his front teeth apart from one, which stood upright in the centre of his gums, gave rise to this graveyard observation. On hearing this name, a stranger to the local area may be excused in thinking we were not very complimentary and quite abusive towards him, but all the jibes and micky taking were always in fun and to be fair to "Tombstone," he always took the joking in good part. He could also give as good as he got, so there was never any real animosity towards him and nobody ever really fell out with him or vice-versa.

After spending a little time asking how each other was fairing, we decided we should all fish down a perfectly "wadeable" and fishable section of the river. Casting would be guided towards the deeper water which, in the main, flowed hard against the far bank. This long pool, or glide if one preferred, stretched for approximately two hundred yards before one had to exit the water next to a large, overhanging willow tree, due to the depth of water increasing.

We entered the water one by one at the top stream, leaving plenty of room between us, my son going first, Tombstone second, with me following at the rear. We fished slowly down the pool like regimental soldiers in perfect line, taking a step downstream after every cast. My son was now just about reaching the exit point, just upstream of this large willow tree. The willow tree stood about two or three hundred yards upstream of an old sandstone bridge which formed one of the main crossing points of the river, the bridge spanning the river with three perfectly symmetrical arches. As I looked downstream towards this bridge, I noticed a considerable disturbance in the water under the centre arch. One has got to remember and appreciate that by now the light was beginning to fade relatively quickly, but the sight I was now witnessing would only allow my brain to compute that what I was seeing was a head of running salmon coming through the arches of the bridge. Again, I reiterate, by this time the sun had gone down and we were now in the "gloaming" stage of the evening. I couldn't quite see clearly enough to confirm what was really making this disturbance, which by now was taking place in the calmer waters just upstream of the bridge.

However, I quietly shouted to my son and Tombstone to take note of what I was seeing. They too appeared to be confused to what we were witnessing. At first, this prolonged disturbance in the water, just upstream of the middle arch, continued for quite a few moments, then all of a sudden the disturbance on the surface appeared to be getting closer. Salmon would have disappeared into the depths of the deeper water by this time. The river bed deepens about thirty yards upstream of the bridge. Strange behaviour for a salmon, I thought. There were now four distinct tracks (bow-waves) being produced in the slower moving water above the bridge, each bow- wave progressing slowly upstream. What was it? By now I had quickened my step and waded downstream towards Brian, picking up Tombstone on the way past and then onto where my son stood. We had all slowly moved towards the bank and took up our hiding position behind a large overhanging willow tree, ensuring we were out of sight from the advancing "disturbance."

*No hiding place*

We were now all standing like statues, totally motionless with all lines back on the reels. Not a movement, not a sound. Brian and Tombstone were side by side, with myself positioned slightly behind and slightly upstream of Tombstone. We were still up to our thighs in water, endeavouring to remain perfectly still and not making a sound as this "disturbance" was most definitely getting nearer. It was just about at this point I realised what was producing this disturbance. It was a family of otters, four in number. By now we could hear the very high-pitched barks and chatter of the otters as they continued to swim up-river. They continuously communicated with each other as they slowly advanced.

The otters were now approximately thirty yards away from where we stood, just at about the two o'clock position as we looked downstream, blissfully unaware of our presence. All of a sudden the lead otter paused for a second or two, looked around, then dived under water and disappeared from sight. However, within a few seconds it quickly became very clear just exactly where the submerged otter was heading. A trail of air bubbles was the give-away and the bubbles were heading directly towards the large willow where we were all standing.

Brian turned and looked at me whispering as he did so, "It's coming for us!" Not as in, it's coming to actually attack us or anything, he just meant it was heading for our side of the river, towards the tree. At this point, a very mischievous thought and action came into my mind. I stooped down, placed my left arm deep into the water soaking the sleeves of my jumper as I did so, I didn't care, and I grabbed the back of Tombstone's leg with my hand. PANIC! All hell let loose. The eerie silence which had been so strictly adhered to during the past five minutes was dramatically broken with an amazingly high-pitched scream, a scream which I thought was not possible from the male gender of our species. Tombstone's rod went flying six feet into the air, the surface of the water erupted, sending a tidal wave in all directions, legs and arms flailing and thrashing the water to a foam. Water spraying everywhere, Tombstone tried to vacate the river as quickly as he possibly could. As he pulled himself out of the water onto the bank, the sound of Brian's laughter resounded loud and clear in the stillness of the dusk evening. Brian had realised what had just taken place. His laughter was vigorously accompanied by much laughter from myself. God knows what the otter thought! It was not sticking around to find out, it too took fright and headed for the far side of the river as quickly as possible, swiftly followed by the other members of the otter family. As one can imagine the air was, shall we say, a little blue, but only resonating from one particular source.

As Tombstone recovered and finally worked out what had just happened, he questioned the origins of my parenthood and said if he had his way I would be condemned to hell for the rest of my life. I have got to admit, of all the funniest experiences I have come across during my angling travels, this particular incident is one of my favourites and definitely is right up there with the best of them. Poor Tombstone!

"What happened to the otters?" I hear you say. Well, once the family had regrouped hard against the far bank they appeared not to be too stressed and none the worse for their experience, which is more than I can say for Tombstone. They just rerouted their "flight path" to swim hard against the far bank and carried on their upstream journey as though nothing had happened.

I think a clean set of underwear may have been required for Tombstone - brilliant!

History tells us that otter presence on the river has been witnessed on a number of occasions over the years, but these sightings were usually few and far between.

However, since about 2004, otters have been an ever-present feature on our water and are regularly seen by numerous anglers. Indeed, during recent years I myself have witnessed and encountered these creatures on many occasions. Watching them just going about their everyday business, every time, without exception, has provided me with a special memory. It is during these times where I'm afraid fishing takes second place, the rod gets pushed to the side and care is taken not to alert the otters to my presence. I usually just sit in awe watching wildlife in action. Fantastic!

Lying deep in the memory banks, there are two further memories of otter encounters which I would like share.

The first memory began as I walked along the high bank heading downstream towards one of my favourite pools. This pool is located on a bend just at the lower end of a big, long, slow-moving canal-like stretch of the river, and as the course of the river bends to the left, a smaller tributary enters the main stream from the north bank. As I progressed closer, I observed a large disturbance in the water; splashes, ripples and bow waves. Was it ducks? Kids throwing stones? Salmon splashing about? I was just too far away to confirm, but experience told me to suspect it might be otters.

I dropped down from the path on the high bank into the adjacent barley field, thus giving me cover, and fortunately, there was an easterly wind blowing, which carried my scent away from the otters. I took my time and carefully approached the point where stood the tree under which the otters were sited. Considering the barley was near ready for harvest and stood quite high, I carefully placed my fishing rod in a safe place on the ground, somewhere I would be able to find it again.

On all fours, I carefully and gingerly crept up the slight incline back onto the high bank and raised my head just above the grass. Sure enough, directly below me there they were, a family of otters comprising of a mother and two of her off-spring. The two cubs (some call them kits, some call them pups) appeared to be fighting, but in reality they were only playing as many youngsters do in the animal world. This type of playing would no doubt stand them in good stead for their future. Diving, swimming, climbing onto the roots and balancing on the overhanging branches of the tree, on occasion they appeared to act out a scene from the film Robin Hood, the scene where Robin duels with Little John on the trunk of a fallen tree spanning a running stream. When eventually one fell off, the other gave chase into the water, screaming and "talking" to each other throughout the whole episode. As for the mother, she had obviously just been out on a fishing expedition. Firmly gripped between her two front "hands" was a lovely, fat brown trout, a fish of approximately three quarter of a pound but with little or no head left. She was obviously enjoying breakfast. Every so often she would stop chomping, raise her head and scan the area looking all around to check on the kids, just as all mothers do! Then she would carry on chomping on her meal and obviously enjoying it. I could hear the sound of the fish being torn apart and the smacking of the chomping jaws - fantastic!

By now I was getting a little uncomfortable and had to slightly reposition myself. Oops! I think they heard me. The mother immediately ceased chomping, let out a loud bark, (obviously a distress call) and the cubs immediately ceased what they were doing. She stared right at me, eye-to-eye contact was definitely made and I froze for what seemed like an eternity, but in reality I suggest it would have been only a few moments.

Eventually, she carried on eating and I slowly repositioned myself into another comfortable position. The pups continued to cause havoc, as kids do. I sat for quite a period of time just observing, but I was here to possibly catch my own fish, not to watch others show me how it's done. I will not succeed if my line is not in the water.

I stood upright and in an instant, Mother and cubs left the scene without a second thought. Good luck to them, I thought. I had just gained one of the most memorable experiences of my life and I feel honoured to have spent this time witnessing this family going about their business in their natural environment. They were totally oblivious to having a spectator. One thing's for sure, I wasn't going to fish in this pool on this occasion. I never even gave a thought to video this on my camera – which just happened to be in my top left hand pocket of my waistcoat – FOOL!

My second encounter involving otters happened as I fished with my nephew, Kyle. At that time Kyle must have been aged about 12, and I remember it was just about "dark o'clock" and we were fishing down one of my favourite streams on the river. Once again the river supported a good flow of water after earlier rains.

We were just about reaching the tail of a stream when about 40 metres downstream of my nephew (25 metres from myself), in amongst the long, overgrown grasses covering the bankside, the sound of cheeping, barking and grass rustling emanated from the same bankside on which we stood. Confirmation of the fact we were not alone was when I noticed the grass moving, and whatever it was, slowly but progressively advanced closer and closer towards me.

I immediately recognised the sound and quickly realised what it was and, once again, froze. Not a sound, not a movement did I make. I didn't want to shout to my nephew as this would have definitely alerted the animal to our presence and the opportunity would have possibly been lost. Within a few seconds, not one but two otters passed within feet of me (I could have reached out and touched them) passing by between myself and the water's edge. All of a sudden they stopped in their tracks, pausing just a few yards upstream of me, obviously becoming aware of my nephew's presence, which is more than he was about theirs.

Sliding from a small patch of sandy bankside, the otters calmly slipped into the river and disappeared into the stream, thus allowing them to continue their journey.

My nephew, still oblivious to what was happening, suddenly shouts, "Uncle Keith, Uncle Keith, look at the salmon." Of course it wasn't salmon, the otters had broken the surface of the water with their backs, which just so happened to be directly in front of Kyle, just out from the tip of his fishing rod. Needless to say, on hearing the shouts of Kyle, the otters quickly disappeared under the surface.

Over the next few minutes I painstakingly tried to explain or convince him (but having a hard job), that it was otters and not, as he thought, salmon, when all of a sudden the otters emerged slightly upstream but across the river on the far side of the stream and onto the riverbank opposite. Point proven! As one would expect the otters had obviously taken fright on hearing my nephew shout and immediately headed for the safety of the far bank.

They hung about for a few minutes giving themselves a shake and a quick rub down and then duly left the scene. My nephew still talks about this experience to this day. It also proves, since the otters appeared 7-8 years ago, the quality and cleanliness of the river must be of a high standard. Otters do not tolerate or hang around in polluted water and there must be a good supply of food for them to remain.

A virtual carbon copy of this event was also repeated on another river located in the south west of Scotland, the River

Cree. One might say the encounter took place right in the centre of the town of Newton Stewart, the only difference being it was not my nephew who accompanied me on this occasion, it was an angling companion of the time, namely John Lindsay. John being much more mature did recognise these animals as otters as they walked passed us.

There's definitely more to fishing than catching fish!

# Wonders of the Riverbank

## THERE'S MORE TO FISHING
## THAN CATCHING FISH.

I make no apology for intentionally using this statement on a number of occasions throughout this book, but what can we take from the statement? I would like to take this opportunity to put forward a few of my own personal thoughts and interpretations.

Surely, it must be relating to Mother Nature? For all of man's inventions, developments and successes in the world, there is nothing, nothing in my eyes, which comes anywhere close to compare with the wonders of Mother Nature.

In many of the chapters within this book, I have mentioned a number of memorable moments involving such wonders of nature. Encountering red vultures, ospreys, otters, wild salmon, deer and kingfishers, to name but just a few. Of course, that's the essence of the book, but the list doesn't stop there. Observing nature in its natural form, with its natural habitat and environment, has always fascinated people, whether one is an angler or not. I just feel anglers (and their like) generally gain more exposure and experience to, and arguably appreciate Mother Nature greater, than most.

Some specific events, experiences and observations I have witnessed whilst spending time on the riverbank are a joy and a memory to behold, especially if that observation involves certain species of animal which are of the kind not frequently encountered on a day to day basis.

Let us consider how we use some of the human senses and how we relate to Mother Nature.

*Follow me - the grass is always greener on the other side*

Kingfishers speeding past like a bolt of orange and blue lightning, deer calmly grazing in neighbouring fields or, if you are really lucky and remain totally motionless, the deer may even pluck-up the courage to come to the water's edge to take a drink, they may even be within touching distance! Numerous aquatic or airborne creatures going about their daily rituals. Damsel and dragon flies continually dancing effortlessly amongst the reeds and long grasses which border a pond or loch, all these creatures cohabit our waterways. Various species of insect life, swarms of may fly or flocks of birds forming dancing clouds of ever-changing size and shape in the sky. Kingfishers, dippers and wagtails continually working hard and foraging for food along the course of the river. Spectacles such as these can be witnessed throughout the four seasons of the year.

Then, of course, there's my own favourite, the King of Fish, Salmo Salar, the Atlantic Salmon. Surely this must be every fresh water angler's dream game fish, often observed encountering and striving to conquer the numerous dangers and challenges as it ascends its own river of birth. Dangers such as avoiding coastal and estuary netting, poachers who use every conceivable illegal method of capture, anglers with rods and line as well as navigating natural barriers such as the strong cascading waters of weirs and waterfalls, which can undoubtedly prove very difficult for the salmon to negotiate. These amazing fish provide such a spectacle, not just for fishermen but tourists and members of the general public alike. Salmon being observed trying to swim over or, indeed, what they can't swim over attempting to leap, time and time again, sometimes 10-12 feet in the air until they achieve their goal, is a sight truly to behold as this spectacle is taking place. One of the most spectacular places I personally have witnessed this was at the Falls of Shin, located in the north of Scotland, but there are numerous places throughout the whole country where these leaping salmon can be viewed.

The salmon's goal? To conquer these obstacles set before them, thus enabling them to continue their journey and reach the clean and crystal clear head- waters of the upper river system. Once successful in defeating all these challenges, only then can the mating ritual begin. The ritual in itself is a sight to behold for those lucky few who have actually witnessed it. Reproduction between cock and hen fish will ultimately take place, thus ensuring the species' survival for the years to come.

**Sounds:**

These are the ever-changing sounds which are experienced; sounds ranging from a deafening silence, only being interrupted by the therapeutic sound of running water as the stream trickles down to the meandering river, to a cacophony of bird songs and calls, for example the sound of geese flying high above in an almost perfect symmetrical "V" formation, such an easily recognisable sight as these birds embark on their annual migrations to warmer climates (or vice-versa).

The unmistakeable screech of the buzzard, and other birds of prey, as they circle high above the tree line; the high-pitched and continuous cheeping of ducklings or signets as their legs frantically paddle, endeavouring to keep up with their mother as they follow in such a regimented single file formation. You might even hear the sound of the bellowing buck deer during the rutting season.

Even the sound of common farm yard animals can bring pleasure. Cows mooing and sheep and lambs bleating on the surrounding hillside. Great!

Foliage and Fauna: a multitude of sights, smells and sounds. Forest, woodland, farmland fauna and flora exhibits, vast arrays of colour and smells with varying degrees of type and species. The yellow of wild daffodils of spring. Yellow flowering gorse bushes with siskins, or maybe the odd linnet constantly flitting from one bush to another, possibly looking for a suitable nest site or searching for an easy meal, picking off the unfortunate insect which just happened to stray into a spiders web. Or hidden under the branches, the rows and rows of autumn brambles and blackberries, red berries lining the banksides and hedge rows. Fauna ranging from the smallest of wild flowers to the tallest of evergreen trees, each one producing aromas from the most fragrant of wild woodland flowers to the colourful and aromatic scent of rhododendron bushes in full bloom.

*Autumn colours line the course of the river*

But without a shadow of a doubt, my favourite time of the year is autumn. Trees in abundance providing such a prolific kaleidoscope of colour, just before they shed their leaves for the winter months. Woodland creatures large and small, too many to list, but each experience encountered having its own attraction and fascination. This can only be described as - fantastic.

Then, of course, there's the good old British weather.

Is there anything good we can say about this? I believe there are many positives we can say! If it wasn't for the British climate being so diverse and unique, I believe we would not have such a wild, pleasant and natural environment for us all to enjoy. It is this mixture and balance, with a combination of weather elements such as sunshine, rain, wind, heat and cold, not to mention the duration and content of each one which Mother Nature provides for us. Every living thing on this earth depends on these elements.

There is nothing nicer than being present on the banks of a flowing river on a clear, warm, dry and mild summer's evening just as the sun is setting. The ever-lowering sun casting long shadows down a slowly darkening pool, or being afloat in a boat in the middle of a Scottish loch watching the setting sun produce large areas of glimmering reflections on the surface of the water and, as the sun eventually does disappear slowly behind the surrounding trees, hills or high mountains, the land becomes nothing more than a silhouette in the background. Such sunsets can be a sight to behold, with the final rays of sun reflecting off the light cloud covering hovering high in the earth's atmosphere. Colours of red and burnt orange fading into the realms of pale yellow, likened to that of an open fire which is well alight with long rising flames and embers floating skywards. The unforgettable and over-whelming sound of silence, apart from the water lapping on the side of the boat or, in the case of the river, the previously mentioned sound of the trickling stream or maybe the sound of your fly line "whishing" through the air or passing through the eyes of your rod as the line shoots. Or maybe, just maybe, the sound of birds preparing to roost and settle down for the night. Then comes the final transformation, daylight into darkness, the silence then being broken with the sounds of the creatures of the night. The hoot or screech of an owl, the rustle of the trees as a slight breeze is formed, the splash of a rising fish, a momentary sight of a bat against the skyline as it expertly avoids collision looking for moths and insects on which to feed. All this is down to the weather and climate (and Mother Nature) – simply wonderful.

These are just a few examples of why the angler so much enjoys participating in this wonderful pastime. I could go on and on and on about the pleasures under this section, but I'm sure many anglers have their own special memories and thoughts of fishing expeditions where it didn't actually involve catching fish! No wonder we say, "There's more to fishing than catching fish."

# POACHING – IS IT
# WORTH IT?

Although the illegal practice of poaching on rivers has been around for decades, there was one period from about the mid-nineteen eighties to the mid-nineteen nineties where poaching on my local river was rife. The effect of this practice on the stocks of migratory fish within the river system, resulted in, or at least contributed to, almost wiping out the salmon in the river. Local club catch returns of rod caught salmon during this period appeared to support these effects. My own personal diary records and statistics undoubtedly prove there was indeed a severe demise in the numbers of rod caught salmon and sea trout on my own club waters.

Historical poaching methods practiced in years gone by, for example "foul hooking" with heavy lead core lines loaded with a series of large hooks attached, and the "gaffing" of fish from many of the weirs on the river appeared to fall out of favour. Although there were still isolated cases, poaching techniques and methods progressed to more effective and lethal methods of illegally removing the salmon (and sea trout) from the pools of the river such as gill netting and poisoning (for example the use of Cyanide). These indiscriminate and ruthless methods of poaching inevitably affected not just the fish caught up in these nets but, if one is to think about it, potentially they will without doubt affect future stocks. A hen salmon is thought to be capable of producing approximately 800-1000 eggs for every pound weight of that fish. So the potential loss of future stocks equates to thousands of fish being lost forever. The poachers were indiscriminately killing thousands, not just the fish in the net.

Over and above all this, particularly with poisoning, the clue is in the word poisoning, other aquatic creatures of the eco-system within the river may also be affected, again potentially wiping out food items such as minnows for the resident brown trout. Cyanide does not just affect the salmon. This was now a major problem on our river.

Some form of policing the river had now become a real need and a major priority if we were to ensure the survival of migratory fish within our river system. A small team of bailiffs had been set up for a number of years, some warranted and some, like myself, (at least in the beginning), just volunteers. But the team needed more.

A few years passed and we "learned the trade" before somebody finally pointed out to me I would be much better advised to become an official warranted bailiff, if not only for the fact of personal insurance. If anything untoward was to happen, then at least I would be secure in the knowledge that I or my family could possibly make a claim for personal injury, loss of earnings or equipment damage, rather than be left with nothing.

After much consideration I thought insurance would indeed be the best policy, especially since I had a wife and such a young family and a mortgage to pay.

Eventually, I made the decision to actually register as a Crown appointed warranted bailiff on our local river. I duly signed along the dotted line and became an official bailiff. A member of a small, close knit-team of Crown Bailiffs, six in number. Incidentally, most of whom had full-time day jobs and some involved in shift work.

Organising full attendance of the team to patrol the river sometimes proved very difficult, especially when patrols had, on occasion, to be organised at very short notice. For example, maybe a club member, or even a member of the general public, had come across something suspicious on the river. Or maybe the weather had caused the river to rise very quickly, producing excellent water conditions encouraging the salmon to "run" and subsequently bringing the poachers out.

It is maybe worth noting at this point, I had been a member of the local angling club since the age of ten and a long-standing adult member, an adult member who had held a number of responsible positions within the club's committee of management. I had never once considered leaving these positions. However, I felt the goal posts had now changed slightly, in that I had signed along the dotted line. Considering I lived in the village and was surrounded by known members of the poaching fraternity, I thought it would be prudent if I were to resign as a member of the committee, making it look as though I had experienced some form of disagreement, thus making it appear as if I had fallen out with the club where, in actual fact, it couldn't be further from the truth. I was actually taking on a role within the club which very few people would take on. Only the club President and the Club Secretary knew the truth and, to their credit, kept this secret a true secret throughout my time as an active warranted bailiff. NOBODY during these years suspected I was a warranted bailiff, but just another ordinary member of the club.

What I had realised by this time, throughout my initial voluntary period, was that taking on a role such as this is not for the faint-hearted. As you patrol the river at unearthly hours in the dark of night, enduring the most inclement of weather conditions, with wind and rain battering your body, unable to see a yard in front of you and with difficult underfoot conditions, things can get a bit, shall we say, unpredictable and uncertain and yes, in some cases frightening. You just don't know what you are going to come across in the dead of night.

Some nights could be likened to a dark, closed room with no lights, it was literally pitch black! As you tried to make your way through the riverside fauna or through a woodland track, a track which you may have followed hundreds of times in daylight without any problem, all of a sudden the task becomes a great deal more challenging, especially when you are trying to keep as quiet and as nimble on your feet as you can. Straining not to step on a twig or something which, in turn, may alert any unsuspecting poacher of your presence. You can hardly see two feet in front of yourself. Other nights may be very, very clear, with a full September moon high in the sky providing so much light you would not be ridiculed if you said it was more like daylight. Your body casting long shadows just to keep you company. This bright, high in the sky, moon posed problems of its own, trying to keep out of sight and away from the skyline of the land to avoid your silhouette giving away your presence or position.

One thing is for certain, the bailiffs were so experienced and knowledgeable they could predict the nights on which the poachers would be active and undoubtedly would be setting their nets, particularly in certain levels of water. Till this day, even after having been retired for a number of years from the bailiff role, when conditions are right, on occasion I still say to my wife, "Aye, the poachers will be out tonight," or words to that effect.

I mentioned earlier, all the members of our team had day jobs and this had a huge impact on our availability and time we could spend as a full team on the river. Many poachers we encountered throughout these years were unemployed and after setting or recovering their nets they could return home and were probably able to catch up on their hours of lost sleep during the following day. We, on the other hand, had our work to go to and after a few consecutive nights of patrolling, tiredness was an issue. However, we did commit to spend as much time as possible on the river (remember this was all voluntary), even if all six members of the team were not available a minimum of two would patrol our beat. Never did we at any time allow a bailiff to patrol alone.

There are a number of nights and experiences to which I can recall during my time patrolling the river. However, I'll just mention a few.

**My First Recollection**

On this particular occasion only three of the team were available; the head bailiff, his colleague and myself. I was the only real "local" for this beat of the river, as the other two bailiffs' "home patch" was further up the valley. They obviously understood and knew the fish which we were trying to protect would eventually reach their patch, so they also had a real interest in protecting this section. Given the water conditions on this particular night we all knew somewhere along this beat poachers would be active.

On meeting up with each other we walked in silence for about four hundred yards along an old farm track which was flanked on both sides with numerous tall trees.

We forded the river by means of an old Bailey Bridge which had been constructed just a few years earlier due to the original sandstone bridge being swept away during severe flood waters.

We decided to head up-river towards a pool where I knew fish would either be running through or resting, experience and local knowledge told me it was definitely one of the better holding pools within the club's fishing, therefore this pool always proved itself to be a prime target for the poachers to set their nets.

As we approached the pool, one of our team noticed movement along the bankside and a disturbance on the surface of the water. We crouched down onto our knees, we waited, we observed for a few minutes and we all agreed the laying of nets was in progress. We were observing at least two people, but who was to say there wasn't more? Remember, it's really pretty dark in the middle of the night. We were also aware there may have been others posted as "look-outs."

We inched forward, step by step, getting closer by the minute and, to be honest, things were going pretty well. The poachers were totally oblivious and unaware of our presence and going about their business as though nothing was taking place behind them. Then it happened, the stalker's nightmare. The sound of a twig or branch breaking under one's feet, the moment of surprise blown. The poachers immediately realised what was going down and took flight, throwing themselves into the pool and swimming right across the deep section of the pool. Now, being local and having fished here for most of my life, I knew that just a few yards upstream the water was only about waist deep and very crossable with waders without getting wet, that's if you were wearing waders, we were not! Only good sturdy walking boots, but nevertheless, that's where I headed straight into the water, swiftly followed by the younger of the two bailiffs who were accompanying me.

Yes we gave chase, yes we crossed the river, up and across the field opposite but unfortunately, only to see three figures disappear over the skyline. If only we had managed to get a few feet closer, or even had our full team with two or three on the other bank we would have caught these guys.

Anyway, it wasn't to be, back to our third colleague. By the time myself and my colleague had returned to the scene of the crime, totally out of breath I may add, he had discovered one gill net completely set, one gill net partially set, a landing net, a rod and reel (which were obviously just for show) and a bag. As a team we then started to remove the net which had been strung across the pool. Guess what? One big fresh-run salmon of approximately 16 lbs had already managed to entangle itself in the net. No time was wasted in retrieving this net as we had to get the fish back in the water as soon as possible.

Eventually, with care, we managed to release the fish from the mesh of the net and one of us spent the next few minutes reviving the fish before its power and strength returned, allowing the fish to swim away into the depths of the river before disappearing from sight, a fantastic sight to see and what a brilliant feeling inside. Knowing this fish will continue its journey none the worse for its experience.

On occasion, speaking as Mr Average Every-day Angler, I have been fortunate enough to have experienced a similar degree of feeling and satisfaction when I have been lucky enough to hook, play, land and RETURN a fish. But I must stress the fish must be handled with respect and with the due care and attention it deserves, without inflicting damage to the fish such as damage to their gills. These released unharmed fish will and do survive to continue their journey.

The story doesn't end here. Once the fish had been successfully released we searched the surrounding area of the bankside, just in case there was anything else the poachers may have intended using for these illegal practices. BINGO! In addition to what we had already discovered and retrieved, but to our horror, we came across another hessian bag which contained a further two gill nets, plus another smaller bag which, on inspection, contained, wait for it, two and a half pounds of Cyanide. Lethal stuff! If the contents of this bag had been introduced into the water God knows what devastation this would have inflicted to the fish stocks, not just at the point of introduction but, more than likely, for quite a considerable distance downstream.

It is a popular misconception that Cyanide takes the oxygen out of the water, hence the fish can be seen gasping for air near the surface or in the faster shallower sections of the pools, thus allowing the poachers to remove these affected fish with ease. This is not the case. In brief, what actually happens is the cyanide attacks the respiratory and nervous system of the fish and the failure of those bodily functions gives the appearance of the fish gasping for air (as if there was no oxygen in the water). It is the failure of the functions that kill the fish, a very similar effect as it would have on humans. It is very difficult to trace cyanide within the flesh or organs of these fish, but would I like to eat a fish which had been poisoned?

Due to the fact we had recovered such a lethal substance we thought it would be prudent to report such an incident to the police. With two of us still dripping water, we arrived at the local police station with our gatherings. After the initial formalities, details and equipment being taken by the officers on duty, we were asked to wait, wait and wait.

We all knew and accepted this was a Friday night and officers were maybe a little scarce on the ground due to a "typical" Friday night in the town, but this was getting ridiculous. As I said, there were two of us absolutely soaking and even though we were inside, it was still very cold and uncomfortable.

Normally, the assistance the bailiffs received from the "boys in blue" was superb, but on this occasion it was really very, very poor. So much so our head bailiff was beginning to get upset and began to lose his cool due to the lack of interest and attention we were receiving from the officers. If the truth be known, he was protesting so much, he himself was warned and threatened with arrest. If my memory serves me rightly, we actually ended up leaving the office in disgust and with no further action being taken. I leave you to decide who were the winners and losers in this event.

It makes you wonder - is it worth it?

**Moving on:**

A number of weeks had passed and success for our team of bailiffs was beginning to falter. Why, we asked ourselves? Were we becoming as predictable as the poachers, in respect to the type of night we patrolled?

The time of night we patrolled? The areas we patrolled?

To cut a long story short, we decided to totally change our routine and activity. Despite the fact the change may prove to be possibly detrimental to the fish, for example nets may be left in all night and we could lose a large number of fish, we decided it was a risk worth taking if it meant we could successfully apprehend the poachers. We decided to patrol in the hours just before daylight in the hope of catching the poachers red-handed as they removed their nets from the river.

We arrived on the water at around 5:00 a.m. patrolled our normal sweep and, low and behold, unsurprisingly there was a net strung across the water just where we expected one to be, so predictable! We unanimously agreed rather than remove the net immediately we would wait until we had movement in the form of the poachers returning. There were five of us on duty on this particular morning. Three crossed the river via an old railway bridge onto the north bank, leaving myself and one other bailiff on the south bank. We settled in to see what, if anything, was to transpire. You don't realise how cold one gets when one stops walking on a cold, slightly frosty, autumn morning - it was a bit uncomfortable.

By now, the morning light was just beginning to creep through when from over the horizon two figures appeared. They stood for some time, quite a distance from where the net was strung across the river, and they were obviously discussing something. We alerted the other group of bailiffs on the opposite bank via our walkie-talkie radios, "roger, figures clocked," was the reply. The nerves and adrenaline were now beginning to flow, hoping we didn't cough or do something which would undoubtedly have warned the poachers of our presence. If we did, the success of our efforts would be scuppered.

Eventually, the two figures separated and one crossed the river by exactly the same means our bailiffs had crossed the river a few hours earlier. Sure enough, our patience was being rewarded. The two figures approached either side of the net and as they started to release the net we moved in. Both parties were successfully apprehended.

We radioed back to base, and our radio controller (local radio ham) immediately contacted the police and instructed them as to where they could meet up with us to take the poachers back to the police station. As we led them away, one of the poachers which my colleague and myself had detained decided to strike up some conversation.

"I thought those things were banned?" he uttered.

"What things?" I replied.

"That thing in your hand, that stun gun."

I shrugged my shoulders and didn't reply. As we walked up the hill heading away from the river and ensuring no names were mentioned, we were constantly talking to the other bailiffs via our radio controller and the radios the other team members had, thus allowing everyone to be kept up-to-date with proceedings.

As we arrived at the agreed rendezvous point, true to their word a police van was waiting to arrest the poachers. We briefed the officers and told them we would follow them to the police station in due course, once we had retrieved the net.

Just before the poacher was put into the back of the van, my colleague caught the attention of the poacher and said: "Remember that stun-gun you mentioned?"

"Aye," he replied.

"Well, it not a stun gun, it's just a big heavy torch," and duly shone it against him to prove it.

My colleague turned to me and said, "If we had let him go away believing this was a stun-gun the next thing we know, we'll be facing a shot gun."

Food for thought in this day and age and as I said before, not for the faint hearted.

As we returned to the water we received a call from the other bailiffs letting us know the net had been successfully removed from the bank. Remember, this net had been set for most of the night and it would be full of fish, a perfect height of water for salmon to run.

Unbelievably, not one fish was trapped in the net. Sod's law! Very mixed feelings about this, absolutely delighted on one hand but so disappointed on the other. Rightly or wrongly I would have gladly sacrificed one fish, allowing us to retain another piece of important and vital evidence to support conviction.

We arrived back at the police station with all the physical evidence we had and each bailiff made a statement.

A number of weeks passed with all of us expecting to be called to appear in court in relation to this case.

However, eventually the head bailiff was contacted to appear at a meeting where he was informed no charges were to be brought against these poachers. Reason given – there wasn't enough evidence. Mostly down to the fact there was no fish kill. They needed a fish as evidence? Not being a lawyer – I don't know if this is true? Once again it makes you wonder - is it worth it?

# ONE OF THE BEST

## RIVER KEN

Any person who has been an angler for close on fifty years will inevitably have fished numerous venues throughout their angling lifetime. Each one of those venues will have their own unique characteristic and unique techniques which need to be considered and applied if one wishes to catch a fish or two. I am sure each and every venue will have its own special memory for the angler.

Indeed, I myself have fished over one hundred different venues ranging from rivers like the small chalk-streams of Wiltshire, to the River Tummell in Perthshire, to the River Alness and Carron in the north east of Scotland, as well as many wild lochs located throughout the Trossachs and Highlands of Scotland and, once I had discovered the art of fishing for pet trout, oh sorry, rainbow trout, numerous small still waters. I really don't mean to belittle the rainbow trout because I have, on many occasion, failed to entice this fish to take my fly but generally speaking, I think it is accepted throughout the angling fraternity, that rainbow trout are considered to be a little easier to catch than their wild cousins. Probably down to the rise and popularity of put and take fisheries.

Who needs to travel abroad when you have such a broad spectrum of game fishing opportunity right here in our own country and on your doorstep? But each to their own, as they say.

For many years as a boy, throughout my teenage years and well in to my twenties, I fished one venue in particular on a regular basis and, in my eyes, at that time, it stood out high above all others. This river was located in the south west corner of Scotland. It was the only venue I can honestly say, hand on heart, I was almost guaranteed to catch fish on every visit. No wonder I loved to fish this venue.

I remember my early visits to this river were as a junior member of my local angling club. For quite a number of years, the club organised an annual bus trip for its members to fish this venue. These trips were always well attended by both adults and juniors alike. It was one of the highlights of my year.

The bus would leave the centre of the village at some unearthly early hour but, to be honest, I personally never appeared to have a problem being there on time. As the bus headed towards the club's chosen venue, spirits were on a high. Most of the senior members of the club would sit near the front of the bus, with us juniors at the rear. I remember there always appeared to be a strange odour of breakfast slowly progressing from the front of the bus to the back, and why were the elder statesmen getting louder and louder as the bus travelled towards our destination? I was always amazed at the number of stories and the number of fish which had already been caught up to this point of the season. These guys must be some fishermen.

As I grew older and wiser I realised the small silver bottles which were being passed around the bus were actually called hip flasks and contained a malt or blended whisky. It wasn't long before I totally understood what that strange odour was! Today, I must be now considered to be one of these elder statesmen! No! I know I am.

For many years after the club ceased their outings to this venue, I personally continued to visit the River Ken as an individual, along with my father and sometimes friends. I was lucky enough to have a father who wanted to spend time with his son and, although he didn't really fish much himself, was always keen to get out into the countryside. As time progressed his interest in fishing grew and it didn't take much to persuade him into casting a line for himself and to visit different venues, he was the one with a car and I was not old enough to drive at this point in my life. Dad made a great taxi driver with great understanding and patience. I say patience as the first time I suggested that I would show him a great river to fish he agreed without hesitation. What he didn't realise was I hadn't a clue exactly where I was going! Well, you don't really pay attention when you are on a bus with your head stuck inside your fly box, worm tin or Mepps box, showing the other boys what was going to inflict damage to the trout stocks, more like them showing me! All I knew was the river was somewhere south of Ayr.

We used an ancient form of GPS, or, more accurately, memory and recognisable landmarks, as the chosen method of navigation. Turning left at Ayr onto the Castle Douglas road, passing through the Ayrshire towns of Patna and Dalmellington, on past Loch Doon which was away to the right then on into the Dumfries and Galloway region.

Earlston and Carsfad Reservoirs now to our left, all of this I could remember seeing, then we came to a junction.

"Which way now?" said dad.

"Turn right," I confidently said to my father, or I guessed.

Travelling just a few miles further down the road we entered the town of New Galloway. We arrived at yet another T-junction in the centre of the town. I knew the place for which I was looking for was very close to New Galloway and it was definitely about here somewhere.

Eeeny, meeni, minee, mo, decision made.

"Go Left dad."

As we left the town boundary of New Galloway I experienced total relief, there it was in the distance. I recognised the bridge spanning across the river with the riverside pub next to it. This was the location I had been looking for, The Ken Bridge Hotel. This was the hotel where we could obtain our permits to fish, exactly 52 miles from home, we had arrived. The fact that we now knew how to get there gave us the opportunity to return for many years to come, which we regularly did. It was not until we had visited a few more times that I realised I didn't need to take the initial right hand turn after Earlston and Carsfad. We could have veered left, continuing on the main road crossing the river and carrying on through the village of St. John's town of Dalry, thus totally missing out New Galloway and taking us directly to the hotel.

The river itself was actually quite a dangerous river to fish as it was flow compensated, controlled by two hydro-electric dams which we had already passed, located a few miles upstream (Earlston and Carsfad). The dam holding back the upper reservoir water would open its gates thus allowing the released water to flow into the lower reservoir, consequently allowing the lower dam to open its gates and deposit thousands of gallons of water into the river system. This sequence was virtually an everyday occurrence to produce electricity via the water driven turbines.

If, at the time of water release, one was fishing downstream of these dams the risk and potential danger to the angler was extremely high. If one just happened to be wading mid-river whilst the water was being released, the angler had only a few seconds to return safely to the riverbank as the river water level and force of flow greatly increased within a very short period of time (just a few seconds). The levels could rise as much as 4-6 feet, frightening and dangerous if you were to be caught unawares. The torrent of water is just like a tidal wave advancing downstream towards you.

Yes, there were warning systems in place, warning the public of potential danger and warning signs posted along the river bank, notification on the permit and a siren would be sounded at the dam just before the release of the water, which, to be fair, could usually be heard for miles around. But on occasion, depending on the wind direction, the sound of the siren would not be heard.

I remember one incident as a junior member at one of these club outings. The incident involved another junior member who just happened to be wading mid-water when the water was released. No siren was heard by anyone. It was the sound of a tidal wave which alerted him to look upstream, only to see this wall of water rushing towards him. Before he knew it he was up to his waist in water and struggling against the strong current to reach the safety of the bank. He threw his rod towards the bank as he shouted for help and fortunately he managed to grab onto an overhanging branch of a tree. Two senior members of the club, realising what was happening, rushed to help the boy, pulling him to safety and clear of the water. It could have been oh so very different.

The funny side to this event, if indeed there is one, is that the boy decided to build a fire, strip to his underwear and suspend his clothes over the fire on a makeshift tripod which he made from the branches of a tree, in the hope the fire would dry his wet clothing. However, after a while there was a strange smell in the air and he turned around only to find flames engulfing some of his suspended clothing. He wasn't having a good day. The only consolation for him on that particular day was that the weather was quite warm, so at least there was no chance of hypothermia setting in. That evening the junior member travelled home on the bus with clothing which was far too big for him, clothes which were begged, borrowed and donated from some of the senior guys. He was looking a right pitiful sight and wondering what he was going to tell his mother. How can one be so lucky and then so unlucky? But I'm sure his mother would only be too delighted that her son had managed to get out of that dangerous river.

There are anglers in the village who still remember and talk about that particular incident till this day. One can never be too careful whilst fishing, danger can creep up on one in a split second, especially when wading.

Back to the actual fishing. I also seem to remember during those early club outings, quite a number of our senior members appeared to spend much of their time during the day in the hotel and not on the water.

Over the years it became perfectly clear that the chances of catching lots of fish from the river prior to the release of the water was classed as pretty average. You had to "fish" for your catch, but fish were there and were there to be caught.

However, once the water had been released and the water level had risen, one might as well forget it. Never in all the years I fished the river did I see fish being caught as the river was in full flood. Maybe that's why the more senior members of the club were in the hotel bar. Even some of the juniors went inside to play pool in the back room of the bar (obviously, no alcohol for the juniors). These periods of high water varied in duration, usually anything from 40 minutes to about two and a half hours and sometimes longer. I assumed the duration of the water release was dependant on the demand for electricity. But, unlike the initial surge and accelerated rise in water level, which only took a few seconds, once the sluice gates were closed, the water level seemingly took an age (but in reality was more like 30-90 minutes) to fine down to its original height.

Once people realised the dam gates were closing, or had been totally closed, a mass exodus of anglers from the pub took place and the river bank suddenly became once again very busy. It was a well-known fact that as soon as the water began to recede, the fish in the river automatically appeared to get immersed into a feeding frenzy. No matter what bait was used, and with a modicum of skill, success was virtually guaranteed. Remember, these were not your normal stew-pond stocked fish, many were totally wild or had been able to "grow on" due to the abundance of aquatic feeding which was obviously available and being stirred up by these controlled spates. On many occasions quality trout were taken. Fantastic sport could be experienced during this period of time. Many entries into my own personal fishing diary during these years bore testament to this.

On one occasion during the month of May, we arrived on the water with less than ideal overhead conditions. The sun was high in the sky and temperatures very warm for the time of year, but the river still produced eight fish to my own rod (fly) and five to my father's rod (spinning). All fish landed were caught above the bridge, all were good quality fish (as in condition), with only a few being retained for the plate. Not bad for a few hour's work. A number of fish were also missed or lost. Great sport, but this was not unusual for the River Ken. No wonder we continued to return for many years. In fact, it was during this visit I carried out one of my own personal experiments.

I had often wondered, do fish feel pain? So, as I had hooked a fish in the crystal-clear water, I dropped the tip of my rod producing plenty of slack line which in effect took away the pressure of playing the fish. To my amazement the fish did not turn and flee to the safety of the centre of the river. It positioned itself just a few yards from where I stood, still clearly visible in the clear water. Facing upstream in the flowing water and lying just a few inches above the bed of the river, the fish lay there holding station in the flowing current as if nothing was untoward. I don't think it was tired out as I hadn't played it too long or too hard. The fish actually lay there for quite a time with me peeling line from my reel allowing the line to flow downstream with the current to eliminate any further pressure being applied to the fish. However, as soon as I re-applied some pressure, off it went into fighting mode once again, fighting like a demon. I asked myself, did this fish actually feel pain from being hooked as it held station? Or did it only react due to the fact it realised something "un-natural" was acting upon it as I once again applied pressure. Probably proves nothing, but it makes you wonder? At this point I quickly landed the fish, unhooked it and safely returned it to the river to fight another day.

As the years progressed, access to the fishing and conditions for this stretch of the river somewhat changed. All of a sudden, the facility to allow the visiting angler permission to fish above the bridge was removed by the local club. Initially, I found this very strange and very disappointing considering my club, my father, my friends and I had been regular visitors and had enjoyed the fishing so much for a number of years. I don't know the reason why the local club made these changes, but I just wonder if it was something to do with the amount of coarse anglers which were now travelling across the border from England to fish for coarse fish. There always was a head of coarse fish in the river (pike, perch, roach etc.) but over the years there were definite signs of an increase in number and species which appeared to move upstream into the river from Loch Ken. As Loch Ken was located just a few miles downstream this enticed increased numbers of coarse anglers onto the river bank.

I am not one to down the coarse angler, everyone to their own, but I do distinctly remember one particular experience which really quite annoyed me. A friend and I had made one of our regular visits to the river. We were fishing upstream from the bridge (before the restriction) when we came across an angler obviously fishing for coarse fish. All his gear was spread around him, umbrella, seat, numerous tubs of bait (worms, maggots etc.), two rods carefully perched on his rod rests each loaded with different bait.

As we approached, as one does we asked, "Any luck?"

"Yes," he said, "but nothing I'm looking for, only these vermin," as he pointed to the other side of his seat.

On looking to the other side of his chair, seven lovely brown trout lay in a pile. My friend and I just looked at each other. Vermin? We were absolutely shocked and disgusted. If he wasn't after trout, why did he have to kill them? This is one angling situation I would rather have not encountered or been able to recall. Was this an early example, or a contributing factor in influencing the decision of the local club to close the river above the bridge to visiting anglers? Being young and lacking in confidence to challenge we didn't pursue the issue, we just walked away in disgust. I think it might have been different today, challenge would definitely occurred.

However, it wasn't long before we found out that the visiting angler could still fish below the bridge.

Downstream of the bridge the characteristic of the river totally changes. It is wider and deeper with longer pools and less streams, but what we did discover over the next few years was that this stretch proved to be just as productive as the stretch above the bridge, with many trout being caught and, yet again, proving to be at its most productive as the water recedes from the hydro-flooding.

Another lasting memory I have regarding this particular river occurred as I was fishing with SKF Angling Club (my place of employment at the time). A good day had been had by all, but it was nearing close of play for the day and a number of my work colleagues including myself were packed up for the day. We had tackled down and changed out of our fishing clothing and were, by now, standing on the bridge looking upstream, waiting for stragglers to come to the weigh-in. It was at this point I bore witness to one of the largest salmon I had ever come across.

One of our members, namely Alastair Dowding, was walking along the high right-hand bank carrying a BIG fish and heading towards the bridge. From a distance you could see the flanks of the fish glinting and shining in the tea-time sun and it looked very much like a large salmon. When he did finally arrive at the car park there was a small crowd waiting to greet him. Salmon confirmed, a beautiful, fresh, firm, clean fish estimated to have been in the region of 20 lbs. But there was a twist! Alastair then proceeded to inform us he had not actually caught this fish but had just stumbled across the fish lying on its side in the shallows, just about a quarter of a mile upstream of the bridge. He just had to walk into the water and lift this very large, very clean fish out of the water.

On retrieving, he found the fish to be dead, but blood was still very fresh and pouring from just below the gill covers (throat) from where a large chunk of flesh had obviously been removed, the form of which got us all thinking, what could have inflicted an injury of this kind? The wound could be likened to that of a bite to the throat from a wild animal, or had some poacher had a go at it with a gaff? Various theories were banded about amongst us but I seem to remember the group settled for the possibility of an otter attack whereby the otter had maybe just bitten off more than it could chew! Well, we'll never know. One thing I do know was at that time, this was the biggest salmon I had ever seen.

The other extraordinary large fish from this river which sticks in my memory is that of a large pike caught by Bert Kelly (Dreghorn Angling Club). Attitudes towards the killing of fish during this era were somewhat different to those of today. This fish, for whatever reason, was not returned to the river, the fish was dispatched.

As we made our way home on the bus, some of the junior members were passing this enormous strange-looking fish around as if playing a game of pass-the-parcel. As it was passed to one particular junior member he decided to see just how sharp these dangerous looking teeth were? He duly placed his fingers deep inside the Pike's mouth and as he ran his fingers around this fish's jaws, one of the senior members of the club duly leaned across the seats of the bus and firmly snapped the jaws shut, clamping the boys fingers inside the fish's mouth. OUCH! The bus rippled with laughter but I don't think the boy found it too funny. The junior member returned home sporting a new ring on a few fingers, rings with a tooth-effect band I think they called it. Other junior members on bus found this absolutely hilarious and, it has got to be said, so did the boy's father who incidentally was also on the bus at this time.

After my father died I still returned to fish the river on a regular basis for a number of years. Not as part of the club, but with a few selected friends or family. We all continued achieving similar success in terms of fish caught but due to the increasing numbers of coarse anglers visiting the river (in their bus loads arriving from just over the border), it was never the same and eventually I stopped going, never to return till this day.

Shame really, but I have plenty of memories of the good times.

At the end of the day, I can honestly say from the times I fished as a junior and throughout my teens fishing with my father, fishing with friends and on into adulthood, this river still holds station in my top five venues, and considering I have fished over 100 venues I reckon top five means I rate this river very highly. I had some great times fishing the River Ken. I often wonder what it would be like to fish the river for trout today, if indeed you still can. Maybe I should leave just as is, memories. But without doubt, one of the best!

Remember the name - River Ken.

# River Monsters

## HOW WOULD ONE DEFINE
## A RIVER MONSTER?

Surely the definition of a river monster must be considered relative. Relative to what, one may ask? The size of the river or lake? The volume of water contained within that river or lake? Of course we also we must consider the species of fish living within that river or lake. Probably along with many, many more searching questions.

Like many anglers, I feel privileged to have seen many hundreds, if not thousands of "monster" fish. If not seen in the flesh, then definitely in a multitude of angling films, videos, magazines and photographs. It must be obvious by now, reading through the previous chapters of this book, my personal preference of monster fish is the Atlantic Salmon. I have spent many hours watching film footage of fishing for salmon and I have sifted through thousands of pictures of these magnificent fish being caught not only in the waters of Britain, but also from numerous famous rivers being mostly located throughout the Northern Hemisphere, surrounding the North Atlantic. Occasionally, even films and photographs reaching to the opposite side of the world, for example New Zealand, Canada and South America, featuring sea trout, rainbow trout and magnificent brown trout.

However, on my little rivers, a salmon of 10 lbs is classed as an unusually big fish, thus deeming it a monster. An average size of 5-6 lbs is the norm. These rivers do not have truly monstrous fish within, or do they?

Over the years, I consider myself to have been lucky enough to have borne witness to some really big monsters for my little local rivers. I have witnessed fellow anglers landing some of these fish and have spent many hours watching these fish fight their way over our dams within our river systems. During my time as a Crown warranted bailiff, I personally have released some of these monsters when they found themselves entangled within poacher's nets.

**Monster Number One:**

The earliest recollection of seeing, what I consider, a river monster was when I was about 12 years of age. At this point in my life I was nearly always accompanied by my father when I went fishing, even though my father himself was not an angler. He appeared quite content to sit on the river bank and watch me do all the hard work. I often wondered why he did this. It wasn't until many years later I realised and actually understood. I'll return to this later.

Fishing was my passion and when I was not at school I could be found on the river bank. I was virtually living on the water morning, noon and night. Although my mother worried about me being down by the river, at least she knew where I was. I wasn't roaming the streets causing a nuisance of myself.

The river had recently been in a spate and I knew there were definitely salmon about as I had seen them leaping and jumping in the pools the day before. I was desperate to get on to the river as early as I possibly could the following morning.

The following morning was a Saturday which meant my father didn't have to go to work, so he also got up early to accompany me to the river. In fact, it was that early it was still "dark o'clock," but no way were we leaving the house before a hearty breakfast. My father was a master at the early morning fry-up. Bacon, eggs, sausage and fried tomato garnished with lovely soft fresh bread to soak up the juices. Brilliant! I can even think back to when I was five or six years of age, watching my father make a breakfast like this at four o'clock in the morning, before he went out in the "paddy bus" when it was his turn to uplift all the other bus drivers and conductors who were on early turn.

Being well fed and watered, we gathered the rods and tackle and walked the short distance to the river, arriving at one of the renowned pools known as Milligan's Pool, a pool which always holds salmon. We tackled up and began to fish. Sure enough as time passed, salmon could regularly be seen leaping throughout the length of the pool. The hours passed with my father and I consistently casting lumps of beautifully designed and colourful bits of metal, Toby Spoons, Devon Minnows, Mepps and Droppen, at these fish. We even tried trotting out old faithful, the garden fly, but all to no avail.

By now it was approaching 11:00 a.m. and we decided a break was in order. We placed the rods down onto the bank and just sat for a while watching fish occasionally break the surface as they negotiated a small weir at the tail of the pool. It was during this break that two of the more senior members of the club arrived, namely Bert Kelly and Wilson Gillespie, and, it's got to be said, both were very experienced and accomplished salmon anglers.

A few moments passed exchanging pleasantries before they asked, "Is it all right to have a throw?"

"Of course," replied my father.

Sods Law! What happens next? On his third cast using a Yellow Belly Devon, Bert Kelly shouts, "I'm in."

WHAT! We couldn't believe it. We had just spent the best part of three hours fishing that exact spot without even a sniff of a fish. Well, at least somebody appeared to know what they were doing. I remember at one particular stage of the fight, the fish taking a very strong run heading for the far bank, stripping line from Bert's reel as it powered across the surface of the river like a torpedo, water spraying from its back like a hose pipe sprinkler system, bow waves radiating across the pool, until the fish literally slammed itself against the boulders of a vertical wall-like face on the far bank.

Surprisingly, the fish remained hooked and after a long, hard fight, Wilson slipped the net. I say slipped, aye, after three attempts he slipped the net under this monster fish. The fish doubled into the net as he struggled to lift it clear of the water. It was a fresh-run bar of silver, fat as a pig, 16 lbs of sheer muscle - a beautiful monster - well it was to me! The fish was about as long as I was tall. How did I feel? Gutted! But it is still a memory I cherish to this day. What a fish!

It's actually amazing just how often this type of thing happens. One can fish for hours and as soon as one takes a break or slightly changes location before you know it, someone else takes the opportunity to take your place fishing down the stream or pool, casts over to the fish you have been watching and trying to catch for ages and then, bang! Success falls to somebody else. I have seen it happen numerous times. Being much older and wiser (I think) all I now say is, good luck to them! There have been numerous occasions whereby I have done exactly the same thing to others. Swings and roundabouts!

*Playing a monster - in the no.11 pool*

**Monster Number Two:**

My next encounter with what I really do class as a "real" monster fish, took place during one of our regular and routine bailiff patrols. The river condition and level were at a perfect height to encourage salmon and sea trout to run upstream through our beat. Once again, the bailiff team decided to patrol a well-known and renowned poaching hot spot of the beat.

The laying of fine-mesh gill nets by the poachers was a regular occurrence in and around this particular section of the river, and experience told us we were virtually guaranteed to come across some nets. As sure as three times three makes nine, it wasn't too long before we located our first gill net of the night, a net which was well staked into the ground and spanning the river from one bank to the other. We didn't immediately remove the net, we took cover and observed for a while, scanning upstream just in case poachers were staking out other nets further up river.

After a short surveillance period without seeing any signs of movement, it was agreed the nets had obviously been set much earlier and we should make a move to extract the net from the water. Normally our team would be split into two sections, two or three bailiffs on each bank. It was an accepted and definite rule within our bailiff team, never at any time will a bailiff be left on his own, possibly leaving him exposed to danger or confrontation with poachers. Therefore, due to the fact only three bailiffs were available for patrol on this particular evening, the three bailiffs were together on the same side of the river. This meant there was no bailiff support across on the far bank, which in itself can pose a few problems. How do you manage to unhook the other stake on the other bankside onto which this net is attached? Maybe the nearest crossing point on the river is a few miles away. With the three of us adding weight to the situation we began pulling on one end of the net as though we were competing in the world championships of the tug-of-war event. Eventually, we could feel the stake on the far bank beginning to give, one final heave and out it came.

As we started to extricate the net and draw it towards us, it very quickly became apparent there were definitely fish trapped in the net. As each fish came to hand, we untangled the fish from the net, often having to use a sharp knife just to cut the mesh. We always endeavoured to release the fish as quickly as possible, thus minimising the amount of stress to the fish. The good news was we successfully managed to release quite a few fish of average size but, as occasionally happens and as one would expect, there were a couple of casualties which unfortunately failed to survive.

Then it happened, a fish of enormous proportions appeared motionless from out of the depths. "Oh my God! Look at the size of this," said one of the team. We lifted the fish clear of the water and it was immediately evident it was too late for this fish, it was dead. We laid the fish on top of the section of net which had already been removed. We did not try to immediately cut this fish free as our priority and concern was still to see if any more fish were entangled within this net. We continued to remove the remainder of the net. A further two fish were successfully cut free and returned to the river before we came to the end of the net. The net was now totally free from the river and could do no more damage.

As the other bailiffs had been retrieving the net, I had successfully managed to cut the monster fish free from its entanglement. I laid the fish out on the grass and we just stood there in disbelief, there was no doubt this was a monster fish for our water.

Unfortunately, as we had already discovered, the fish was well and truly dead, dead as a door nail. It had obviously been stuck in the net for some time and had failed to release itself. Guess who got the job of carrying the heaviest fish back to the car? By the time we reached the car I was knackered.

What were we going to do with it? Considering we had not managed to apprehend anybody for the crime, we didn't need the fish for evidence. We obviously reported the incident to the appropriate authority and it was eventually decided and agreed the fish should be donated to one of the local care homes for the residents to enjoy. Some would argue this gesture was the wrong course of action, as fish recovered from the nets of poachers were usually incinerated after being used as evidence against the perpetrators. As I said, we didn't catch the perpetrators so on this occasion it was felt that it's nice to be nice and the fish was donated as suggested. The only regret I have is I don't think anybody thought of taking a photograph of the monster. However, I still have the picture firmly embedded in my memory.

A true river monster for the River Irvine. The weight of the fish was 27 lb 1 oz. The author's best to date.

*Best of two for the day – 15 lb 8 oz of pure power.*
*(The second fish was carefully returned to the water)*

**Monster(s) Number Three:**

It's 3 December and the season is long finished, when the
bailiffs received a telephone call reporting a multiple fish kill
in the vicinity of the Laigh Milton Mill. A number of hasty
phone calls were initiated to quickly assemble the team of
bailiffs. Within a very short period of time, the team had
gathered in the car park of Laigh Milton Hotel (formerly an
old water wheel powered mill). Recent weather conditions
had ensured the preceding weeks and days leading up to 3
December had been devoid of rain and temperatures had
plummeted to well below freezing. Therefore the river was
left with abnormally low water conditions for this time of
year and the surface of the water could only be likened
to that of an ice-rink, with the covering ice being many
inches thick.

But we were not there to admire the lovely winter scene,
there was work to be done investigating the reports of a fish

kill. Sure enough, as we started to patrol the water's edge, there lying under the ice were many large salmon, motionless and staring skyward, these fish were obviously dead.

To be honest, the size of some of these fish at this time of year didn't really surprise me. I knew fish of this size ascended the river after the official closing date of the season. I truly believe I am one of only a few people who realised this at that time. Remember, the season had long since closed, so no anglers should or would be on the river during December. Therefore, most would not have known these really big fish ran the river at this time of year. The reason I was aware of these fish came to light many years ago, to be precise, during the years 1972 -1976. During these years I was serving my time as an apprentice engineer in one of the local factories, a factory which just happened to be located not a million miles away from Drybridge Dam (Girtridge Mill), where salmon could often be viewed negotiating this weir.

During the early part of my apprenticeship, and once I had finished my shift, I would regularly walk up to the dam and wait for a period of time to watch these fish running the slopes and ridge of the weir, even though the daylight was beginning to fail. Once satisfied I had seen enough of these fish (sometimes not), I would leave Drybridge and follow the course of the river downstream until I returned home, by which time it was usually dark.

On many of these visits I witnessed large river "monster" salmon running at this time of year. I remember thinking at the time, if only I could fish for these fish but, obviously, it was not possible. Many of these fish I estimated to be somewhere between the high teens and into the low twenties in terms of poundage weight. It was a great sight to see, exceptionally fast moving like torpedoes, as the fish left the deeper water of the pool below to ascend the first part of the weir. Water jets spraying over their snouts, head and back parting the water like the bow of a ship. One could actually hear the fish running as their powerful motor (tail) propelled them up the incline of the dam through the fast flowing water. These sights and sounds still remain with me today and are as clear now as they were then.

These magnificent beasts! They were so powerful, so strong, so able to fight against these fast flowing river currents. Nothing could stop them! An unforgettable sight!

As I stood looking through the ice I was faced with the other side of the coin. These magnificent fish lying dead in such numbers, I found it very difficult to accept the sight which stood before me. I pondered on the nature in which these majestic fish met their fate. Some may argue the thought that these fish were kelts, salmon which just didn't survive the rigors of spawning and had failed to make their way back down the river to return to the sea. I can assure you, these were not spent fish (kelts). I am sure the other bailiffs and those present on this particular occasion would also bare testament.

But we were there to do a job, we had to recover the fish and try to find out why these fish died. To successfully remove these fish it was pretty obvious gaining access to them was going to prove very difficult, not to mention dangerous, but we had to if we wanted to send samples away for analysis and investigation. However, at this point in time we were not really kitted out for the task in hand, to break through the thick ice.

As one or two of the team went in search of appropriate tools to break the ice, the rest of us went fish spotting. We continued to search upstream and downstream of the Laigh Milton Dam. Needless to say, more dead fish were located. Many of these fish were of a more normal and average size, up to 7 lbs. It wasn't just "monster" fish which had suffered.

Eventually, appropriate tooling was sourced allowing us to gain access to these fish. A substantial number were recovered, but others were just out of the bounds of our own safety, these had to be left where they lay.

However, enough fish were recovered to provide samples. Quite a number of the fish recovered weighed in at between 18- 22 lbs. These are very big fish for our local river, true river monsters, substantiating those sightings which I had witnessed during the early seventies.

Samples were indeed duly sent away to the appropriate laboratories for analysis and, in due course, the club received detailed reports of their findings. Although I personally didn't read the report, I am led to believe there was no evidence supporting foul play (pollution, poaching or poisoning etc). The report concluded that death occurred due to natural causes, the effects of extremely low water levels and weather conditions, coupled with the lack of oxygen in the stream, could not sustain these fish at this time. This was the official recorded cause of death. I am not clever enough to argue this point but I believe we just have to accept the findings and say death was just a freak of nature on this occasion.

I must admit, seeing all these salmon lying dead is not one of my favourite memories.

# Ultimate Computer

## THE FLY ANGLER – WITH
## INFINITE MEMORY

It's amazing the amount of information and analysis an angler has to mentally process before he reaches a conclusion or an answer to the question - how do I catch a fish? If he is really lucky, he might even end up with a desired result, actually catching a fish. There is so much information the angler has to gather, analyse and evaluate before he can actually formulate a plan of attack which may just enable him to catch this creature. A plan he then has to convert from theory into practice, even then on too many occasions this technically well thought out and professionally performed plan does not always work. It's then back to the drawing board. In comparative terms, is that not some of the essentials of a computer system? Computers require input of information, analysis and evaluation of such information, formulation of information, recording of information, memorising information, recalling information and sometimes may even come up with a possible solution.

Let us consider some of this information and thought processes which force us anglers to dig deep into the old grey matter to formulate a successful, methodical process to which we can entice, trick or annoy a wily old trout, or a very stubborn lazy old salmon, into taking our fly, lure or bait. This is where past knowledge and experience is invaluable. This analytical process is usually developed and deployed long before the angler even casts a line onto the water. Careful planning always plays a very integral and important part in transforming hours of unproductive fishing into that moment of success.

Although I refer to the fly angler, other methods of angling, for example bait and spinning, also require much similar analysis and planning. One should see the connection as I work through the following questions, which are posed to the budding (fly) angler. You can modify as you deem fit.

1.  What species will I be fishing for?
    Trout, salmon, grayling, pike, other?

Every angler knows that every species of fish has its own specific and unique attraction to the angler, its own animal instincts and its own environmental conditions in which it lives. These fish must constantly practice whatever skills are required by whatever means possible to ensure its continued survival. Survival, this is the bottom line for these creatures. We, as anglers, have got to figure out a way of defeating these natural instincts of survival if we want to be successful in fooling the fish into taking our bait. Man against beast.

Every angler has his or her own preference as to which species of fish they choose to fish. I personally have had a life-long love affair with the freshwater game fish. In earlier years, my fishing revolved around the wild brown trout. However, in recent years I have had a tendency not to fish as often for these beautiful creatures but, for one reason or another, I find myself fishing more for rainbow trout at some of these put and take fisheries. However, I still prefer to fish the more wild, hill-loch type fisheries, rather than just the man-made hole in the ground. Yet without doubt, as I have grown older, I love fishing for salmon on my local river, particularly during the latter part of the season when attention turns to salmon as they ascend the river to spawn. Fishing for rainbow trout most definitely takes a back seat.

Each species has its own well-deserved merits, a place in my heart and in my memory. There is nothing nicer than fishing a compact little river shrouded by overhanging trees, rippling streams and flowing pools. Watching a wild brown trout constantly rise to the surface to sip an unsuspecting insect off the water, as this little morsel of trout food drifts past the trout's feeding zone. Delicate casting of your fly is imperative (if only to ensure your fly does not get caught in the overhanging branches), landing your tiny artificial fly just upstream of the rise, seeing that all important disturbance on the surface of the water as the trout is fooled into taking your fly, line tightens, strike, fish on, or maybe not? Whatever! Sheer adrenalin, excitement and heart stopping stuff anyway. That's why we do it!

Then there's the rainbow trout which I class as a fun fish, big and burly, a strong and greedy fish. In this present time they are abundant, large numbers being stocked in many lochs, lakes or small still-waters throughout the length and breadth of Britain, indeed throughout the world. Due to their insatiable appetite and willingness to take the angler's offerings, it is generally accepted rainbow trout appear to be a little easier to catch. Just as easily, however, one can draw a blank and catch absolutely nothing, but what fun one can have fishing for these fish.

But to me, successfully catching and landing the king of fish beats them all. Why do we even manage to catch a salmon at all? Why does it take a fly in its mouth? What we do know as fact is that salmon do not feed once they leave the sea and enter into fresh water. They fast throughout the duration of their time in fresh water and throughout their journey to the head waters of the river and back to sea. I once again ask, if salmon do not eat in fresh water, how can we catch a salmon with flies or lures that are, in many cases, produced to be representational of food? Man against the mysterious beast. If or when one is fortunate enough to successfully hook and land old "Salmo-Salar," what a fantastic feeling inside. It is really "the cream on the milk," especially if one returns the fish to the river for it to live and fight another day.

Yes, I firmly believe I should have every right to retain a fish or two for the table, but returning a fish to the wild river feels – fantastic! Brilliant! These words seem to be understating the real pleasure and feeling one does experience inside when returning this beautiful creature back to its natural habitat. Supporting and holding the fish with its head facing upstream, thus ensuring a good flow of oxygenated water passes through its gills, watching the fish's gill covers for the first beat of recovery, eventually pumping like bellows and getting stronger with every beat. Remember, usually this fish has been fighting for its freedom to the point of near exhaustion so patience is often the key to ensuring this fish fully recovers, even though the water temperature can be very cold, numbing your hands and fingers. As the moments pass you feel (through your own hands) the life and power returning into the fish's body. Initially, maybe just a slight tremor of the wrist just above the fish's tail. Eventually, you feel a strong kick of both tail and torso. The tail kicks again, a little stronger this time. The fish is now holding station by itself and receiving very little manual support. Then, all of a sudden, the fish really kicks its tail and swims away, sometimes swimming away at a fair rate of knots, other times swimming away at a nice and gentle pace as it disappears into the depths to continue its journey, none the worse for its experience. My advice to any angler, bid the fish farewell and give thanks for the memory. This is the pinnacle of salmon fishing. A brilliant feeling!

*Carefully releasing salmon (grilse) - River Irvine*

On the other hand, if the beast wins (gets off after being hooked), man shakes like a leaf seemingly losing his reason all together, curses and swears, stamps his feet, jumps about, takes the huff and eventually dissects his own actions as if he was performing a post-mortem and thoughts of suicide run through his mind. I would argue that no other freshwater fish when lost, has this effect. Salmo-Salar.

Sorry, I got side-tracked! Back to the Human computer.

2. What type of venue am I fishing?

Is it a small stream or river, a large river, a wild Scottish hill loch, a man-made reservoir or small still water?

3.  Where in the country is the venue located?

Different locations throughout the country support different and varied forms of food for the trout to eat, plus not one part of Britain appears to enjoy the same climate at any one time. This obviously does affect the choices the angler has to make in relation to what technique he is going to adopt to catch his fish at a particular venue.

4.  What are the water conditions?

Yet again, another factor which undoubtedly affects the willingness of the fish to play, and indeed what methods and techniques the angler should use. Is the river fast flowing? Is it slow and canal-like? Is it high or low? Is it dirty or clean and clear? Shallow or deep? Is it flat calm, slight ripple or big wave? Water temperature - is it warm or cold? OH MY GOD!

5.  What rod should I use?

Is it suitable? What species will I be fishing for? Where and what type of venue will I be fishing? What conditions do I intend to fish (including weather). Length of rod, weight of rod, action (soft through, mid to tip, fast), make and manufacturer? Will it be comfortable and enjoyable to use?

6.  What reel?

Many centre-pin fly reels are on the market with varying specifications and configurations, dimensional sizes, line capacity sizes, models, varying capabilities and performance (for example drag) and varying costs. Does it match and balance the rod? But most importantly does the user have confidence in the reel and does he like using it? Just a multitude of considerations the angler has to endure in deciding what he requires from the reel.

7. What line?

Ask yourself, do I use a floating, sink tip, intermediate, rating Di3,4,5,6,7? Weight forward or double taper? What length of leader, what breaking strain of leader, what make and colour of leader? Decisions, decisions!

There is no doubt a well-balanced and compatible fly fishing outfit (rod, reel and line) will, and does, indeed enhance your own personal performance and probably make it easier on yourself. However, my personal belief is you don't need to break the bank to achieve this. There is a large, wide and varied range of outfits out there in the market which do not cost the earth. There are many quality and lower affordable priced outfits which will perform more than adequately for the job in hand.

8. Time of year and time of day?

Every experienced angler knows that this issue does have a profound effect on one's success rate. Experience has shown this, with reference to my own personal diaries, dating back to 1970. I have experienced more success during the periods of morning (8 a.m.-12 p.m.) and late evening, just about an hour or so before darkening until about an hour or so after dark, with much less and limited success experienced during the afternoon. There is one period of the day whereby I never appear to have caught many fish which is really early morning, when the mist is still hovering over the surface of the water. It isn't until the mist clears and lifts that I begin to experience some success. I have found this to be true no matter what species of salmoniod I fish for (others may very well have other experiences). With regards to afternoon success, I think the fish must be like the Spanish, siesta time. Although, it is more likely that the fault lies at the thick end of the rod.

As for the time of year, my fishing in the early to mid-season is always predominately for trout, with April and May proving to be the most productive months. With regards to salmon and sea trout in my local rivers, they do not really start to leave the sea and enter the river system, in any great numbers, until mid-July and August. Even this event in recent years appears to be changing, with the best month for salmon and sea trout return now being September. On the very rare occasion, it has been known for the odd fresh spring salmon to be taken in the early weeks and months of the season, but I restate, this has been very much a rarity.

9. The fly itself.

This is one area which is mind-blowing. There are literally thousands of flies produced which supposedly will catch fish for the fisherman.

Where do we start? Basically, there are only two categories of artificial fly, those that float (commonly referred to as dry flies) and those that don't (wet flies, lures, nymphs). Why so many different patterns? Flies are generally accepted to be either close imitations of actual insects, or are tied to be representational of a fish's food item. Some may argue that all flies are representational, are they wrong? Others? Who knows?

But what does the angler need to think about in relation to what fly or lure he is tying onto the end of his leader?

- His quarry - species of fish.
- Do I fish imitation or representational?
- Consider time of year and therefore what natural insects are about (for example may fly, duffers fortnight).
- Do I fish surface or sub surface (dry fly or wet fly)?
- If I fish below the surface, at what depth do I fish?
- What size of fly?
- Does the colour of the fly matter? I believe, very much so!
- What action will this fly have on and in the water?
- How many flies do I fish with? (Point fly and droppers.)

Hairy Mary

Silver Butcher

Silver Invicta

Black and Yellow Tube

Blue Charm

Peter Ross

Black and Yellow

Dunkeld

These are only a few of the questions surrounding the fly selection, I'm sure other anglers can think of many additional considerations in terms of fly selection.

10. Weather and overhead conditions. Bright, dull, changeable, calm, windy, gale, rain, dry, warm, cold? Air temperature and humidity, is it clammy and thundery, for example. All of these aspects have to be considered if the angler is to be successful. Again, experience and the angler's memory banks have a big part to play in the evaluation and choice of what techniques need to be employed to compliment the weather conditions.

11. Retrieve - do I fish the fly fast, slow (figure of eight), varied, fast and erratic (stripping) or static?

A fish's diet almost certainly comprises of mostly eating natural, moving, living creatures, whether it be snails, beetles, flies, insects or small fry. All of these, without doubt, are usually taken by the fish as the food item is still living and moving. Therefore, an angler will try to imitate, or at least try to replicate, the natural movement of the food item through his line down to the fly. This definitely enhances the angler's chances of being successful.

I'm sure the issues mentioned above only scrape the surface of the information needing to be evaluated to ensure success. In my opinion, there is nothing in this technological world that compares to the human brain and its ability to memorise and recall information to give success to the angler. However, in angling there is no guarantee for catching fish. It should go without saying, if after all this you have not caught a fish on the fly, fish the worm!

There is a poem I once read and noted many years ago. I have no idea who wrote it and I can't remember where I first read it, but it goes something like this:

> *Sometimes o'er early*
> *Sometimes o'er late*
> *Sometimes nae water*
> *Sometimes a spate*
> *Sometimes o'er dirty*
> *Sometimes o'er clear*
> *There's aye something wrang*
> *when I'm fishing here.*

This is very close to the truth. But, in reality, the fault usually lies firmly with the angler himself.

# FAVOURITE VENUES

Fishing since the age of ten, and with close on fifty years angling experience, one invariably gains the opportunity to fish many venues and locations, I am no different.

Throughout the past forty or so years, I have been fortunate to have been blessed with good health and the ability to travel, which in turn has allowed me to fish many different angling locations, albeit some only a few times with others on a more regular basis. In actual fact my records show I have drowned worms, chucked numerous forms of beautifully shaped metal spinning lures and cast thousands of artificial flies over one hundred fishing locations. Each one of these individual locations sports its own unique aura, special characteristic and inviting appeal. However, the majority of these venues I have fished are mostly located in and around Ayrshire, radiating out into the regions of the central belt of Scotland. However, occasional visits to further outlying locations and venues are also included. A compilation referring to these venues has provided the nucleus for this book.

Unfortunately, with reference to salmon fishing, I have never had the privilege of being in such a financial position whereby I could afford to fish on a regular basis on some of the more famous and most prolific salmon waters of Scotland, waters of such kind Scotland has many. Therefore, I had to resign myself very early on to the idea that I was only able to fish lesser renowned waters, whereby I could just about afford to wet a line or two. On the other hand, I believe some of these lesser waters offer a far more difficult and challenging experience to bring a fish to the bank. Arguably, the sheer volume and numbers of fish within these smaller rivers do not compare to those numbers of their larger cousins. There's no local or full time Ghillie to put you into the right position at the right time and no Ghillie to attach the tried and proven fly or spinner to the end of your line, to name just a couple of scenarios. Most of us have had to depend on those well-learned well-practised methods and techniques of trial and error, with the odd sprinkling of previous knowledge and experience to help us pinpoint just exactly what are the most productive catching methods and techniques, not to mention the regular "taking" points at these locations.

It would not be practical for me to write in detail about all of the venues I have fished, but I would like to share some memories relating to a few of my favourites. With reference to my diaries, and considering the information contained within, I noticed I could split these angling venues into three distinct categories:

a)  Rivers
b)  Large wild lochs or fisheries
c)  Small reservoirs or fisheries

Many years ago I decided to apply a very simple rating system to every location where I have been fortunate enough to fish. I allocated a number rating system from 1-5 against each venue.

**Rating - as follows:**

1. Would not bother me if I never fished this venue again
2. Nice to have fished, but wouldn't go out of my way to fish again
3. Always willing to pay an occasional visit to this venue
4. Impressed and enjoyed fishing - would like to fish regularly
5. Would always fish the venue at every opportunity

Using this scoring system, I was able to identify my favourite all-time top ten river venues. Not necessarily most fished with most success, but the ones I enjoyed fishing.

**Top Ten – Rivers:**

| | |
|---|---|
| 1. River Irvine | 2. River Annick |
| 3. River Clyde | 4. River Annan |
| 5. River Alness | 6. River Eden |
| 7. River Ken | 8. River Ayr |
| 9. River South Esk | 10. River Wylye |

Some of these rivers I have previously mentioned in earlier sections of the book and related some experiences encountered at these locations such as River Irvine (my local river), River Eden in Cumbria and River Ken in Dumfries and Galloway.

From the outset I think I should expand on the rivers to which I hold right at the top of the tree. Number one and two have to be the rivers on which I was raised and, I like to think, the rivers on which I "served my apprenticeship." Indeed, it is the banks of the River Irvine and Annick Water which are still my local rivers. The Annick Water is the major tributary of the River Irvine until it reaches the harbour at Irvine. The Annick Water is generally classed predominantly as a brown trout stream, although over the years this little river has also supported a number of sea trout and salmon. But let me talk about the River Irvine first, I will return to the Annick shortly.

I have mentioned the River Irvine in great detail during my introduction of the book, but I think it is worth mentioning a few other points with regards to the Irvine. As you have probably worked out already, the river's main inhabitants with regards to fish are brown trout, salmon and sea trout. Unfortunately, over the past 25-30 years the sea trout population within the river system has severely declined which, I believe, is said to be true for many rivers throughout Scotland. This to me is a worrying sign for the future. There is no way I would like to see the sea trout become extinct in our British waters. In my opinion, pound for pound, the fighting qualities of these fish are second to none. I know the "powers that be" have done extensive research into why the sea trout has declined so dramatically, but I believe more could and should be done to protect this beautiful species.

A number of areas stick in my mind when talking about the River Irvine. There is absolutely no doubt throughout my lifetime the Irvine has been a fantastic brown trout water, not just for myself but for many other members of the other clubs scattered along the course of the river.

It's not the easiest water in which to catch a fish, one has to work very hard to experience success. In fact, I've often heard it said, "If you can regularly catch fish from the Irvine you can catch fish anywhere." Indeed, a number of local anglers have gained Scotland international honours by "serving their apprenticeship" on the banks of the River Irvine and Annick Water, thus perfecting and honing their skills. And that's where we'll go next!

Annick Water is arguably classed as one of the best little trout streams in Ayrshire, particularly before the building of Bourtreehill housing estate in the new town of Irvine, and even taking into account the amount of past industry throughout its course. Historical competition records of Dreghorn AC can verify that this little river, on many occasions, out-fishes its mother river and a great number of competitions were won by those who caught trout from the Annick Water. Annick water rises well above the town of Stewarton, meandering through miles of arable farmland before it reaches the ever expanding boundary of Irvine town. Its characteristics throughout its length vary little; streams, pools, streams, pools, rocky bed and heavily tree-lined banks, but to fish the river, particularly with the fly, requires a high degree of skill in successfully negotiating these natural obstacles and extracting a fish or two from its depths.

During the first half of my angling life, I fished the Annick Water on a very regular basis, particularly during the early part of the season. However, in recent years my visits to this little stream have somewhat dwindled to virtually nothing, but there are those who still fish this little river regularly and know this water like the back of their hands. These anglers find much success. Apparently, the Annick Water still fishes really well in a falling spate (some things never change).

I mentioned earlier that salmon and sea trout are also present in the Annick Water, in fact one of my earliest memories of witnessing the capture of a large sea trout (I should maybe have included this fish in River Monsters) is when I came across an old stalwart of the local club, a real "old style" gentleman who went by the name of Sanny Turner, a master of catching sea trout on a trotted worm. On this particular occasion, Sanny was walking home down Dundonald Road in the village of Dreghorn. Sanny had been out fishing on the River Annick where he had met up with another local angler, a Mr Willie McEwan. Willie was accompanying Sanny as they lived reasonably close to each other, not quite neighbours but near as damn it. What was Sanny carrying? An enormous sea trout. With his fingers placed through the gill covers and with the fish's tail scraping the ground it was obvious he was struggling to carry this magnificent fish, a fish which when officially weighed came in at 10 lb. In all my years since that day, I have not witnessed a sea trout of this size no matter where I've fished, and that includes large sea trout which I have released from poachers' nets during my time as a warranted bailiff. I feel totally privileged to have witnessed such a fish. I know for a fact this fish still stands till this day as a club record for a sea trout, a truly memorable sight! Where was it caught? The River Annick!

With reference to the amount of migratory fish within these two rivers - as previously mentioned - there is NO doubt these little spate rivers cannot be compared to the likes of the Tay, Tweed and Spey. They do not "hold" the same amount of migratory fish within their system and realistically they can't even be compared to those neighbouring rivers of South Ayrshire such as rivers Stinchar and Doon, for example. But, to me as a lesser mortal, the River Irvine and River Annick are my rivers and I treasure them.

The River Clyde - what a river! Predominately trout and grayling in the crystal clear waters of the upper reaches. Although in recent years, due to the purification of the water in the lower reaches, salmon can now be found cohabiting alongside a modicum of coarse fish.

Salmon can once again enter many of the lower tributaries, but still cannot ascend to the headwaters of the main river due to one man-made obstacle (which in reality would not take much modification to allow passage for the salmon) and one natural unsurpassable feature, Cora Linn (The Falls of Clyde). This is a natural waterfall with a vertical drop of 84 foot. A fantastic spectacle and sight when the river is in full flood and totally impassable for the salmon of course, no matter how high they can leap. There has been talk of building a salmon pass, even at this location, but I believe many of the anglers who fish the upper reaches of the River Clyde do not want the building of a salmon pass to take place. They believe it would be detrimental to the natural and prolific trout and grayling fishing which is available in this area. I must say, it is a view to which I can totally sympathise. I have witnessed and experienced on numerous occasions the excellent trout fishing to be had above these falls. However, in recent years my visits to the River Clyde have also somewhat "dried-up." At this stage of my life I have a tendency and personal preference to wait till the latter part of the season and fish for salmon at other venues, instead of fishing for trout on the River Clyde.

In my experience, the prime and most enjoyable time to fish the River Clyde is just as darkness is falling on a summer's evening, I remember on a number of occasions fishing evening sessions up and around the villages of Crawford and Abington. As you approach the river you can observe numerous fish gorging themselves on the prolific insect life (which the River Clyde appears to have in abundance). Insect life which has spent most of the day airborne but is now floating on the surface of the water and in the process of laying eggs for their next generation. This is when, all of a sudden, the big trout appear. A massive bow wave shoots out from under the bank on which you walk, the wake cutting into the centre of the main stream. Obviously a fish of some substance and I can tell you, there are some extraordinary large trout in the River Clyde at this time of the evening which begs the question, where do they hide during the day? One never seems to see these fish during the day. One thing is for sure, they are definitely present and sure do come out to "play" during these short hours before darkness.

Over and above this, as darkness descends, other creatures of the night make their appearance. Bats fleeting past so close and so quickly they give one such a fright, but yet never collide into you. A Ghost Owl (Barn Owl) glides past silent as a graveyard and if one had not been looking in that direction at that particular point in time, one would have missed it, never knowing or being aware of its presence. The sound of the rippling water appearing to be magnified in the stillness of the evening. The sound of trout slurping and splashing as they attack their prey - fantastic! I'll move on...

Apart from the Crawford and Abington stretches, there are a number of other locations on which I have fished this lovely water. Upstream and downstream of the Wolfclyde Bridge, near the Lanarkshire town of Symington, and the Gordon Streams located just a short distance downstream of where the Douglas water flows into the Clyde and just upstream of Cora Linn. The Gordon Streams just happened to be the first location I ever fished the River Clyde. This visit was away back in 1969 just a couple of years before I started keeping a fishing diary, but I remember it as though it was yesterday. I was just a young boy of 12 when my friend's father (Mr McEwan) asked would I like to go fishing with him, his son (John - my pal) and John's Papa (Mr Melon).

"Aye, great." No idea where we were going, but it was a day away fishing.

We set off early the next morning, I remember it was just beginning to get light, no matter, I was wide awake so excited and raring to go, but it seemed like hours before we got there. In reality it was only about 40 miles away from home and at that time of the morning it probably didn't take us that long at all. Of course, the conversation in the back seat was all about the number and size of fish we were about to catch, no problem to us young ones.

We arrived on a nice, calm, clear morning with a tiny breeze. Mr McEwan suggested we all fished the fly. Now remember, John and I were just beginners at this fly fishing game. All I had was a brand new, but broken, nine foot Greenheart rod, new because my parents had just bought me the rod at the start of the 1969 season and broken because on my very first outing using the new rod, I lifted the top section by the thin end and SNAP. My parents were non-too-pleased, but dad being dad spliced it together, bound it with some form of twine, varnished the whipping and guess what, it worked.

Anyway, after talking in the car of all those fish we were going to catch, the fish appeared to have other ideas on that particular morning. Although to be fair, John did get a couple of small ones. We all stopped for lunch and returned to the car for something to eat, only to find out I was the only one not catching fish, I was down in the dumps. What was I doing wrong? Mr McEwan came to my rescue - he obviously knew what was wrong - it wasn't me, it was my flies (I think he was just being kind), but I believed him, even though there were hundreds of big Yellow Sallies floating downstream and I had tried yellow flies with no success. He opened his fly box and selected one single size 14 Iron Blue Dun wet fly and told me to tie that onto my leader. I duly listened to him and on went the killer fly to my line. We finished lunch and went back to the riverside. Guess what? Within a few casts I hooked a fish, not a big fish but it was a fish, surprisingly it wasn't even a trout, it was a grayling, my first ever.

As the afternoon progressed, I was getting more and more offers, although missing many of them, but I was now enjoying myself. Tea time approached and it was time to pack up. My total for the afternoon: two brown trout and three grayling, not one of any decent size but I didn't care, I was still catching fish on the fly - great!

As for the others, both Mr Melon and Mr McEwan had caught decent fish and, if I remember, John also managed to catch one good fish plus a couple of smaller ones. I thoroughly enjoyed my day, well the afternoon at least.

It wasn't until a few years later before I returned to fish the Gordon Streams, but this time it was my own father who accompanied me. Once again, I had no idea how to get there. I obviously hadn't been paying attention on the previous visit with John and his dad, all I knew was it was towards the town of Lanark so we drove about in the general direction along country roads just off the A74 main road. I tell you, my dad had some patience.

All of a sudden I recognised a junction. "Turn left, turn left," I excitely shouted, to which my dad duly did and low and behold, just a little further along the road we had arrived at the water's edge. What a memory (it was years before satnav).

What fly did we use? The Iron Blue Dun of course! Over the following ten years or so I returned to the Gordon Streams with a few of my friends. Willie Stewart of Cal-Air Angling Club, Jim Hek, with whom on occasion I still fish today, and you know what? Which fly always brought success? Yes! You've guessed, the Iron Blue Dun. Uncanny!

Even if one is not an angler, my recommendation to everyone is if you get a chance, visit New Lanark and the Robert Owen Mills Experience. Take the time to follow the short woodland walk upstream to view the Falls of Clyde (Cora Linn), especially if the river is high and flowing full tilt. It is a fantastic sight and even if you are 100 metres away you will feel the spray upon your skin. More so if the wind is blowing in the right direction.

The River Annan has very similar characteristics to the River Clyde, with both rivers rising not a million miles from each other in an area of Southern Scotland. The only difference, apart from flowing in an opposite direction (the

River Clyde flowing due north and the River Annan flowing due south), is that salmon can and do ascend right into the upper reaches and headwaters of the River Annan and just like the Clyde, the Annan also plays host to exceptional quality brown trout.

I frequented the River Annan on many occasions during my early teenage years, fishing with my father and my Uncle Tom, who lived in the small Ayrshire village of Muirkirk. It was he who introduced us to the Annan. He regularly travelled down to the Annan upon his old trusted blue Vespa scooter to fish for trout and salmon. However, when we arranged to fish together, the trusted scooter was left in the shed. My father always picked him up in the car on our way through the village of Muirkirk.

During my really early years of angling, Uncle Tom was my angling hero. He appeared to be a very successful angler and on many occasions when I visited my auntie's house, a brace of salmon were regularly to be found lying in the bath, salmon obviously caught by my Uncle Tom earlier that day.

Unfortunately, I was pretty inexperienced in the art of angling during these early years, but listening to my uncle and seeing the fruits of his labour must have been a totally inspiring and encouraging experience for me. There was no doubt about it, seeing these big fish and having these long, searching discussions with Uncle Tom most definitely contributed to my life-long passion.

Apart from the fish lying in the bath, another everlasting memory of my Uncle Tom and our fishing trips together is when we eventually did arrive at our destination he was never in a hurry to get started, but instead, the first thing he had to do on arrival at the water's edge was to take time out and make us a brew. Not from a pre-filled flask though, instead, I was sent to collect a small clump of dry grass and a few twigs. On my return from this very important duty he had, as usual, already formed a small circle of stones on the bankside with a crudely manufactured tripod towering over the circle of stones. Two or three bits of paper and some light flammable materials (such as my dry grass, small light twigs etc.) and he carefully lit the fire, fuelling it by gently blowing it to encourage ignition.

Once the flames had taken hold, out it came – Old Billy. Retrieved from the darkest corner of his bag, an old, battered, black bit of a can - a Billy-can - more like an old burnt bean can to me. The hook attached to this can was made from an old wire coat-hanger and was roughly shaped to allow suspension of said can over the fire. Again, I was the "Go-fur" - "Go for some water will ye son." I was sent to the river's edge to fill up the can with water from the "burn." By this time, the fire was usually well alight and was going great guns. He carefully placed the can on the hook and suspended it perfectly onto the tripod. Each leg of the tripod was seemingly measured to perfection to allow the can to sit squarely over the fire, thus allowing the water to boil in the optimum time. It's amazing how good a cup of tea tastes when made from the natural waters of the stream and over an open fire.

When my uncle passed away our excursions to the Annan ceased and for a few years my attention turned to the River Nith in the vicinity of the Elliot Bridge, south of Sanquhar. Unfortunately, these outings to the Nith never appeared to have the same attraction or excitement, nor the same success. It was only a few years after this our source for daily permits on this beat of the River Nith dried up, uncannily just before my father passed away in 1983. Hence, my visits to the Nith also ceased. I have not returned to the Nith to fish for salmon since, and have only returned to the Annan on a few occasions. But the memories of the Annan most definitely live on.

Another memory from the Annan which is embedded in the old grey matter took place just after I had started my engineering apprenticeship with SKF Bearing Company. Within days of starting my employment in August 1972, I had joined their fishing club. I was fifteen. The club had only one more outing planned before the end of the season and guess where? The River Annan. Wow! How good was that? Not only that, but the outing had been arranged for the same beat as I had already fished with my uncle and father on numerous occasions before, above the Red House Hotel, Newton and Whamphray.

I was not old enough to drive, so I was to travel with a chap called George Angus, accompanied by two others, Jim Annal and Alex Wallace. On arrival, we picked up our permits and headed for the river. We proceeded to drive to the top boundary of the beat, parked the car and tackled up with great expectations. We started at the top boundary where a large railway bridge of metal construction crossed the river, the bridge forming part of the main West Coast Rail Line connecting England and Scotland. Just below this bridge is a fast-flowing stream at the head of a lovely long, deep, clear-water pool, the deeper side of which hugged the right bank as you look downstream. A line of young tree saplings lined the length of this pool on the very same bank, thus restricting access, so fishing really had to take place from the left bank, the shallow side, allowing casting into the deeper side under the bushes.

From previous experience, plus stories relayed by my uncle, I knew this particular pool always held salmon, particularly this late in the season. Yes, on occasion, and as the morning progressed, the odd fish could be seen "head and tailing" at various points down the pool. We fished hard with no success, then somebody suggested a recce from the far bank. With the clarity of the water being so good, we may be able to see the exact points where these fish were lying within the pool. However, that would require crossing the river, either by wading across above the head of the stream or crossing the railway bridge. In times gone by I had witnessed my uncle crossing the river at this point, but he knew the bed of the river and the exact path to follow to get him to the other side, I didn't. To cut a long story short, but on reflection, two of us were very stupid as we decided to take the bridge route. It was really quite a distance along the track from one side of the bridge to the other. We went for it anyway. Fortunately, we didn't meet a train. I think if we had we might have been fishing a river in the sky.

Crossing the bridge successfully negotiated, we headed the short distance downstream to the pool in question. Taking care to avoid the trees and bushes, we reached our position overlooking the river. Sure enough, there below us lying in about six feet of water were a couple of salmon, their tails wafting with the minimum of effort, gently moving from side to side thus holding the fish in station in the flowing current, breathing easily with the minimum of effort. We quietly moved a few yards down the pool, separated the bushes and again there below us lay more fish. We repeated this action right down the length of the pool and, although we didn't count the number of fish, there were a few scattered about.

On a number of occasions Alec had cast his spoon (if I recall correctly I think it was a Toby) right in front of a fish's nose, only to be constantly ignored. Then on one occasion one of the fish decided enough was enough. The fish was for it, a quick burst of speed in the direction of the lure retrieve and with just a few inches before the fish caught the lure it hit the brakes. The fish halted in mid-stream as if it had hit a brick wall and turned away, only to gently return to the very same lie from where it started. Both of us had witnessed what had just happened, but of course this all took place below the surface. Poor Alec was totally oblivious to what had just happened. Needless to say, once we had explained what had just taken place, Alec hammered this place for ages afterwards but the fish never moved again.

By now time was getting on and I could see George breaking down his rod and putting all his tackle away. Once done, he appeared to retrieve what looked like a toilet bag from his fishing bag - it was a toilet bag - followed promptly by a small hand towel which was also retrieved from the depths of his fishing bag. Stripping off to the waist and entering the water, applying some form of cream to his face and then producing a razor, he shaved there in the middle of the river, put on his aftershave and proceeded to change the rest of his clothes. No wonder his fishing bag was so big!

"Right lads, are ye ready for the off?"

What's all this about I thought? Like little tin soldiers under orders, Jim and Alec immediately ceased fishing and started to pack away their tackle. I had no option, I just followed. I hadn't a clue what was happening. We loaded up the car and set off for home, with no fish, I may add. The next thing I knew, we were in a pub in Moffat.

"What do you want to drink Keith?"

Now remember, I was fifteen years of age and drinking habits of young people back then were totally different to those of today. I had never been in a pub, let alone had a drink in one. The only drink in which I had ever dabbled was pinching a sip or two out of my father's can of pale ale at Christmas or New Year.

When I eventually returned to the bar area from the toilets, the guys asked again, "What do you want to drink, Keith?"

I had no idea what to say. My only saving grace was earlier in the day I had overheard the guys talking of something called "pints o' heavy" and as quick as lightning, "half a pint of heavy" was my reply. I had four of them before we left, and felt it.

We left Moffat and headed home up the A74, through Douglas and into Muirkirk when all of a sudden, the car veered right and into the car park of Muirkirk Miners Club. Oh no, I thought. What if my uncle is in the club? What if I bump into him and he tells my parents?

Fortunately, I never did see him that evening, but the penny was beginning to drop! Working men's club, live music, drink, women - now I know why George got washed, shaved and changed.

I think I had another couple of half pints that night which is a lot less than Alec and Jim had. However, George couldn't drink a lot due to him having to drive. Do I remember what time we left the club? Even with only a few more small beers I think I slept for most of the way home.

Many years later I fished exactly the same pool with members of Dreghorn AC at one of their annual river

outings. The two gentlemen who were with me on this
occasion must have been fed-up listening to me telling them
how much I knew about this stretch and pools thereabout.
Nevertheless, they put up with me. As I mentioned earlier,
the River Annan is also renowned not just for its runs of
salmon and sea trout, but also for its large, hard-fighting,
quality brown trout. I was just about to unexpectedly prove
this. Fishing the same stream and pool below the railway
bridge, I started casting my fly at the head of the stream,
slowly progressing downstream every two or three casts.

About one third of the way down the stream, a strong take,
and what a take! The line screams off the reel and the fish
takes off downstream, words of, "well done Keith," echoing
behind me. But the fish was not yet landed. It fought deep
and dogged, and there was no clue as yet as to the size of fish.
Although something told me it wasn't massive, and it wasn't
a salmon, but it was definitely a good fish - but how good?
What a fight it was giving me, the fish using the current to
its every advantage. Eventually, the fish began to tire and as
it came to the surface for the first time this gave me my first
glimpse. It was a cracking Brownie and as it cruised past in
the crystal clear water, I could tell it was a cock fish. A few
moments later it was in the net. Not a huge Brownie, but a
really good one, a truly wild fish and in perfect condition
for this time of year. I have got to admit, during the early
part of the fight with the effect and influence of the strong
current, and the way in which the fish first reacted when
initially hooked, it led me to believe it was much bigger
than it actually was. Nevertheless, a beautiful fish of 1 lb 12
oz was landed. I carefully unhooked him, held the fish for
a few moments facing upstream until he got his strength
back and the fish was returned safely to the river, none the

worse for the experience and fit to fight another day. I know of, and have seen, bigger brown trout caught from the River Annan, indeed I had seen my Uncle Tom catch Brownies of three and a half pounds, but this was my fish and what a good account it gave of itself. It deserved to be returned and given its freedom - great memory!

The River Alness (Averon):

Over thirty years ago a very good friend of mine, and former secretary of my local club, decided to up-root and move to the north of Scotland in his quest for a new working career in pastures new. Until July 2015 we still met two or three times a year to go fishing while the wives went shopping. Over these years Bill has taken me to fish a few rivers north of Inverness, but there is one little river, a relatively short but fast flowing river from source to sea, which supports a healthy run of migratory fish.

The tidal water and town water is controlled by the Alness AC, with the remainder of the river fishing being controlled and managed by private estates. The river fishing is split into a number of beats, each beat supporting a limited number of rods. Thanks to Bill, I have now had the pleasure of fishing this lovely little river on a few occasions, particularly in the earlier days when my wife and I would travel north for a holiday break and, on many occasions, we would call in to see Bill and his wife Elspeth. Bill always appeared to somehow manage to secure permission to fish on a few of these rotating beats on a day ticket basis. I have been fortunate enough to fish the town water, beat two and beat four.

From what I can remember, the river was just what I imagined it would be. A small, compact little highland spate river tinged with colour - "tea colour" being the nearest comparison – fast-flowing, tumbling through narrow gorges creating short, deep pools with the occasional longer pool. I was not disappointed. No need for a big double handed rod, well maybe at most a 12 foot, if one must. The River Alness is my type of river. Not too wide, not too daunting, just a pleasure to fish. Casting and coverage of its full width is no problem.

13 August and the river is in perfect order, that tea colour again and a falling spate. Changeable overhead conditions with long spells of cloud cover. We headed to beat four, crossed the river via a bailey bridge, walked slightly upstream to a pool which, in my eyes, definitely looked "fishy." As I tackled up I couldn't take my eyes off the water. That probably explains why, after feeding my fly line up through the eyes of my rod, attaching my leader of 10 lb nylon and tying a size 10 Dunkeld on the dropper and a small Ally's shrimp on the point, I had to start again. I had failed to feed my fly line through one of the eyes, I hate doing that! However, I sorted it.

The excitement and feeling of anticipation had the heart beating fifteen to the dozen, well maybe just a little faster than it normally did, which was probably down to the fact I had already witnessed, even in this short period of time, a number of fish entering the pool and "moving" in the tail of the pool. It was very difficult to resist the temptation to head directly to the tail of the pool to cover these fish, but I stuck to my plan to fish the "head" and to systematically fish down the length of the pool covering all the likely looking taking points which, I must admit, seemed to be quite a few. A number of larger type boulders, or something of that nature, formed a major characteristic of the river bed. Every part of the pool looked as though there was the potential and possibility of hooking into a fish.

Now, being the gentleman that Bill was, and considering I was the visitor, Bill invited me to fish through the pool first. I immediately accepted his invitation, totally appreciating the gesture. The decision to ignore the fish in the tail of the pool appeared to pay off. By now I was approximately half way down the pool and quite visible, just a few feet out from the far bank, a small disturbance was being created on the water's surface.

This ripple was created by something lying just below the surface, subsequently causing the water flow to be deflected towards the centre and main stream of the river. I cast my fly across and down to the far side of the disturbance, my fly landing hard against the bank and just a couple of yards above this disturbance. I took care to mend my line immediately as it landed on the water, thus compensating for any drag or skimming which may affect the speed and course of my fly. Hoping, of course, I could safely guide my fly past whatever was below the surface, successfully avoiding hook-up on this possible snag, my fly appeared to swim past perfectly, allowing my flies to sink to the desired depth.

As the flies approached the point at which I expected a fish could possibly take, yahoo, the line tightens and shoots away! I gently raise my rod to set the hook, no sense in striking into the fish too hard, this would just increase the risk of ripping the hook out of its mouth and the fish would be missed. It was as if the fish immediately realised it was hooked, up and out of the water by at least two feet, obviously a fresh run grilse, a bar of silver.

I shouted to Bill, "fish on!" Bill, by this time, had entered at the head of the pool and had started to fish down behind me. The fish went airborne again and again! Fortunately, I managed to keep my wits about me and keep the fish on. A couple more long runs and the fish began to tire. I was now in total control, but I have had that feeling numerous times before, only to find the fish bidding farewell. Must keep focused, concentrating and watch the fish's every move, must stay in contact.

Keeping my rod high, but being very aware of the overhanging branches of trees which were blowing perilously near to the tip of my rod, I began to lead the fish towards the waiting net where, by this time, Bill was poised like a heron patiently waiting to pounce on its next unsuspecting fry. Needless to say, when Bill did eventually pounce, he expertly netted this little bar of silver and a beautiful grilse lay securely in the root of the net. It had taken the dropper, a size 10 single hook Dunkeld. Although not the biggest salmon (grilse) ever caught, it definitely was a worthy adversary. What a fight, what excitement and satisfaction it gave to me.

Personally, I think a 4 lb bar of silver straight off the tide is one of the nicest fish you will ever see, shaped like a torpedo, glinting in the sun like a mirror and, pound for pound, (just like a sea trout) what fighting qualities! On this occasion I felt this fish was a perfect size for the dinner table, so out came the priest to administer the last rites as humanely as possible. It's only fair. I think, no I'm sure, the hip flask made an appearance at this point.

After we had gathered ourselves together, I thought it was only right and proper to let Bill fish down through the remainder of the pool and finish with the first crack at the fish in the tail of the pool. Fish were still showing as they entered the pool from the stream below. Lo and behold, as he reached the final yards of the pool, his line went tight, fish on! This was a carbon copy of the fight I had just experience a short time before, the only difference, Bill had to be careful he did not allow the fish to fall back into the stream below because there was no way he could have followed with the contour of the river bank and the overhanging trees below him.

Eventually, I had the pleasure of returning the compliment of netting Bill's fish. Although ever so slightly smaller, the two fish were as alike as two peas in a pod. As I hinted earlier, it is not always the biggest fish which gives one the most pleasure.

What's that I hear Bill? Oh sorry! It's the hip flask calling. We sat for a while just enjoying the moments.

We fished on for a while with no further takes, so Bill suggested we should move further downstream to fish other pools. I think Bill just wanted to show me other parts of the river which, by the way, I fully appreciated.

"I suggest we should go and fish the tidal [town] stretch for the last hour or so," said Bill.

So, off to below the town of Alness it was. I remember there was a strong smell of whisky in the air, no seriously, I thought I had not closed my hip flask properly and maybe it was leaking. But no, we were fishing adjacent to a Scotch Whisky distillery, the fumes from which wafted in the air and across our noses. Lovely!

Still with the same flies on my cast, I fished through a couple of pools where again fish could be seen moving, confirming fish were still leaving salt water and entering the river system in a pretty steady stream. To be fair, by this time, I was just going through the motions as I had already experienced a fantastic day fishing. Fishing new waters, experiencing various beats, catching a beautiful wee grilse, good water and overhead conditions, good company - what more could one ask for? Just as I was reflecting upon all of this my line once again tightened, it was immediately obvious it was a fish of much smaller proportions but nevertheless, a very welcome little sea trout (herling) which had actually taken the Ally's shrimp. A fish of approximately three quarters of a pound but all credit to the little fish, it didn't want to be landed. I carefully brought it to hand and released it without lifting the fish clear of the water, this action made easy due to the fact only one point of the treble hook had embedded in the fish's lower jaw. It was easy to release.

It was now time to leave this lovely little river, we dismantled our tackle, loaded the car and, for a brief moment, just stood there admiring the two fish lying side by side in the boot. We then bid the water farewell and thanks for the memory, before heading back home to Bill's place.

On arrival a brief photo session took place in Bill's garden with the Kessock Bridge acting as the backdrop. It was then down to us to prepare the fish for the table ready for dinner. There's nothing like fresh salmon (couldn't be fresher) well prepared, well cooked and well presented, washed down with a lovely white wine followed by an evening of relaxation, good conversation amongst friends and oh aye, a few wee "goldies." Fantastic memory. Thanks Bill!

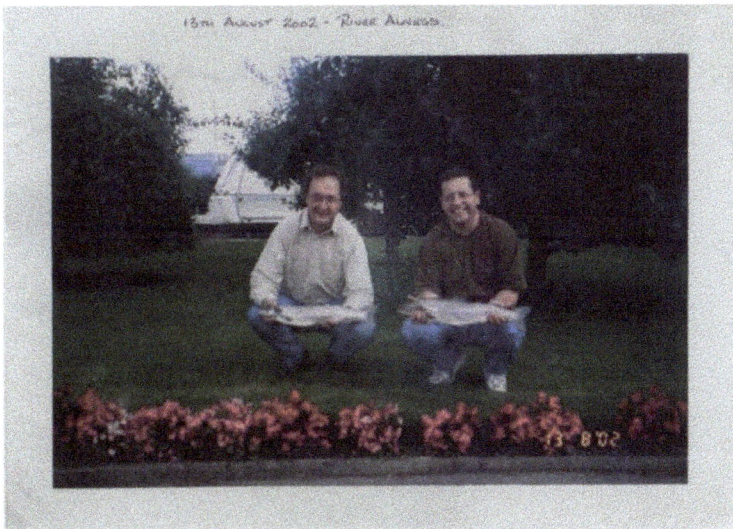

13th August 2002 - River Alnwick

*Like peas in a pod – I mean the fish*

**Record of Fish**

| Date | Species | Location | Length | Weight | Method | Conditions | Total on visit | Accum Total | Notes |
|---|---|---|---|---|---|---|---|---|---|
| 05/05/2010 | Brown Trout | Holmes Streams | | App. 1lbs 2 onz | Fly – Black spider & Winged Olive | Water very low **(1)**, clear & clean. Overcast evening with slight breeze – temp. drop after 8:00pm. | 3 | 3 | Caught 1 fish – caught 40 – River is absolutely stuffed full of Salmon Smolts. Also, many very small trout fry, once again proving succesfull natural breeding is taking place. Plus quite a number of trout between 7"-9". –1st. outing |
| 22/05/2010 | Rainbow Trout | Middleton – Largs – left hand platform on dam-back. | | 3lbs 12onz | Fly – Yellow Dancers | Water starting to show signs of Algae – Blistering warm day | 2 | 5 | JWAC – Fished until lunchtime with a degree of success, caught two, dropped two, broken out once, and raised one, went really dead at lunchtime – went to pub to watch football. 2nd outing. |
| 26/06/2010 | Blue Trout | Craufurdland | | 2lbs 1 onz 1lbs 11onz | Fly – G/H Damsel Black Buzzer | Flat calm, muggy atmosphere – Difficult to fish | 2 | 7 | JWAC – Few other offers/takes which were missed and was broken out once. Lochan very busy but few fish caught. However Grant managed four. 4th outing. |
| 17/07/2010 | Brown Trout | River Irvine | | | Fly – | Early morning – Spin/Fly level falling to great fly water in the evening.**(6/5)** | 4 | 11 | Although fishing for Salmon – caught a few trout. Only seen one Salmon going over dam mid afternoon. All trout returned |
| 20/07/2010 | Brown Trout | River Irvine | | | Fly – | Still a great fly water after rains had raised the river the day before.**(5)** | 3 | 14 | Still no signs of Salmon. All trout returned |
| 23/07/2010 | Brown Trout | River Irvine – Bogie br. & Burnt wood. | | | Fly – | Good fly water – **(5)** | 2 | 16 | Only fished for two hours – still no signs of Salmon. One trout an extraordinary deep fish – absolutely stuffed. Both trout returned. |
| 30/07/2010 | Rainbow Trout | Harelaw dam | 20" (510mm) 8.5"(470mm) | 2lbs 12onz 1lbs 6onz (Total 4:02) | Fly – Yellow Dancer | Very breezy – overcast. | 2 | 18 | Fished evening with JWAC – fish caught just before dark within last half hour of daylight. Also caught a small pike and two Perch. |

| Date | Species | Location | Length | Weight | Fly | Water conditions | | | Notes |
|---|---|---|---|---|---|---|---|---|---|
| 21/08/2010 | Rainbow Trout | Pinbraid – Left bank – two from just above outlet – two from bottom of Island | | 8lbs 14onz | Fly – Mini Black Fritz shimmy (3) – Pink tailed Pennell Intermediate line. | Water level higher than normal – Strong westerly breeze, early cloud changing to sunny spells later. | 4 | 22 | Fished with Johnnie Walker AC – Very relaxed day – Started with full Scottish breakfast, soup and roll for lunch, alcohol and good company – Excellent customer care from the fishery staff – Jim & Pauline – oh aye! The fishing was quite good too.This is what a days fishing should be like! |
| 25/08/2010 | Brown Trout | River Irvine – Above Gibsons pool & No. 11 | | | Fly – | Water conditions perfect (5/4) – Nice weather conditions also. | 2 | 24 | First signs of Salmon – Seen one guy catch one of the smallest Grilse I have seen (3lbs if lucky) – nice wee fish. Thought more Salmon would have been caught. |
| 26/08/2010 | Salmon (Hen fish) | River Irvine – No. 11 stream | 24.5" (623mm) | 4lbs 12onz | Fly – Size 12 treble, Blue Charm varient – (Gold body) – | Water still with a reasonable flow, with a touch of colour (4). One short heavy shower clearing to a clear sunny evening. | 1 | 25 | Good night on the stretch tonight – 3 Salmon caught and one missed. See August notes. |
| 17/09/2010 | Salmon (Cock fish) Brown Trout | River Irvine – Tail end Red Bridge Pool – Streams below Red Bridge | Salmon 23" (580mm) Brown trout app. 11.5" | 3lbs 4onz app. 10onz. | Fly – Size 12 treble, Blue Charm varient – (Gold body) – | Water level and clarity in perfect order after three days of big spates (5/4).Clear, bright evening. Dark at 7:45pm | 2 | 27 | Enjoyed this evening's fishing – see end of season notes. Also caught a number of smaller trout – all returned |
| 18/09/2010 | Salmon (x2 Cock fish) | River Irvine. – Bogy Bridge stream | Salmon 1 Unk. Salmon 2 – 26" | App. 3.04lbs & 5lbs 13onz | Fly – Size 12 treble, Blue Charm varient – (Gold body) – | Water level slightly lower than last night – still good clear flow (4). Clear bright afternoon. | 2 | 29 | See end of season notes. Also lost one Salmon and caught a couple of smaller trout which were returned. What a couple of hours fishing – great. |
| 19/09/2010 | Rainbow Trout | Lawfield | | Total 9.01lbs Heaviest fish 3.10lbs. | Fly – 3 x Black Fritz 1x Yellow Dancer | Clear windy day most of the time with one short rain shower. | 4 | 33 | Final outing of JWAC – Six members attended – won the outing. |

| Date | Species | Location | Length | Weight | Fly | Conditions | No. | No. | Notes |
|---|---|---|---|---|---|---|---|---|---|
| 21/09/2010 | Salmon (cock) Brown Trout x 2 | River Irvine – Top side Red Bridge. Trout, Red Bridge Streams. | | Salmon – App. 3lbs Trout App. 10onz each. | Fly – Blue Charm Varient again. | Perfect spate after big dirty spate **(5/4)**. Clear bright sunny intervals. Starting to go dark now around 7:30pm. Can only get a couple of hours fishing. | 3 | 36 | Only down five minutes when hooked Grilse – Slightly coloured fish, not fresh from sea. Returned unharmed – photos taken of release. |
| 24/09/2010 | Salmon (cock) Brown Trout x 1 | River Irvine – Red Bridge streams | | App 4.08onz B/T App. 6onz each | Fly – Black & Yellow size 10 treble | Again a perfect spate, just on the turn from spinning water to fly water and falling **(5/4)**. Bright sunny evening with a slight northwesterly breeze. | 2 | 38 | Fished all the way down from No. 11 with only some small trout. Decided to try streams below bridge. Now 4:00pm – Changed fly to Black & Yellow, immediate success — fish took about a third of the way down stream. Single photo taken, then fish released. |
| 25/09/2010 | Salmon x 2 (Hen fish) Brown trout x 2 | River Irvine – Carmel mouth & Tail of No.11 | First fish – 25.5" (650mm) | First fish – 5.07lbs Second fish app. 5.04lbs | Fly – size 10 treble, Black and Yellow & Size 12 Blue charm varient. | Great tea-coloured flow – perfect fly water**(4)**. Bright & sunny with slight breeze as last night. | 4 | 42 | Arived on the water at 11:15am. Started opposite Carmel mouth. Within minutes hooked into first fish. Landed safely. Worked my way down through No. 11 pool and on reaching the tail of the pool at 12:00noon I hooked my second fish. Both Hen fish and virtual carbon copy of each other.Photo's taken then second fish released. The real story of today — See end of season notes. |
| 01/10/2010 | Brown Trout | River Irvine Red Bridge Streams | | App 12onz | Fly – | Excellent fly water **(4)** – no signs of Salmon. | 2 | 44 | Fished for 2.5hrs. — Also caught 4/5 smaller trout — all fish returned. |
| 05/10/2010 | Salmon (cock fish) | Wires pool | 26" | 5lbs 3onz | Fly – Size 12 treble, Yellow Dog | Good spin water earlier in the day – afternoon seen water fall to good fly water **(5/4)**. even the wind had dropped. | 1 | 45 | Arrived on water at 4:30pm on a falling water. At 6:30pm hooked this fish in the Wires pool (between Red Bridge and the Silver pipe).Darkness closing in at 7:00pm. |

**Season Notes 2010**

**February** - Extra stocking of fish took place – 650 x 12"-14" (£2000)

**March** – After long periods of low level waters during January and February, March saw a number of high waters enhanced by snow melt – reports of a number of Kelts and a few Spring Salmon during first few weeks of season. Brown trout fishing very slow – even stocked fish proving hard to find – too cold.

**April** – Again early part of month saw long dry spells with low water levels. Weather still very cold. Later in month, air temperatures starting to warm up and a few trout starting to feed on flies.

**May** – Ventured out for the first time on **Wednesday 5th**. Water levels really low, but river is absolutely teeming with Salmon Smolts and very small Brown trout fry – fantastic – no real rain throughout the month, water levels as low as I have ever seen. Still no water on last day of May. Fished Lake of Menteith on **29th**. Blanked, although Bill Gibson broke his duck with two fish for 4lbs. Weather really changeable – very windy.

**June** – Had two short showers this month – but did not make any great impression to the river water levels – lowest levels I can ever remember. Trout fishing non-existent so far. Only fished the river once to date.

**July** - Even though it had been trying to rain for about ten days, **July 14th** saw the first real rains which made any difference to river levels – first real spate. A few Salmon witnessed going over Drybridge dam early Saturday morning of **17th**. During the following week the river was up and down like a yoyo – still no signs of Salmon. By the end of the month water level back down to low.

**August** - By mid month (20th), there had been a number of heavy, flash rainfalls but again not enough to give the river any great rise in water level, although a number of "freshening flows" were evident. Some reports of Salmon in the mid-upper reaches of the river – must have run through Dreghorn during July spate. **Tuesday 24th** – heavy rain producing a big brown spate. **Wednesday 25th** – perfect water – heard of a couple of fish caught and witnessed one myself. **Thursday 26th** – Water now really fining down, but still with a reasonable flow. As I started to fish the No.11 stream I had just finished saying to Hugh Skeoch that I had not caught a Salmon from this particular stream for a few years, when the line tightened and after a short but exciting fight, Hugh netted the fish. Nice fresh hen fish but not a bar of Silver. Just as darkness fell John Linsay caught a lovely bar of silver grilse at the tail end of Red Bridge pool – this is definitely the smallest grilse I have ever seen – 2.5 lbs – if lucky (found out later 2 lbs). But what a beautiful wee fish. Hugh also had an offer earlier, but missed and Hugh's work colleague managed a fish from the Holmes stream using a Rapala.

There were also some signs of some larger trout rising tonight which have not been evident so far this season.

**Sunday 29th.** Received reports of diesel pollution on the river Irvine. After investigation the source of pollution was sited between Crosshouse and Knockentiber on the Carmel water. Phoned SEPA. Apparently this oil/diesel has been running since **Friday 27th** and SEPA are aware of but will still investigate further. Await feedback. Water levels back down to low level. No signs of fish kill as yet. Definitely need rain now to flush out pollution.

**September** - It's now **Monday13th.** First rains for over a fortnight. However, early AM and still no difference to water level (well maybe a freshening). Hopefully the rain will continue for the remainder of day to give a rise in water which will allow fish to run and hopefully remove the remnants of the diesel spillage. SEPA located source, shut off and placed various bunds on the Carmel burn and River Irvine at the Red Bridge. Heavy rain did continue throughout Monday.

**Thursday 17th.** - Arrived on the water at 5.30pm. Water conditions perfect, fining down after three days of high dirty spates. Absolutely no signs of the diesel contamination. Prospects looked good. Started at the Carmel mouth and fished right through the pool with no success, nor signs of Salmon, fished through No. 11 stream whereby I caught my biggest Brown Trout of the season – even though it was only 10 onz but it was in prime condition and very welcome. Fished down Willow flats and had a short period above Red Bridge.

Approaching 7.00pm – I move to below Red Bridge to the tail end of the pool. Five minutes later I hook a Salmon, right on the lip of the streams. A short exciting fight took place before I slipped the net under the fish. A beautiful little bar of silver, fresh run, sea-liced Grilse of 3.04 lbs – a cock fish shaped like a torpedo. I continue to fish down the streams catching a few small trout on the way. I approach the end of the run just in front of the protruding clump of grass on the far bank when within two casts I get two good offers from, what were obviously good fish, and I missed both. All in all I really enjoyed tonight with catching fish and receiving offers on a regular basis. I finished at around 7.45am. What was really surprising, I only met two other anglers on the water.

**Friday 18th.** - Arrived at the Bogie Bridge at 1.30pm to find the river in excellent order, a little lower than last night but still with a good clear flow. The day was bright with a slight westerly breeze. I entered at the top of the stream and started to fish my small Size 12 Hairy Mary/ Blue charm silver and gold bodied flies. Half way down the first pass through the stream I caught a nice little Brownie which was duly returned. A Salmon jumped a little further downstream, just under the overhead wires crossing the river. Encouraging I thought. On reaching a well known lie near the tail end of the stream, the time now being 1.45pm, the line tightened and after an exciting fight a beautiful bar of silver, sea-liced Grilse of about 3.04 lbs was safely netted. You could have been excused for thinking this might have been the twin brother of the fish I had caught the night before. After a short period of admiration I duly returned the fish to the river to continue its journey upstream. It's a fantastic feeling to return such a beautiful creature. I gathered myself together and continued to fish to the end of the stream.

On weighing the fish at home – It recorded 5 lbs 13 onz on the digital scales and measured 26" long. Footnote – The search for a new net now begins.

I started "backing-up", still casting, still fishing when BANG – the line tightened very quickly and a fish, for a brief moment was on, until it jumped clear of the water only to release itself from the hook in the process – as I caught a good look at this fish I know this was a much bigger fish than the Grilse I had returned 15 mins earlier. An onlooker from the bridge shouted – "did it come off?" – "Aye it came off." Time now 2.05pm. Continued to fish, finishing my backing-up technique to the head of the stream. I thought I'll have one more pass down the stream, then I'll maybe move location. Five minutes later, with the onlooker from the bridge still watching, the line once again tightened. It immediately became obvious this fish was also a heavier fish than the one I had returned earlier. Again I played out the Salmon and brought it to the net – only to watch the fish burst through the mesh but fortunately, got caught in the strands just behind the dorsal fin – yet another cock fish safely landed. This fish, estimated at around 6 lbs, was fresh run but not a bar of silver. I decided to keep this one. After catching another few small trout I returned home at 3.45pm well satisfied with my last two visits to the river.

**Saturday 19th.** - Fishing the last ever outing of Johnnie Walker Angling Club at Lawfield Fishery. Yet again another breezy day at this venue. Clear for most of the time but had one shower during the day. Hooked my first fish within the first 30 minutes of starting – a nice Rainbow Trout of 3.10 lbs on a Black Fritz goldhead. Within the first hour had three on the bank – then all went quiet for a number of hours, although I still got some offers when I changed to buzzers on the surface, but missed them all. Eventually went back to the intermediate line using a Yellow Dancer, bringing success and my fourth fish to achieve bag limit. Total weight of fish – 9.01 lbs – enough to win the very last ever outing of Johnnie Walker Angling Club. What a fantastic three days of fishing. **What a fantastic three days of fishing.**

**Tuesday 22nd** – This extraordinary fishing period

continues. After a big, dirty and, in my opinion, unfishable spate yesterday, the water conditions are now once again perfect. Overhead conditions consisted of broken cloud with sunny periods. There was a slight westerly breeze but wasn't cold. Arrived on the water at 5.10pm and decided to start just on the top side of the Red Bridge. Within five minutes of starting my fly swung round in front of the middle arch and the line tightened, fish on. It soon became evident, it wasn't the biggest Salmon ever hooked and I had some fun trying to locate and dispatch my camera from the top pocket of my waistcoat. Had intended to try and take some action photos whilst playing the fish. This proved more difficult than I thought and after a few failed attempts to secure a good photo, I gave up with that idea and just concentrated on landing the fish. Photos can come later. Eventually, a lovely fish of around 3 lbs came to the net. Surprisingly the fish was not a bar of silver. It had obviously been in the river for some time and had shed its sea silver coat. Never the less, still a fresh fish and nowhere near full spawning livery (see photos).

Once photographed, I nursed the fish back to strength before safely releasing it to continue its journey. Yet again the same size 12 Hairy Mary variant (treble) claims another fish. That's now fish number four on this particular fly. I have now equalled my personal best for any one season with five Salmon. Surely, this success can't continue. Hopefully it will, because there is still plenty of time left to the season end. Over and above this Salmon, I also caught a few other small trout and hooked two reasonable sized trout in the streams below Red Bridge, all of which were safely returned to water. Post note – The following night, the river had yet again risen to a big, dirty spate due to heavy rain – didn't venture out.

**Friday 24th** – Arrived on the water about 2.15pm to find water in excellent condition after another two days of rain and big, dirty spates. After fishing from the No.11 to the Red Bridge with only a few trout (one reasonable) caught, I decided to try the streams below the bridge. I also decided to change fly, to a Size 10 Black & Yellow treble to try and get a little extra depth due to the heavier hook. I started at the top of the stream and within minutes the fish took. Excellent fight in the heavier, streamier water but eventually the fish came to the net – a cock fish of 4.08 lbs. After weighing and photographing the fish it was duly returned to fight another day – Great!

**Saturday 25th** – What the hell is going on? I can't believe this purple patch I am having. However, there is a twist in today's proceedings, which will be explained later in the memo. Arrived on the water at 11.15am to find the water conditions absolutely perfect for the fly – still a good flow and what we call tea-colour. Within minutes of starting (11.18am) I hooked into a fish in the lie just below the Carmel mouth. Fish hooked on the same Black & Yellow as last night's fish. As usual a good fight ensued. A few minutes later the fish was safely netted. A hen fish of 25.5" long and weighing 5 lbs 7 onz. Decided to keep this fish. I continued to fish through the No.11 Pool and, on reaching the tail lye, I hooked my second fish. Again a good steady fight before the fish came to the net. A virtual carbon copy of my first fish. Another hen fish, similar condition and colouration and, after weighing, found to be only 3 onz difference in weight. After photographing the two fish together, I duly stood nursing the exhausted fish, facing it upstream in the flowing water. A few minutes passed and I could feel the life and power returning. I let the fish go submerging my arm to let the fish lie between my feet a few inches off the river bed, the fish by now holding its own in the flowing water. I didn't move and just stood watching this fish. Eventually with a kick of its tail the fish swam across the gravel and into the depths, none the worse for wear. Fantastic sight to see the fish slowly swim away fully recovered from its encounter.

The time was now 12.15pm and I continued to fish to the Red Bridge. Point of note – by this time I had also caught a number of smaller trout. I took a break on the bridge speaking to Colin Bismor, reminiscing on days gone by when Colin also fished as a boy and young man. He asked where I was heading. I reminded him of an occasion when he lost a Salmon below the Wires pool and I informed him I hadn't caught a fish from that lye for a few years, but I always fish it through. As we parted I continued down the streams fishing towards the area discussed with Colin. This is where the real story begins. It was now 3.45pm and as I fished past the rock on the far bank just at the tail of the pool Colin and I had discussed earlier, my small Hairy Mary fly swung round, my line just stopped. I honestly thought I was stuck. As I pulled to free my line, low and behold, did it not pull back with a vengeance and tear off downstream – fish-on. I didn't even feel the take. It immediately became apparent that this was a much larger fish than I've hooked/caught all season. Eventually, I managed to bring the fish into the pool with some degree of control at which point the fish then duly decided to become airborne, which gives me my first real good look at the fish. Definitely a double figure fish and a bar of silver. So much for me being in control. Then the fish decided just to lie dormant in mid-stream, 11 foot rod severely bent but seemingly not making an impression. Just applied constant pressure. Eventually fish moved, only to take off downstream again. Followed fish until I managed to turn it back upstream. Gradually coaxing the fish back into the pool the fish was now beginning to show signs of tiring, so much so, fish now lying parallel to me virtually on the surface, giving me a second good look at the fish. Suspicions of a possible double, in my mind, now confirmed – you just know. Look at the tail on her. I could even make out it was a hen fish. After a few moments, fish decides to move slowly into the depths again. No panic. Just keep applying steady pressure I thought. This fish is definitely tiring. Now I'm in control.

Fish again waning and lying close but still not quite ready for the net. Not be long now I thought to myself. Then, after about nine/ten minutes of playing, guess what, fish decides it's not ready to give up yet. Fish turns tail and decides to head for the faster water beside a rock on the far bank. Knowing there are a few weed beds over that side, I decide to apply a little extra pressure to turn the fish, and to a certain degree successfully, but as the fish turns, the tail comes clear of the water and appears to land back on itself and onto the line. Fish lost. Maybe expecting to land a third fish was asking too much, but it still doesn't ease the pain. I would have loved to have netted this fish after such a fight. I returned home, wondering why it is always the ones you lose that you remember in such great detail and not the ones you land. Oh by the way, I also caught quite a few Brownies, two of which made acceptable length. All Brownies returned to water of course.

**Anyway, I can't complain. Eight fish landed to date**

**(four of which returned)** and two fish lost. What a fantastic period of fishing. Long may it continue.

**September** – Ending with heavy rain and high waters. Receiving good fish catches throughout the river system – Kilmarnock, Galston etc.

**October** – Tuesday 5th – The Saga does continue. The river was once again dropping to a fishable level for the fly. I had fished for a short time in the morning but felt the river was still a little too high for the fly, so I returned home and decided I would try again later in the day. I returned to the river at 4.30pm to a much better level. I quickly fished through No.11 and Willow flat. Fished down through the streams below the Red Bridge and down into the Wires Pool. At 6.35pm I hooked a Salmon. A good strong fight was experienced before bringing the 5 lbs 3 onz cock fish to the net. The fish had taken a small size 12 treble – Yellow Dog in mid pool. This fish had a little colour but was certainly still fresh enough to keep. After considering whether to put the fish back, I decided that the fact of the matter was that this was a cock fish and there was obviously a large number of cock fish in the system this year. Plus I have returned a few fish during this "purple patch". I felt I should keep this fish for the table. With darkness now approaching at approx 7.00pm it didn't leave much time to continue fishing, so I left the river and returned home a very satisfied angler – again.

**Thursday 13th** – There's been no rain throughout the past week, and water levels are low. Haven't ventured out and have not received any reports (via the grapevine) of fish being caught.

**20th October** – the rains returned and during the final eleven days of the month saw three totally unfishable spates.

When the river did fall to a good height it was on the last two Sundays and therefore couldn't fish. With the darker nights, which left no time for fishing anyway, I did not venture out for the last three weeks on the River Irvine pools and with the water at a perfect height.

However, on **Friday 29th I** fished a new stretch of water to me, on the River Ayr – the lower reaches of the Muirkirk water. What a fantastic mile of water. Streams, pools, streams pools and with the water at a perfect height fish were showing everywhere. I fished with Fraser Strachan for four hours in the morning and during this time I saw one Salmon caught, two Salmon lost and I even managed to miss a take from a Salmon myself. I saw more Salmon jump in the space of four hours than I have seen on the Irvine over the past six/seven years. What have I been missing for the past umpteen years? A stretch like this, virtually on my doorstep. I will definitely try this stretch again in the future, although I do accept it will have to be quite late in the season, considering the beat is so far upstream. Both Fraser and myself did catch a few small trout (even on the Salmon flies) all of which were returned.

**November** – Extension period on River Irvine. First eight days of the month started with some real unpleasant weather in terms of rain and wind etc. which in turn produced very high waters, these being for all intent purposes unfishable except for the last three Sundays of the season where the water levels were perfect on the day. But guess what – we cannae fish because the law does not allow us. I even took a holiday on the eighth but couldn't fish, again due to the high water levels. If the truth be told, I haven't fished since the **9th October** due to water conditions. Doesn't look as though I'm going to get the chance of making double figures in terms of Salmon caught. Last day will be Saturday coming (13th). As suspected, never managed last few days due to water conditions – yet again, water levels far too high.

**Season Summary -**

a) Fantastic amount of Smolt/Parr during April/May

b) Long dry summer with low water levels – first real rise in water 14th July

c) On a personal basis, September provided excellent Salmon catches. Nine landed, four of which were returned – two lost and one take but missed.

d) Unable to fish the final five weeks of the season due to water conditions and timings all wrong – final four Sundays had perfect water levels but by law, cannot fish for Salmon on a Sunday.

e) For the second year in succession – still a distinct lack of good sized Brown Trout – why?

f) For the second year in succession – yet another pollution incident affecting the Carmel Burn/River Irvine. SEPA building a case for possible prosecution.

g) After two years of encouraging signs of Sea Trout returning to the river, this year turned out to be very disappointing – never saw one sign of a Sea Trout.

h) Yet another good Salmon run – This is the third year running which has had a definite increase in the number of Salmon in the system – Is the hatchery work paying off? Although it still goes on, it appears there is less poaching on the river, than there was a few years ago.

| Species | Qty | Total Weight | Heaviest Fish | Average Weight |
|---------|-----|--------------|---------------|----------------|
| Salmon | 9 | 40.07 lbs | 5.13 LBS | 4.08 lbs |
| Sea Trout | nil | | | |
| Brown Trout | 22 | unk | app. 10 onz | app 6 onz. |
| Rainbow Trout | 14 | 29.07 lbs | 3.10 lbs | 2.02 lbs |
| **Total** | **45** | | | |

| No. | Venue |
|-----|-------|
| 31 | River Irvine |
| 2 | Harelaw |
| 2 | Craufurdland |
| 0 | Menteith |
| 4 | Lawfield |
| 4 | Pinbraid |
| 2 | Middleton |
| **45** | |

Blanks – Kyle of Sutherland, Bonar Bridge.

Lake of Menteith.

## Water Level Grading - River Irvine

Very Low – Bare bones, virtually no flow between pools.

Low – Some flow but, very little carry-through.

Normal height – Constant flow between pools, fishable.

Good flow – usually second day after big spates (if no further rain) – tea coloured – good fly water – can be coloured if no higher spate (i.e. just enough rain to bring water level to this height).

Small spate – Excellent fly water – slightly coloured but can still take a fly. Verging on spinning conditions.

Spate – coloured – Spinning/Worm can still be fished.

Big Dirty Spate – Verging on unfishable – maybe worm at some locations.

Extraordinary big spate – Very high and unfishable – rubbish being washed down.

# River Ayr

It is only in recent years I have re-associated myself with the River Ayr. As referred to earlier, I often visited relations in Muirkirk, a village where the upper reaches of the River Ayr flow. I remember as a young boy going down to the river with my older cousin, Tom, to play, rather than to fish. If our parents had known where we were, I'm quite sure they would have been non-too pleased, but boys will be boys and to the river we went.

I remember seeing shoals and shoals of fish in the clear shallow waters, shoals numbering anything from five to fifteen and finding out later these were actually shoals of grayling which were once very abundant in these waters. Grayling and loads of brown trout could be seen darting away as we played along the river bank, well you couldn't really call it fishing. No wonder there were so many fish in this little stream, Muirkirk Angling Club, at this time, ran their own fish hatchery, stripping eggs from the female trout during their spawning season and fertilising these eggs with the milt from the cock fish. The hatchery had many successful years of rearing young trout, then releasing the fry into the main River

Ayr and into the Greenock burn. Brown trout was the main resident at this time, salmon and sea trout were virtually non-existent in these upper reaches due to the practically impassable weirs sited in Catrine and Sorn. Many years passed and eventually these dams were modified to allow the unhindered passage of migratory fish into these upper reaches of the river around Muirkirk. For some reason as I grew older and became more interested in fishing, I never did seriously wet a line on the River Ayr. Maybe it's because my cousin was never really into fishing, who knows?

It wasn't until 2011 I ventured back out onto the River Ayr and by this time I knew salmon were well established in the upper reaches. A work colleague, who also fished, had been fishing this area for a number of years and wondered if I would like to spend a day with him. Great, I thought. No problem.

He secured the day permits and off we went, heading for an area between the village of Sorn and Muirkirk. It was late October and recent rains had swollen the river earlier in the week, but by now the river had returned to just about its normal height. Things looked promising.

We crossed the river by an old swing bridge. We decided to walk upstream and fish our way back. We walked for about half a mile, passing a feeder stream which entered the main river across on the far bank. At this point the river appeared to narrow down quite considerably, but the river still contained a number of deeper pools and streams. I walked a little further upstream than my colleague into a nice looking pool about 100 yards long. On arrival a fish rolled – very encouraging!

I started at the head of the stream, taking a step down with every cast. It took me about 30 minutes to fish through the pool and as I did so, I witnessed quite a number of fish "showing", not one having the decency to take my fly, I may add. I moved downstream fishing as I went. Finally catching up with my colleague, he too appeared to be having the same luck as I. Seeing fish but no takers!

As we approached the next pool he pointed out that this section was somewhat of a renowned taking pool and suggested I should fish through first, considering I was the visitor. I duly obliged, once again fishing down the pool taking a step with every cast. Fraser entered the pool behind me and once I had moved to a safe distance downstream he began to cast.

We slowly progressed down through the pool, by this time I was reaching the final quarter at the tail end of the pool. It was at this point, just downstream of me but well within casting distance, a salmon moved in mid-stream just behind a rock.

"Did you see that Keith? Big fish!" Fraser shouted.

"I did so," I replied.

I cast my fly just upstream of where I had seen the fish. Seconds passed and the line tightened and I raised the rod, rod bent, fish on!

"Well d..." shouted Fraser, but before he could finish, the fish was off. Missed the chance! But it provided a few seconds of excitement.

We fished for a further three hours without success, that was the only chance of the day. However, I can honestly say, I saw more salmon leaping and showing in the short time we were there than I've seen jumping on the River Irvine in the previous five years. I was well and truly hooked on the River Ayr. Why have I never seriously fished this river before? Definitely missed opportunities!

Still with the memory of 2011 fresh in my mind, I once again returned to this stretch of the River Ayr during the late season of 2012, this time along with my son Brian. Needless to say, I headed straight upstream from the bridge and once again right back up to the top pool.

This time, however, the water was a little higher and the early morning mist was thick, visibility down to about fifty yards at times and cold to boot, but by 10:00 a.m. the sun was beginning to peep through and the mist was clearing. I had fished my way down through the upper pools and had reached the exact same spot where I had interested a fish twelve months before.

Honestly, without a word of a lie, as I cast towards the very same spot, the very same boulder, my fly lands virtually in the same place as before. I mend my line and within moments my line tightens.

"Brian, fish on," I shout, but there's no reply. I shout again, still no reply. I look around and glance upstream where I fully expect to see Brian as he had been following me down through the pools but there was no sign of him, the mist was still too thick. I realised at this point I was not going to receive any assistance to net the fish, if indeed the fish were to stay hooked of course. I played the fish for a few minutes then through the mist came a figure.

"Were you shouting me?" asked Brian. Considering the bend in my rod, he quickly realised it was indeed me who he had heard shouting.

As he approached he didn't ask for the net but instead he said, "Where's the camera?"

"Top left-hand pocket of my waist coat," I replied.

He fumbled about in my pockets for a moment until he found it and began to film, once he had figured out how to use it. By this time the fish was beginning to tire quite rapidly, but Brian still managed to capture a few brief moments of video footage before he thought of unhooking the net.

I could see the fish was pretty coloured and I immediately stated to him, "By the way, this fish is going back," even before Brian slipped the net under her.

If anyone has ever caught a salmon and released it at this time of year you will know the water temperature is pretty cold, freezing in fact. Holding a salmon in position facing upstream to aid recovery can, on occasion, take quite some time and before you know it, your hands and fingers become pretty numb due to being submerged in this freezing water. The coldness appears to travel up your arms and into the core of your body leaving you cold for the rest of the day. This is where experience counts.

I turned to Brian and asked, "Would you like to release the fish and I'll film you?"

"Oh yes," he replied.

 I thought - result!

After taking a few still photographs, still cradling the fish Brian scrambled his way down the bank and into the water where upon he duly proceeded to revive the fish.

"This water's chankin," he said.

"Aye ya wimp, why do you think I've got the camera?" I was laughing as I made the reply.

After a short time, the fish regained its strength and strongly moved away and disappeared into the depths.

*Brian releasing a coloured fish on the River Ayr*

Twelve months passed and once more we were back, but this time we had company. One of Brian's friends had just taken up salmon fishing during the season before and, believe it or not, actually managed to catch his first salmon, he was hooked.

We arrived and the water was at a perfect height but unfortunately as the day progressed the rain became more torrential. Salmon could still be seen moving throughout the stretch however, and indeed it was on this particular day I witnessed one of my life-long dreams. I witnessed a hen salmon cutting her redd in preparation for spawning. I just sat and watched. The flanks of the fish were flashing in just a few feet of water as she dug out the nest with her tail, she would then turn and circle around, drop back maybe a five or six feet radius and return to the exact same position and then repeat the process of forming the nest to receive her eggs. Nature in real time.

After a while, we all moved downstream to a likely looking pool. By now, the water had slightly risen and had slightly changed colour. Davy entering the pool first, Brian second with me to follow. Me? No way!

Three in the one small section of the pool? Instead I moved to the tail of the long pool in the hope of hooking a fish as they came over the lip of the next small weir which, in reality, was just a row of boulders stretching across the width of the river from one bank to the other. A few minutes passed and I turned to look upstream, just to see if the guys had settled into the head of the pool. Brian's rod was bent and Davy was scrambling back up the bank with a net. I shouted, "Brian, are you into a fish?" Stupid question really, it was obvious he was playing a fish.

I reeled in my line, attached my fly to the rod ring and proceeded to walk back upstream to where Brian and Davie stood. I removed the camera from my waistcoat pocket and began to film. Three seconds of filming were what I achieved before the batteries ran out. I fumbled about in the rest of my pockets where I knew I had a fully charged set of batteries and I eventually found them, removed the originals from the camera and inserted the new batteries. Right, filming back on. I raised my head only to see Davie slip the net under the played out fish.

Preparation and timing is everything! Brian had already decided during the fight that if he was lucky enough to land the fish he was going to release the salmon back into the river. So, after a few moments of admiring the fish with the obligatory still photographs I then heard those familiar words via Brian's lips: "Davie, do you want to release the fish and I'll film it?"

I couldn't help but smile and have a quiet giggle to myself, needless to say Davie agreed. Déjà vu. Brian always was a quick learner. For the next five to eight minutes constant grins and chuckling were passed between myself and Brian, unless of course Davie happened to look up at which point the serious faces were deployed.

"This bloody water's freezin', ma hands are numb," exclaimed Davie.

"Is it? Are they really?" said Brian, sounding surprised. There's no substitute for experience, experience counts!

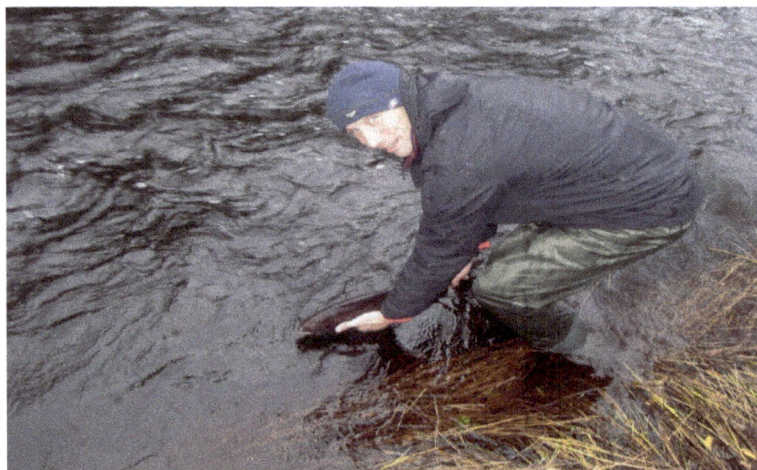

*Another salmon successfully returned to the river*

Reference to the Rivers of Ken, Eden, South Esk and Wylye have already been mentioned earlier in this book so I don't intend harbouring on, but there were so many good memories relating to all these rivers (and others). I so enjoy fishing rivers.

**River Venues Fished**

Rating - (Right hand column) as highlighted earlier in the book

1.  Would not bother me if I never fished this venue again

2.  Nice to have fished, but wouldn't go out of my way to fish again

3.  Always willing to pay an occasional visit to this venue

4.  Impressed and enjoyed fishing - would like to fish regularly

5.  Would always fish the venue at every opportunity

## River Venues Fished

| | | | | | | |
|---|---|---|---|---|---|---|
| 1 | Alness | 5 | | 18 | Irvine | 5 |
| 2 | Annan | 5 | | 19 | Ken | 5 |
| 3 | Annick | 5 | | 20 | Kyle of Sutherland, Bonar Bridge | 3 |
| 4 | Avon | 3 | | 21 | Leven | 2 |
| 5 | Ayr | 5 | | 22 | Lune | 3 |
| 6 | Black Water of Dee | 2 | | 23 | Nith | 4 |
| 7 | Bladnoch | 3 | | 24 | Ribble | 3 |
| 8 | Carron | 4 | | 25 | South Esk | 5 |
| 9 | Clyde | 5 | | 26 | Spey | 3 |
| 10 | Cree | 5 | | 27 | Stinchar | 3 |
| 11 | Doon | 3 | | 28 | Teith | 3 |
| 12 | Earn | 3 | | 29 | Teviot | 5 |
| 13 | Eden | 5 | | 30 | Tummell | 4 |
| 14 | Ewe (Estuary) | 1 | | 31 | Tweed | 4 |
| 15 | Forth | 3 | | 32 | Urr | 4 |
| 16 | Garnock | 4 | | 33 | Wylye | 5 |
| 17 | Girvan | 3 | | | | |

# Larger wild lochs, lakes or sizeable fisheries

| | | | | | | |
|---|---|---|---|---|---|---|
| 1 | Ardgowan | 4 | 21 | Hillend Res. | 2 |
| 2 | Awe | 4 | 22 | Invar (Galloway) | 3 |
| 3 | Brack | 4 | 23 | Ken | 1 |
| 4 | Bradan | 4 | 24 | Kirriereoch | 3 |
| 5 | Buidhie | 3 | 25 | Lake of Menteith | 5 |
| 6 | Butterstone | 3 | 26 | Leven | 3 |
| 7 | Carron Dam | 4 | 27 | Linlithgow | 3 |
| 8 | Chon | 3 | 28 | Lubnaig | 3 |
| 9 | Clatteringshaws Res. | 2 | 29 | Muirhead Res.(Largs) | 3 |
| 10 | Craigendunton Res. | 3 | 30 | Northird Res. | 5 |
| 11 | Doon | 4 | 31 | Ochiltree | 3 |
| 12 | Dornal | 4 | 32 | Pinbraid | 3 |
| 13 | Drumlangford | 2 | 33 | Pinwhapple Res. | 3 |
| 14 | Earlston | 2 | 34 | Portmore | 4 |
| 15 | Earn | 2 | 35 | Roscobie | 3 |
| 16 | Fad | 5 | 36 | Soulseat | 2 |
| 17 | Fitty | 3 | 37 | Tay | 2 |
| 18 | Fruid | 2 | 38 | Vennichar | 3 |
| 19 | Garve | 3 | | | |
| 20 | Harelaw Dam | 3 | | | |

## Top Ten

| | |
|---|---|
| 1. Lake of Menteith | 2. Northird |
| 3. Loch Fad | 4. Pinbraid |
| 5. Harelaw Dam | 6. Ardgowan |
| 7. Dornal/Drumlangford | 8. Roscobie |
| 9. Carron Dam | 10. Butterstone |

I have already referred to a number of the venues listed above, but I believe some venues are worth an additional mention.

## Lake of Menteith (LOM)

One of Scotland's premier trout venues, indeed some would argue THE premier fishery in Scotland, but surprisingly it is not known as a loch, it is known as a Lake. I absolutely love this venue, not just for its fishing qualities but also for the total aura of beauty at this picturesque venue with the surrounding scenery second to none.

The facilities and organisation are more than acceptable and the lake is large enough to be formidable and challenging in terms of actually catching a fish or two, and when you do catch, the quality of fish undoubtedly matches the scenery.

The lake is set on the southern edge of the Trossachs National Park, sandwiched between the towns of Callander and Aberfoyle. This magnificent fishery represents the cream of rainbow trout angling, but it also has another claim to fame which attracts and intrigues hundreds of visitors. Standing on an island in the middle of the lake is Inchmahome Priory. This is a much-visited Scottish historical tourist attraction and the priory is where Mary Queen of Scots sought sanctuary during her time before being transferred south to England where, as recorded in history, she was beheaded. For a small fee one can visit Inchmahome Priory by making use of the regular ferry crossings transporting foot passengers throughout the day from the Port of Menteith.

The other major visitor attraction which the lake lays claim to, weather permitting of course, is the famous Bonspiel. For those who do not recognise the name Bonspiel, this is an open-air winter event which involves the sport of curling being played on the frozen surface of the lake if and only when the lake completely freezes over naturally. The ice needs to be of such thickness it will support the heavy loads then, and only then, will this event take place. When conditions are right people flock from all over the country to either take part or to witness this event. At the time of writing, the last time the "unofficial" Bonspiel took place was in 2010. I say unofficial because the authorities at that time would not sanction nor would give the event blessing due to health and safety concerns. In reality it didn't matter, the event went ahead anyway. Furthermore, and better still, my wife and I were there to witness it. We walked from where we parked the car in a siding on the Callander to Aberfoyle road and onto the frozen lake, past the trout-rearing cages and on to Inchmahone. On leaving the Island we once again walked across the ice to the Lake of Menteith Hotel.

It was like a grand winter fair! The atmosphere was buzzing with numerous makeshift curling rinks having been formed on the ice on which many teams were competing. There were sledges being pulled by dogs, supporters and members of the general public were skating about the ice, even a Land Rover was being driven on the ice adjacent to the shoreline! Television cameras were filming the event and burger bars and BBQ's were serving hot foods located on the snow covered lawn at front of the Port of Menteith Hotel and in front of the fishing lodge. A quick drink from the hotel bar and then a leisurely walk back across the ice to the car. Who says we can't walk on water?

As for the wildlife which frequents and resides around Menteith, it is wonderful. So varied and second to none. Deer on the slopes of the surrounding hills and, if you are lucky, one may venture to the water's edge. Ospreys soaring high above the lake, then all of a sudden plunging into the water in the hope of catching lunch. Great-crested grebes swimming and disappearing as they dive under the surface and the unmistakeable signs of feeding fish breaking the surface right across the lake, it's little wonder why the lake attracts so many people from all walks of life, visitors from all over Scotland (and beyond) to experience these offerings.

*The unofficial Bonspeil 2010 – Lake of Menteith*

Back to the angling! Anglers flock to fish the depths of Lake of Menteith, I use the word depths due to the fact it can only be fished from a boat, the management and land owners do not allow fishing from the shoreline. For the occasional visiting angler Menteith it can be quite a challenge to catch a fish or two, it can often prove somewhat difficult. The lake is large and sometimes daunting, especially in rough or inclement weather conditions, but on the other hand many good, enjoyable and profitable days are also possible and if one is fortunate enough to have a good day (in terms of catching fish) these days totally out-weigh the odd blank day or two.

In reality, it took me five visits to the lake before I started catching fish and even now it's more than likely that on the odd occasion I will experience a blank day. But that is part of the fascination, challenge and enjoyment of the Lake of Menteith. However, I believe to experience the odd blank day stops one from getting too big headed and too overconfident, maybe just reminding oneself, you are not as good as you thought you were!

I mentioned the lake is fly fishing only and even though I have been tying my own flies for many years I am not the most proficient and my flies are not what one might call the neatest. In fact, some of my friends and fellow anglers look at them in despair. Many of these flies are supposed to imitate or represent natural flies and insects to fool trout into thinking your fly is a tasty natural meal, but do mine? I sometimes wonder.

I recall one occasion, fishing with the Crown Fly Fishers, and my boat partner for the day was Robert Irvine, really likeable and a well-respected angler to boot. We were fishing as usual with teams of flies when all of a sudden my line went tight, not in the water but actually in mid-air. Within a fraction of a second the water in front of the boat erupted. What the hell? It was not a fish, it was a bird, a swift to be precise, fighting with all its might trying to stay afloat ensuring it didn't drown. I carefully "played out" the bird, I didn't need to adjust my drag on my reel or even deploy the landing net, I just lifted and retrieved the poor little bedraggled thing by hand lining and brought it on board. To my amazement, I discovered the bird was not fouled or entangled in my fly line but actually hooked in the beak, honestly! The swift had taken the dropper fly in mid-air, a small Bibio, tied by myself.

I carefully unhooked this poor little creature which potentially had just made one of the biggest mistakes of its life, how lucky it was to have been landed. It was immediately obvious the bird's plumage was totally water-logged and just as obvious it wouldn't be able to fly until it had dried out. I passed the bird to Robert who in turn opened the zip of his fishing waistcoat and carefully placed the bird inside, hoping the heat from his body would aid the recovery of the bird. Fifteen minutes or so elapsed, it seemed a lot longer, and by this time the bird's plumage appeared to have dried out enough to attempt release. We felt it was ready to take flight so we headed to the shore to carefully place the bird on a high branch of a tree. A swift needs height to be able to open its wings to take flight and swifts find it very difficult, if not virtually impossible, to take flight from the ground.

As the bird sat on the branch it was obvious it was still in a state of shock, it just sat there motionless on the branch, but at least it was upright and self-supporting. We watched for a while with no sign of the bird wishing to take to the air, so I returned to the boat. I once again settled into my fishing position as Robert slowly rowed the boat back onto the lake, stopping just a few yards from the shore. Still keeping the bird in our view we waited a little while longer, still no movement from the swift, but we were here to fish and we had waited long enough. At this point, as if the bird knew we were about to depart and as Robert started the engine to motor, the bird took flight - result! There's more to fishing than catching fish!

One feature arising from this story, I thought, was that my fly tying can't be that bad. Even the birds think my flies are real! A point which, on a number of occasions throughout the remainder of the day, I made my fellow anglers (or doubters) well aware of.

Orders on a post card please - only kidding!

If you are lucky enough to be in the right place at the right time at the Lake of Menteith, you may be so privileged to witness another species of bird which visits our shores during the summer months. I, of course, refer to the magnificent and spectacular osprey. Imagine, this bird often migrates anything up to 3,000 miles from the continent of Africa just to breed and feed upon British shores. This magnificent bird of prey fishing for lunch provides us with such fantastic viewing, certainly beats sitting in front of a television. This is live action!

After many years of fishing the lake both during day and evening sessions, I recently had the opportunity to fish the lake for the first time, closely followed by a second opportunity, during an early morning summer session (4:00 a.m. – 9:00 a.m.). I absolutely loved it. Overhead and weather conditions on both occasions were very good, tranquil and peaceful, and there were very few boats on the lake which meant no other boats were cutting across your drift, a good boat partner and yes, the fish were on, on both visits. I will definitely look forward to fishing these limited sessions again next summer and hopefully beyond.

As a total package, fishing at the Lake of Menteith is not just about catching fish. I would unreservedly recommend it to everyone, a visit to the lake is well worth it.

**Ardgowan:**

Located high in the hills above the town of Greenock, west of Glasgow, is Loch Thom with Ardgowan forming the smaller compensation reservoir lying adjacent to the larger Loch Thom. Ardgowan is surrounded by beautiful scenery and is skirted by a well- known rambler's walk known as the "Greenock Cut," running parallel to the northern bank of the reservoir. Located at the west point of the reservoir is Cornalees Visitor Centre which acts as a start or finish point for these walkers (depending on which way they walk the cut of course).

Ardgowan is over-shadowed by the highest hill in the area, namely Dunrod Hill, and if one is reasonably fit and able to climb to the cairn on top of Dunrod Hill, one will not be disappointed. On a clear day your efforts will be rewarded with a 360 degree view second to none. Views to the west overlooking the Firth of Clyde in which the Islands of Cumbrae are located, with a backdrop of the larger Island of Arran in the background. As you turn clockwise you will witness the views towards the Cowal Peninsula and the Arrochar Hills, moving on to views over the city of Glasgow and the most southerly of Scotland's Bens, Ben Lomond, with an elevation of 974 metres.

Continuing a clockwise rotation, moving through east to south, taking in the sights of Renfrewshire and most of Ayrshire, you now reach a stage where you virtually face due south and if you are really, really lucky and have a perfect clear day, in the far distance you might see (although very faintly) what I believe is the Merrick, the highest hill in the Scottish Southern Uplands. The Merrick lies within the Galloway Forrest and National Park Dumfries and Galloway. Moving from south to west, your eyes sweep across the Clyde Estuary as it opens out into the Irish Sea, Ailsa Craig (Paddy's Milestone) protruding from the sea in mid-channel in the shape of a Christmas pudding and finally, rotating back to where one started looking over the Cumbraes.

Ardgowan's fishing lodge and Cornalees Bridge Visitor Centre are, as I said, located at the west end of the reservoir and from here one can follow a single track road which winds its way down through the wild moorland-like landscape of Brisbane Glen, before reaching the popular Ayrshire seaside holiday town of Largs.

At 37 acres, I class Ardgowan as a larger, wild-looking fishery and I rate it very highly. I have fished this venue as a visitor on quite a number of occasions and, I must admit, with a fair amount of success for my efforts. Although my successes have been predominately catching rainbow trout in the region of 1.5-2.5 lbs, I know there are much larger fish to be had in Ardgowan. Indeed, I have been in the company of people who have caught much larger fish; trout in the region of 7-8 lbs, for example, but to me, catching these bigger fish might be nice but it's not the end of the world if you don't. It's the fuller picture and aura of this venue that I like and if one is in good company catching the odd fish and experiencing and enjoying the environment in which you are fishing must be the ultimate pleasure in terms of angling. All this makes Ardgowan one of my favourite venues. There's more to fishing than catching fish.

## Small Still Waters - Ratings as previously

| | | | | | | |
|---|---|---|---|---|---|---|
| 1 | Annbank | 1 | 18 | Orchil Fishery | 3 |
| 2 | Arranview | 1 | 19 | Raithe Res.( Prestwick) | 3 |
| 3 | Bowden Springs Fishery | 2 | 20 | Regal Fishery Drumclog | 3 |
| 4 | Burnfoot Res. | 4 | 21 | Rough Loch | 1 |
| 5 | Burns Fishery(Tarbolton) | 3 | 22 | Solway Fishery | 2 |
| 6 | Cowans Law | 2 | 23 | Springwater Fishery | 3 |
| 7 | Coyle Water | 3 | 24 | Stable Lakes | 2 |
| 8 | Craufurdland | 3 | 25 | Swanswater | 2 |
| 9 | Dalvennan | 2 | 26 | Troon Res. | 3 |
| 10 | Drum Fishery | 2 | 27 | Unknown Lochan- J Pape | 3 |
| 11 | Fintalla Loch | 2 | 28 | Unknown Lochan- Crocketford | 2 |
| 12 | Glenburn Res./ Fairlie Moor | 4 | 29 | Waterside Fishery | 1 |
| 13 | Howwood | 3 | 30 | Morton Castle- Drumlanrigg | 4 |
| 14 | Kilchrist Fishery | 1 | 31 | Achagour (Tain) | |
| 15 | Loch Heathe- Glen Clova | 2 | 32 | Achagour (Tain) | |
| 16 | Middleton | 2 | | | |
| 17 | Northcraig Res. | 1 | | | |

**Top Ten**

| | |
|---|---|
| 1. Burns Fishery | 2. Glenburn/Fairlie Moor |
| 3. Middleton | 4. Morton Castle |
| 5. Swanswater | 6. John Pape's private Lochan |
| 7. Orchil | 8. Springwater |
| 9. Howwood | 10. Craufurdland |

Small put and take fisheries didn't really come to my attention until the early to mid-1990s. I was quite happy fishing rivers and large wild lochs, but once I discovered the potential of catching fish relatively easily on a regular basis then I can honestly say, it whetted my appetite for quite a number of years.

Fishing for rainbow trout at these smaller venues was something different and yes, initially a challenge, not only in respect of a different species, but applying different techniques and flies of different form. Tying flies and lures such as Cat's Whisker, Damsel, Black Fritz and so on was all alien to me and initially I found it very hard to accept I was tying flies of such proportions to entice trout, I did not even tie salmon flies to these dimensions. As the years have progressed I have learned it does not have to be big ugly lures you need to catch rainbow trout, indeed, I have caught many, many rainbow trout on very small flies, including many "traditional" trout fly patterns. Nevertheless, rainbow trout fishing can still produce some very challenging days! I mean blank days. Even the most experienced of rainbow trout anglers can have off-days. However, angling for rainbow trout can be very enjoyable whether fishing with big lures or small imitation flies.

One typical scenario, which appears to get my adrenaline flowing whilst fishing for Rainbow trout, is when my fly is on or just under the surface. My line is a fair distance out and I start to retrieve the fly, when all of a sudden a bow wave appears just a few yards behind the fly. Sometimes you can even see the fish's dorsal fin and much of its back breaks the surface of the water. The fish follows for what seems to be an eternity, will it take or will it not? The heart beats faster, the fish closes in and nips at your fly but at the last second decides not to take with any conviction, certainly not enough to hook-up, what do you do? Some would say speed up your retrieve, others would say stop, slow down, just do something different.

In my experience, if the fish wants to take on that particular retrieve it will, if it doesn't want to take, it will not! No matter if you speed up or slow down, I've tried them all. I am now going to slightly contradict myself and say "sometimes these techniques do work, but not always!" It's still worth a try, do something different!

Many times, I have witnessed a fish follow like this, and for some considerable distance, only to turn away at the last moment, but for those few seconds the fish is chasing the fly and the thrill and the feeling of anticipation that one experiences is brilliant. If the fish does not take, cast out again into the same vicinity and perform a similar retrieve to see if the fish comes back. If it does happen to take this, follow-up and cast well and good, but one has to accept it is now a totally new set of conditions. The initial follow and chance has gone, probably never to be repeated. However, another follow is another chance and occasionally the techniques mentioned might just work on the very next cast.

As the years have progressed, my understanding of rainbow trout fishing has improved and a modicum of success has become a regular occurrence. I don't fish as much for rainbows now, but I still enjoy the opportunity. There are indeed some lovely little fisheries scattered throughout Ayrshire and beyond and, just like rivers, they all have their own character and attraction. If you are lucky enough to visit a fishery which is well managed, well maintained and supports a good head of fish it all adds to the overall pleasure of fishing.

There's one little fishery in South Ayrshire that sits in a small remote valley in the hills, close to the village of Colmonell. The first time I fished this venue I approached the lochan from the north along a single track road. From this single track road one can look down onto the lochan, a lovely setting and if the sun is in the right position virtually every feature of the bed of the fishery can be seen. Sand bars, deeps and weed beds, all are recognizable. However, at this point the road is too high above the lochan to pick out any individual fish below the surface, but one might see circular ripples on the surface of the water as fish gorge themselves on the local insect life.

As the road descends towards the southern end, a sharp right hand dog-leg turn takes you into the fishery lodge and car park, taking care to avoid the mixture of free roaming wildlife, rabbits, ducks, pheasants, geese and free range chickens. A particularly warm welcome greets you in the form of a lovely maturing lady who cannot do enough for her fishermen. On a number of occasions friends and I have telephoned in advance just a few minutes before our arrival, only to have a full Scottish breakfast and cup of coffee awaiting on a few set tables within the fishing lodge.

I say lodge, it's more like a large hut, but very homely and clean and tidy with freshly cooked food, good company and friendly conversation with the older gentleman who tends to the business end of the fishery. What a great way to start the day fishing for rainbow trout and brown trout.

It's then down to the business of catching fish and, I can tell you, there are some bumpers of fish in this little venue. I myself have experienced some successful days in terms of catching fish but I have never managed to land anything bigger than 4.5 lbs, but I can verify and have witnessed colleagues who have landed Rainbows of 13 lbs and Browns of 5lbs, although the fishery do ask anglers to return all fish over 6lb.

Come lunchtime, it is time to retire to the hut for homemade game soup and a roll. Who knows what goes into it? Does it matter? It's most welcome and "awfi guid", especially if the weather has not been too kind. Soup made by whom? Who else, but the more mature lady mentioned earlier (I hope she doesn't mind being referred to as more mature, as I said she's a lovely lady.) She is probably the only one who knows what goes into it!

Fed and watered yet again, it is time for round two. I don't know what it is but I personally, no matter where I fish, do not seem to be as successful during the afternoon sessions as I do in the morning sessions. I do catch the odd fish, but just not as many as I do during morning sessions.

It's weigh-in time by now and guess what? The proprietors are more than willing to help with the weigh- in and provide yet another end of day cuppa, duly supported with some lovely home baking. All of these facilities come at a very reasonable cost and just as you take your leave and bid farewell until the next time - aye go on - half a dozen free range duck and pheasant eggs for the house. There's more to fishing than catching fish! Oh, and I nearly forgot - the name of the fishery – Pinbraid.

# Morton Castle

## WEDNESDAY 7 SEPTEMBER

I received an invitation to fish for rainbow trout on a small lochan within the Drumlanrig Caslte Estate, near Dumfries. The invitation was offered by, believe it or not, a junior member of our local club, the son of a good personal friend Jim Hek, Jim himself being a very good angler. By this time, young James had been fishing for a number of years, since about the age of six, and was coached and ably taught by his father. As James was growing up, he and his parents frequented numerous game fairs throughout the country and during these visits the young James had been encouraged and invited to occasionally take part and compete in a number of casting competitions. So much so, that by the age of 12-14 years he was starting to seriously compete against adults (adults with much more experience than he) and give them a run for their money. In particular, his forte was now casting with a fly rod, target casting, distance casting, demonstration casting, you name it, he could do it and would compete alongside the best. He must have been very good because during this period some of the main tackle manufacturers were beginning to take note of this young man's talents, supported by the number of prizes and trophies he was now winning on a regular basis at these gatherings. Prizes of which were, by now, numerous, but the pinnacle of all this success culminated in him gaining Junior International Honours in the form of representing his country, fishing for Scotland at a number of international events and venues throughout Great Britain.

Winning competitions at one of these game fairs gave him the opportunity to fish with two invited guests on the Drumlanrig Castle Estate. The Estate stood on the banks of one of Scotland's most famous salmon rivers, the River Nith, just north of the town of Dumfries. Good on you James!

Where did James learn his trade? On my two local rivers, the River Irvine and Annick Water of course, under the mentoring and guidance of his dad, Jim, and other members of Dreghorn Angling Club.

Anyway, onto our day at Drumlanrig Castle.

Not fishing for salmon, as one might expect, but fishing for rainbow trout at Morton Castle Lochan, to be precise. We arrived at Drumlanrig Castle on a dull and not so pleasant morning with rain threatening and most probably imminent.

Prior to making our way to the lochan, James had a duty to perform. He was to be the subject of a prize-giving presentation and photo-shoot in front of Drumlanrig Castle with all his trophies he had recently won at the local game fair. Photos were duly taken, with his dad and I standing in the wings wishing they would hurry up and get on with it. Didn't they know we had an appointment with a fish or two? Sufficient photographs were successfully taken and, with departing pleasantries exchanged to the manager of the estate, we finally made our way to the loch. It was 10:00 a.m. by now, I know this because I looked at my watch. Driving along the old track which meandered through the trees, all of a sudden we had arrived. There in front of us sat a lovely little dog-leg lochan and to my right stood the ruins of an ancient castle (Morton) of yester-year, towering and standing guard over the lochan as if to protect it from any unwanted intruders.

Apparently, there was a small, well-hidden boathouse located at the top left hand corner. So well hidden, I couldn't even see it at first, but Jim assured me it was definitely there. The threatening rain had now started falling so we all opted to start our day's fishing from the bank and meet back at the boat house for lunch at 1:00 p.m. James and I had made up our minds to make our way back down towards the Castle which left Jim to decide where he was going to fish.

I noticed there was a small bay, not much of one I must admit, which was sited between the castle and the dam back. On our approach I had spotted a few fish rising within this bay. Encouraged by this I stopped for a moment just to watch. A fish broke the surface and another a few moments later, then another a short time after this, there were obviously fish in the area. James had continued to walk past the small bay and onto the dam back itself. Still scanning the water surface, I proceeded to unhook my flies and cover these rising fish. Five minutes had not passed when I hooked my first fish of the day. I raised my head to look across towards James and lo and behold, he too was also playing a fish at the same time. The biggest difference was he landed his, I dropped mine.

As time passed throughout the next couple of hours, both James and I experienced some degree of success, hooking and catching fish all of which were around one and a half to two and a half pounds in weight, with most of them being returned. But, how was Jim senior performing from the boat? He was fishing at the top end of the lochan and for much of the time was out of sight from where we were fishing. Therefore, we could not alert him to the success we were having.

Just before 1:00 p.m. we noticed Jim and the boat appearing from behind the dog-leg bank. He had obviously found the boathouse. I immediately noticed Jim was under much paddle power (no outboard motors allowed) and to be fair, an outboard on this size of lochan wasn't really necessary. Torrential rain was now falling and Jim, good old Jim, was steaming towards us to collect James and myself to take us back to the boathouse for lunch. Beats walking!

"How are you doing?" was the shout from the boat, as he approached the bank on which we stood.

"Surprisingly well actually," I replied. "How about you?"

"I've got the dinner on," he shouted. Tells a story, I thought, as he evaded the question.

James couldn't wait to tell his dad of our success, "I've landed three with a few other offers missed and Keith's also got three, two of which were returned, plus two fish lost. What do you mean dad, you've none?"

James must have taken pity on old dad, as when we clambered aboard James said, "Move to the stern dad, hold the rods and I'll row." Good on you James.

We rowed back up the loch and into the very well-hidden boathouse. No wonder I couldn't see it earlier, it was hidden under a very large chestnut tree which was in full dress and severely overhanging, nobody would have seen it. James carefully docked the boat and we tied off and disembarked to find Jim wasn't kidding when he said he had lunch on. Jim had already carried the camping stove, food bags and drinks to the boathouse from his car, then proceeded to organise and prepare for the cooking. As the minutes passed there was a lovely aroma filling the air, the smell of venison sausages and venison burgers cooking. This was going to be a great lunch, unless Jim burnt them of course. Fortunately, no such disaster materialised and lunch was served. Great! Who cares if it's raining out there?

It wasn't long before young James started, and seemed to be enjoying, giving his old dad some abuse, sorry advice, in the form of what were the non-catching flies.

Turning to me he said, "What about you Keith, what are you catching them on?"

I personally was gaining success using small Black Nymphs or Bob Bits type flies, fished slowly just below the surface. I duly lifted my rod to show Jim what was attached to my cast. The next few minutes were spent with Jimmy searching his own box of flies for something similar. As luck would have it, he had none!

Lunch over, cooking equipment and utensils put away and discussion then turned to who was going back out in the boat, as in reality the boat could only accommodate two anglers. James intimated he did not want to fish from the boat, he was quite happy fishing from the bank, so the decision was easy. I would join Jim afloat on this lovely wee lochan.

We loaded the boat with my tackle, cast off and set sail into the centre of the lake. Within minutes of the restart I was into another fish and, by the sound of it, so was young James. Shouting across to us as he played the fish, "My net's not big enough for this fish," which we could believe because we could see the fight from a distance. With his rod severely bent, one could see the fish was leading him a merry dance, even swimming between him and the bank on a couple of occasions, round and round he turned before the fish headed back out into the centre of the loch. Eventually, after quite a while, the fish was subdued and James managed to land a fish of 6 lbs. A fish of pure Rainbow muscle.

*Young James Hek - this fish led him a merry dance*

All of a sudden the silence surrounding this peaceful area was dramatically broken with the sound of gun shots filling the air. Peace shattered. Clay pigeon shooting? No, I think it was an actual duck shoot, whatever it was it sounded pretty close. This shoot appeared to carry on for ages but although the peace and quiet was shattered, it didn't seem to effect the fishing any.

Both James and myself continued to catch fish, what's wrong with Jim? This was not like Jim! Eventually, he managed to hook and land his first fish, a nice Brownie of approximately 1 lb which he duly returned unharmed to the water, but his success was short-lived and he continued to struggle, whereas James and I just kept catching. It was obvious Jim needed help. Into my box of tricks and I pulled out a carbon copy of the fly I was catching most of my fish on, a black Bob Bits. I had only one left in the box, but friends being friends I had no reservations about passing this last fly to Jim. Jimmy tied it on and within minutes he finally had some success in the form of a beautifully conditioned Rainbow. These fish were all in prime condition and they had the fight to match.

Then came the mother of all takes and fight as a fish took my fly. It turned and stripped me down to the backing within seconds and at the end of its run, the fish jumped clear of the water giving us a good look at it. We both turned our heads and looked at each other, WOW! Obviously a better fish we both agreed, and estimated the fish to be in the region of the size and weight to that of the fish James had caught earlier (I think it was bigger, well that's what I told James later). Concentrate Keith! Fish now under control and gathering line back onto the reel. Under control? No chance, I spoke too soon! The fish turned and decided to take a run once again into the backing. Once again I managed to stop it and brought it under control, no problem. The fish was now tiring and just fighting as one would expect from a normal fight, just a matter of time now. Then, for no apparent reason, disaster, line went slack and the fish was off. Oh bother! I think my words were.

"Well, some you win, some you lose," I said, gritting my teeth.

Jim, by this time, had managed to double his tally and was beginning to get the hang of this fishing game, bringing another couple of Rainbows to the boat.

Meanwhile, young James had once again disappeared out of sight to another part of the lochan and we didn't see him again for quite a while. Jim and I worked it out and concluded he must be catching fish, or he would have reappeared before now. Then, as I was paying more attention to the surroundings, rather than watching my line, all of a sudden bang! Another good fish hooked. Guess what? It broke me out! I hate it when that happens, not really for the fact of losing the fish, but for the fact that the fish is away with a hook in its mouth. For the fish's sake I don't like that happening. Apart from that I knew I didn't have another fly like it in my box, I had given it to Jim earlier. Silly me!

I fished on for about an hour without catching another fish although I did have a couple of offers, but nowhere near what I had experienced earlier. The time was now approaching 5:00 p.m. and we thought we would go and find James and have a short break. I rowed back up the lochan and we once again all met up. Tally for the day so far: James - nine fish, Keith - nine fish and Jim - four fish, with numerous fish lost and missed.

After a short break we decided to fish on, but would call it a day around 6:30 p.m. James still didn't want to go out on the boat, so Jim and I once again set afloat. For the last hour or so I decided to try something totally different, a real change, a small gold-head black Fritz shimmy lure on a slow-intermediate line. We set adrift close to the bank, following the contour of the bank which would in turn take us right past the castle. There was one solitary large tree overhanging the water and I saw a fish move under these branches. With the direction and speed of drift I should cover that fish within the next two casts. Careful not to hook the tree, I cast my little gold-head into the region of that rising fish. Two short sharp pulls and just as I was about to start a figure of eight retrieve, my line tightened yet again, I had a fish on. I gently played it and duly brought it to hand to be unhooked without lifting the fish out of the water. Jim by now was having more regular success and catching yet another decent trout. I ended the session with one more fish, just before it was time to pack up for the day.

We rowed back to James who had continued his good fortune, he had caught a further seven during this final session. "Another great session," he said.

What a day! Stats for the day:

34 fish caught between us, 32 Rainbows, all quality fish averaging between 2-3 lbs (except James's fish at 6lb) plus two brown trout. 8 fish retained between us, 26 returned unharmed.

James - 16 Rainbows and 1 brown trout

Keith - 11 Rainbows with no brown trout

Jim - 5 Rainbows and 1 brown trout

It was a fantastic day's sport with good company.

I sincerely hope I get a chance to return to Morton Castle at some point in the future. But there again, things might prove to be very different the next time. However, I have the memory of this time and that is what counts.

## Small Fisheries - Ayrshire

Ayrshire and the surrounding area abound with small fisheries, so much so that one might say we in Ayrshire are spoiled for choice. I have so many different memories from these smaller fisheries it would be virtually impossible to list them. I never became a real regular at any of these venues, I preferred to "do the circuit" during any one particular season, fishing each between 1 to 5 times per season. But once the salmon and sea trout came onto the scene, fishing small Rainbow fisheries takes a back seat. What I would like to do is give a brief resume of just a few.

## Burns Fishery - Tarbolton

Prior to being introduced to rainbow trout fishing, I can recall passing this venue as my father and I returned from fishing the River Ken. Occasionally, instead of keeping to the main road heading for Ayr, we would take a right onto the country road at the hamlet of Polnessan, just north of Patna, this road eventually taking us through Tarbolton before reaching home.

At that time the fishery consisted of one small rectangular reservoir of about the size of a football pitch and only facilitated bait fishing. This rectangular pond was also totally surrounded by nothing more than fields of marshy, bog-like ground. However, over the years the fishery has grown and now supports a number of ponds of varying size and character. One aspect of the fishery I have learned over the years is that Burns Fishery is by far the best value for money in terms of number of fish allowed to be retained, session times and ticket prices. But don't be fooled, it can also prove to be quite challenging in respect of actually catching fish.

There is no doubt the fish are definitely present in the ponds, but getting them out can be another matter. I'm sure some of the local and regular anglers may agree.

I have always found the staff at this fishery to be very accommodating and very helpful when it comes to encouraging junior anglers. On a number of occasions I have contacted the fishery and asked them if they would consider acting as host for my local club to hold their "End of Season Fish and Presentation of Prizes" for the juniors. This event was organized for our junior competition winners plus all junior members who actually participated in any of the club's competitions throughout the season.

With immediate agreement, Burns Fishery could not have been more accommodating, nor more encouraging, towards our junior anglers. The day basically comprised of breakfast on arrival (warm filled rolls and a drink); a 10:00 a.m. start with two hours fishing; lunch (snacks provided by the Fishery and Angling Club) and finally, two more hours fishing. This was followed by weigh–in and presentation of trophies. For the years that Burns Fishery accommodated our juniors, I, on behalf of Dreghorn Angling Club and myself, would like to thank them most sincerely.

The only downside was that like many small fisheries, it can suffer from overwhelming weed growth during the late summer months. The staff have to work very hard trying to keep the ponds weed clear and sometimes you wonder, are they winning? No matter, many a good session can be had in the right conditions and like every fishery I have visited, I eventually found my favourite "hot spots" - places where you seem to have more success in catching fish than others.

The largest lake (fly only) has two islands in the middle which gives the lake a bit of character and, depending on the wind direction, these islands give rise to some good feeding channels, or wind lanes as they are sometimes called. If you can work these out, sport can often be very good. There is no doubt that Tarbolton is one of my favourite small venues.

### Springwater Fishery – near Dalrymple

What has happened to Springwater? In my early years of fishing for rainbow trout this small fishery was definitely right up there with the best. Well managed and well maintained, crystal clear water and acceptable facilities with the fishery comprising of a bait pond and a much larger fly only pond. Excellent quality and hard fighting fish were there for the catching. Renowned as a "top of the water" fishery, catches could be great during the early part of the summer. However, lures are not to be ignored, indeed my heaviest Rainbow of seven and a half pounds was caught on the old favourite – the Cat's Whisker.

Springwater can be challenging and sometimes very frustrating. Fish rise everywhere but do not always take your fly which, to be fair, is a situation I personally quite like in a small water fishery. You have to use your experience and work hard for your fish. On the other hand, if one does manage to find the fly the fish want, sport can be exciting and very productive.

Springwater was a place where one would often find the professional fly tier David McPhail in attendance, performing off-the-cuff demonstrations especially for clubs who had organized outings to the fishery. On a few occasions, David was kind enough to provide such demonstrations for the junior members of Dreghorn Angling Club during a number of their annual junior prize giving outings when held at Springwater.

Then, all of a sudden, the fishery began to deteriorate. The banks appeared to be left to grow wild, compared to what they were previously. On one particular occasion I had a bit of spare time on my hands, so as I passed the entrance to the fishery I decided to call in, not to fish but just for a nosey. I couldn't believe what I was seeing.

The water was over-run with weed and, in my opinion, was virtually unfishable, indeed, there was only one gentleman fishing. He had come down from Paisley and he now felt he was wasting his time. He had hooked fish but had lost every one to the weed. Just as we were discussing this he hooked yet another and even though he tried as he might to keep the fish away from the weed, he couldn't and the fish was lost.

"See what I mean?" said he. "One thing is for certain, I'll not be back unless the fishery gets its act together and improves," he added.

From that point on I stopped visiting Springwater for a few seasons. When I did decide to return, there was some improvement evident along the banks and casting platforms, but it was still not near its former glory. Over and above this, a third pond had been stocked with coarse fish, obviously accommodating those anglers who were so minded. Not a problem. Still, determined to visit this venue as improvements were evident, I visited again only to find I was catching roach on the fly within the main pond. Talking and listening to other anglers, as one does, I was not altogether convinced that Springwater was now actually providing an attractive package and I have not fished there since. No doubt I will return sometime in the future, but hopefully I will find it restored to a former state. It still lies in my memory as one of my favourite venues during those early years of fishing for rainbow trout.

Middleton Fishery near Largs, Craufurdland near Fenwick, north of Kilmarnock and Glenburn (Fairlie Moor), all in their own right are worth a cast or two. These are just some of the numerous small fisheries within my local area and I can tell you, I have had many a good day or evening session on these fisheries. However, in recent years I appear not to be fishing these venues for a full day, I now fish for approximately four hours at any one session. I believe, and this may sound a little over-confident, that if I haven't caught fish in four hours then I'm not going to, and I generally head for home. But at least I've had some measure of relaxation and enjoyment just being out in the countryside and if not catching fish, one always seems to be able to find someone to "talk a good fish." There's more to fishing than catching fish!

# JWAC

## (JOHNNIE WALKER ANGLING CLUB) 1960–2010

What can I say about Johnnie Walker Angling Club? So many experiences, so many memories - a book totally dedicated to this club could surely be written. I joined the club in 1991and it immediately became apparent the club was not just an angling club, but bordering more on a social club. Three ingredients were required by the members of this club.

*An interest in fishing*

*Must be sociable and friendly*

*Most of all - as the title suggests - an ability to partake in a few measures of the amber nectar (but of course it had to be their own brand).*

I qualified for two and a half out of three, I had to change from drinking my preference at the time, Grouse whisky, to, what else but Johnnie Walker Red Label or Black Label, it didn't really matter. I was versatile anyway and to be honest, the transition was not that hard.

The club membership comprised of employees and a few former employees of the JW Kilmarnock plant. In terms of actual membership, it wasn't a really big club when I joined in 1991 but maybe, just maybe, that is why there was an undoubtedly strong and obvious close friendship between the members. The number of venues fished throughout any one season could be anything from six to eight, finishing off the season with a presentation dance for members and their invited guests. Trophy winners would be presented with their prizes for catching the heaviest bag of fish on that particular outing on the day. The dance and presentation always took place in the Barcastle Social Club in the small Ayrshire town of Galston. I say trophy winners, yes there was indeed a trophy for every outing, plus a trophy for the heaviest fish caught throughout the season.

One aspect of the club became very apparent, very quickly to me - none of the members were that serious or competitive enough to give the impression that they must win at all costs. There is a saying: "It's not the winning, it's the taking part that counts," and I can honestly say right from the outset of my JWAC membership, I immediately realised this statement was never so true. I was going to really enjoy fishing with these guys. Considering the club was formed in the early sixties and with me not joining until 1991, it doesn't take a genius to work out that by the time I joined the club had been in existence for close on thirty years since its inception. A few of the founding members and long-term serving members were still hanging in there such as John Hall, Reg Archibald, Charlie Patterson and Ian Grant.

My first outing with my new angling buddies was quite late in the season and they had only one venue left to fish, the River Tweed near to Galashiels. With respect, it also didn't take me long to figure out who were the real fishers and those who were just there using angling as an excuse. Some were more interested in just a day out, supported by copious amounts of whisky and Irn Bru, so patriotic! Our two national drinks mixed together tasted just fine!

There was not many fish caught that day but as an introduction to new friends it was worth every cast and swallow.

## Loch Fad

My first real participation as a true member of the team descended upon me the following season. I attended the AGM fully expecting a very serious well-planned, well-structured, business-like meeting. I was so wrong! The meeting really turned out to be a story telling session. The only part of the meeting which came close to resembling what is usually expected at an AGM was when the forthcoming season's venues were discussed and agreed. It was my first meeting and I was determined to make an impression. I was going to make a suggestion.

I had joined JW from my previous employer where one of my former colleagues just a couple of years previously had decided upon a complete career change and embarked along with his wife on a new venture. Tommy and Christine opened a hotel in Rothesay, located on the lovely Isle of Bute which is situated in the middle of the River Clyde estuary on the west coast of Scotland. The Isle of Bute was home to a loch of some repute - Loch Fad. On a number of previous occasions, I had failed to persuade members of my former employer's Angling Club to support Tommy and his wife Christine in the form of pre-booking the fishing on Loch Fad for the Saturday. Book the ferry crossing, book the hotel for the Saturday night and return home Sunday afternoon, but my suggestions always fell on deaf ears, nobody backed my idea. However, as soon as I suggested this to the guys of JWAC, wow! They bit my hand off. A weekend away from work and the wives, go for it!

It was decided there and then at that very meeting, Rothesay and Loch Fad would be the second outing of the year and would take place during the month of May. Needless to say, I was left with the organising. No problem.

With hotel, ferry, car transport and fishing booked and organised and overall costings calculated down to the last penny, we were all set for the weekend away.

The day arrived and we assembled at Wemyss Bay Ferry Terminal and, if I am not mistaken, there were three car loads of members. Everybody who said they would attend was present and correct. As we waited on the quayside, awaiting the go ahead to embark onto the ferry, "Big Reg" summoned us all to form a circle and just like a flock of sheep we followed his instructions. Reg stood well over six feet tall and had a build to match, so who would dare argue anyway. He then proceeded to make a small speech of congratulations aimed towards Charlie Paterson who had been fortunate enough to win the first (April) outing of the year, and in doing so had won a lovely big bottle of JW Red Label. As we were applauding Reg leaned forward to present Charlie with his prize, but for some reason the prize didn't quite reach Charlie fully intact. As the bottle traversed forward, the cap and seal of the bottle were inadvertently cracked and opened.

"OOPS!" said Reg with a big smile on his face. "Well, it's open now so I suppose we better drink it." Inadvertently opened? Not a chance!

The bottle was then ceremoniously passed around those present as if communion was being taken in church and before long, the bottle was empty. This, by the way, all happened before 8:00 a.m. What a breakfast! It certainly perked one up for the rest of the day. I was now beginning to get a real insight into what I could probably expect in the years to come. As time and the years passed I found it to be very much the case. Fishing, friendship and copious amounts of fluid of the alcoholic kind definitely went hand in hand.

Time to go! It was safe to embark onto the ferry and proceed to our destination. Across the Firth of Clyde then reaching the lovely Isle of Bute and onto Loch Fad.

What a place! I had often heard about it, but had never fished this venue. Loch Fad is a long, narrow loch of approximately 175 acres. With the hills of Arran and Goat Fell acting as a distant backdrop as you look down the length of the loch, it is a beautiful setting. Fishing from boat or bank is permitted on Loch Fad, so some of the group decided it was a boat for them and others opted for fishing from the bank. Since it was our first visit to the loch as a club, the fishery management team offered to transport some of us to the top end of the loch using the large flat-bottomed boat they used for stocking, drop us off, and then return to pick us up approximately 30 minutes before the end of the day's fishing. Great service! Who could turn down this offer? A few members had no hesitation in taking advantage of this unusual offer, those few being Reg Archibald, Hugh Cummings, Allan Strachan and myself. We could not ask for better service than this.

Iain, Craig and Willie set sail and George and John decided to fish from the bank just along from the lodge. We bid each other "tight lines" in the usual manner (think about it) and off we went to fish.

True to his word, the fishery manager propelled us up the middle of the loch at a fair old rate of knots, the speed being produced by the big powerful outboard engine attached to the stern. As promised, the fishery manager dropped us off in a lovely little bay on the right hand bank of the loch, just where an old stone dyke disappeared into the water and a small trickle of a stream flowed into the loch. We alighted, thanked the fishery manager most sincerely and hoped he would not forget to come back for us at or around the agreed time. It was a very long walk back if he didn't.

"A toast to the fish," bellowed Reg. We didn't disappoint! Toasting completed it was time to set up our tackle and it became immediately clear that Reg, Allan and Hugh preferred to fish using only bait methods. I was the only one who appeared to be kitted out with a fly rod. It also quickly became apparent this was the "extra sociable" section of the club.

Allan stood out like a sore thumb, obviously and definitely not a fisherman, dressed, shall we say, somewhat differently, more likened to a garden gnome. Reg at least looked like an angler and at least appeared to have some idea of what he was doing and Hugh – oh Hugh! Hugh set up his rod, reel and line, half-filled his bubble float with water and attached the float accordingly. He decided maggot was the order of the day and according to him, this was going to be the "killer" method. Rods were now all ready for action – so we had a drink.

Hugh lifted his rod, walked to the edge of the water and as he got there I heard the words, "what the **** is wrong wi' this?"

He had forgotten to ensure the bale arm on his reel was in the right position before feeding up his nylon through the eyes of his rod. "s***, I'll have to strip it all down again."

"Hold on Hugh, I'll show you a quick way to resolve that problem," said I.

I took his rod from him, removed the spool from its spindle, switched over the bale arm, placed the spool back onto its spindle and set the tension. Then, with a turn on the handle, re-engaged the bale arm into the line retrieve position.

"There you go pal – you're ready for action." He stood staring at me in amazement which really meant, "huh, smart *******."

Accepting his rod back, Hugh once again approached the water's edge. He took up position to cast, the rod thrust forward, PING! The bubble float went skyward as if it was going to fly all the way across to the other side of the loch, but it didn't have any line attached. The "ping" was the sound of his line breaking due to him not releasing the bale arm on his reel. Back to the drawing- board for him. It wasn't long before Reg was into his first fish of the day, a nice well-conditioned rainbow trout. Big smiles for Big Reggie.

Half an hour passed and Hugh was once again ready. I think he managed about three casts before "ping" bubble float number two gone.

"This is "S***. I'll just have another beer," said Hugh.

Back to the drawing board, again! It was myself who managed to hook and land the next fish, another Rainbow caught on a Cat's Whisker. Reg was into yet another fish, all bodes well.

Hugh was ready to go again and about an hour passed without incident until, "Ping."

"Right," I said. "What are you doing wrong?" I reeled in my line, lay my rod to the side and went to his assistance.

I observed him tackling–up the full assembly. By this time he had to borrow another float from Reg. It became quickly apparent to me that the main contributing factor for this many breakages may have been down to Hugh having no idea of how to tie a knot. The method he deployed was nothing short of a Granny Knot. We all know how weak a granny is but there was something else! During the conversation, I realised his monofilament line was so old and perished it was breaking even if you sneezed at it. Fortunately, I had a new spool of 5 lbs leader material over and above some spare casts which I had in my cast wallet. I duly proceeded to attach this line to his reel. Set up once again and bingo, he was now fishing.

He had a drink.

Reg by this time was excelling himself by managing to land another couple of fish. Allan, he was still sitting like a little garden gnome, constantly telling me he wasn't really a fisher – "NO, I don't believe you!" I said with a little sarcasm. Finally, it all settled down and we managed to give the fish a run for their money.

By the end of the day Reg had landed six lovely trout, four for me and Hugh a couple. Allan, well there's always next year.

It was now 4:30 p.m.in the afternoon and we could see the manager's boat approaching as he powered his way up the loch towards us. Time to stop fishing and put the fishing tackle away, we had a pre-sail drink.

Reg was on a high and totally convinced he had won the "competition." Six lovely fish like that, "nobody, but nobody, will have caught more" he said. He began to repeatedly sing at the top of his voice, "Championy, champion, olay, olay, olay." I'm not sure, but I think the Old John Barleycorn was beginning to take effect.

The boat duly arrived and the manager shouted, "Had a good day I see boys." I don't think he meant in terms of fish caught. We scrambled aboard the launch. "Good fishing?" asked the fishery manager.

"Championy, champion, olay, olay, olay," was the reply. The manager just shook his head.

All accounted for and with the equipment secured, we powered our way back towards the little harbour and the fishing lodge. As we did so, we passed Willie Barnes and co rowing their little boat like mad, hoping to make the weigh-in time. Well actually, it was young Craig Grant who was rowing.

"Championy, champion, olay, olay, olay," once again resounded as we waved to them on the way past.

A few hundred yards later we were passing the bank anglers, George Smith and friends who were still fishing, taking advantage of the final few minutes before stopping time. They were only a few yards along the bank from the lodge by now.

"Championy, championy, olay, olay, olay!"

"Reg!"

"What?"

"Shut-up!"

We cruised into the small harbour, tied up the boat and alighted in a fashion. Looking after Reg's fish was priority, no way was he going to drop them over the side at this stage. He was the winner of the competition and that was that. Ten minutes passed and all the guys were back at the hut.

"Championy, championy, olay, olay, olay!" Then it was onto the weigh-in. After a few more nips from the remnants of each-other's hip flasks of course.

We took it in turns to weigh our catch, Reg intentionally waiting until last, by which point, undoubtedly, his six fish were indeed the heaviest bag. He turned away - "Championy, champion…"

"Hold on Reg, there's still one person to weigh-in their catch."

"What?" exclaimed Reg.

Up steps George with a sack full. One fish, two fish, three fish…eleven fish, twelve fish. Bag limit achieved.

Reg's face was a picture, we were all in stitches, sides sore with laughing. Reg wasn't happy and used words the likes of which I had never heard – what a shame!

On hearing Reg chanting all the way down from the top end of the loch, George made a point of telling everyone how many he had caught but for nobody to let on to Reg. He would wait until everybody had weighed in, then he would spring the surprise. Fantastic! It certainly worked.

Reg has never been allowed to forget about this first visit to Loch Fad.

As for the Saturday night's entertainment, Rothesay didn't know what hit it. Three o'clock Sunday morning we made our way back to the hotel in our shirt sleeves - it really was such a mild and warm night, or morning.

Over the next few years JWAC organised quite few more visits to the Isle of Bute, each visit with its own special memories. In fact, it was the following year that Reg was the centre of attention again, only this time one could argue it was for his angling prowess, being crowned "King Perch." 34 perch, which would have been some achievement if he had been fishing for perch, but he was after Trout. Brilliant!

## JWAC

*L-R – I Grant, H Cummings, W Barnes, J Hall, K Lynch, C Grant, R Archibald, G Smith and A Strachan.*

I also seem to remember it was during this second visit another one of our party experienced a similar come down. I have already mentioned the fact that quite a number of the JW members were more orientated towards fishing with bait rather than the fly. "El Presidenti" and founding member, namely John Hall, was no different. At the start of the day, and before the group separated to go their own way, it was evident some of the members would like to maximise their options, fishing from the boat and at lunch time swapping over with some of those fishing along the shoreline. This suggestion was agreed. John Hall had expressed a preference to fish from the boat in the morning session and from the bank during the afternoon. No problem. Boat partners and bank teams all set off to do the business. Lunch time approaches and it is nearly time for John to row to the bank to changeover. His grand catch during the morning session from the boat – zero - no fish! So changing his option made sense, but not before coming up with an idea.

As he headed for shore, he just happened to be passing the trout rearing cages which were located in the middle of the loch. He thought, if I drop my worm over the side of the boat and row into shore, allowing line to peel from my reel, I may be able to tempt a feeding fish from below or around these rearing cages. At this location his bait would be in such a position where it would not normally be, due to the fact his bait would be well out of casting distance if he were to cast from the shoreline.

So be it! Down went his bait as he let the line free spool from his reel as he headed for shore. The bow of the boat slipping gently onto the shingle shore, he disembarked and set his rod down onto a make shift rod rest. The usual pleasantries and greetings were exchanged asking if anyone had any luck. "No," replied John, but then stated with confidence, "but I will in a minute." He then proceeded to explain what he had just done, dropping his bait under the fish cages where it was more than likely that a trout from below these cages would be feeding on any loose feeding pellets which had not been snaffled by the trout in the said cages. Well that was his theory - man loves a thinker!

A few moments passed and sure enough his rod tip began to bounce rigorously. He jumped up off his backside and sprinted to catch his rod before it was pulled into the loch. "Fish on," shouts John, his rod bent double as it bore the strain. "Must be some size of fish," he says. "It's certainly pulling and fighting hard."

As usually happens, all the other guys standing watching were offering him advice on how to play and land this fish. It was obvious he had no intentions of listening to these incompetent fellow anglers (his club mates). He stood winding in as slowly as he possibly could, his rod remaining bent under the constant strain. He was grinning from ear to ear as if someone had pushed a banana into his mouth sideways, and even then with probably enough room for another. With his chest sticking out like a strutting peacock, he was ensuring all others around him were aware, HE was the man. HE was the King fisher.

Due to the amount of line he had allowed to peel from his reel, it wasn't surprising it was taking an age for him to wind in, and OH BOY was he milking it! Eventually, the monster fish came close to the shoreline, never once having showed its head or even broken the surface during the extended fight.

"Will one of you ******** get the net ready instead of offering stupid advice and making me nervous, I don't need your advice anyway." By now, the number of spectators surrounding John had swollen quite considerably, anglers from all directions had gathered to see this monster fish. BUT, I was the ******* who was given the privilege and honour to net this gigantic fish. John trusted me!

I waded out a little into slightly deeper water to accommodate the net. Then I saw the fish under the surface, a fish of about two and a half to three feet long. At this point I had a quiet chuckle to myself before turning and telling John, "I'm not netting that."

"Aye, just get it the first chance you get." John replied.

"I told you, I'm not netting that."

"Why no'?" asked John.

"Because it's a big dirty ugly eel, ya dumpling," I said with great delight.

The crowd erupted into uncontrollable bouts of laughter. John's face was a picture. I've seen a look like that before and I immediately had memories and recollections of Reg's face from the previous year. Who says lightning never strikes twice?

Poor John, what a disappointment! After all his effort and performance convincing everyone he was fighting one of Loch Fad's legend monster rainbow trout, he ended up with a big dirty slimy eel and, of course, egg on his face. Oh dear!

**Lake of Menteith:**

Every club has its characters and I suspect you have already worked out who was the character of JWAC. As I was now a well-established and accepted member of the Johnnie Walker Angling Club, the members once again agreed to fish and go along with another one of my suggestions, to fish another one of my favourite venues, enter LOM. Most of them had never heard of LOM, let alone fished it. If nothing else, it would be an experience for them.

The day arrived and the members duly gathered at the Port of Menteith Fishing Lodge in plenty of time allowing us to obtain our permits for the day session ahead. Once again, I was paired up with Big Reg as a boat partner. By this time the "big yin" was becoming not just a close work colleague, working in the engineering department, but was quickly becoming a personal social friend. Well, somebody had to take him under their wing. We loaded our rods, tackle bags, nets, lunch bags (carry out) into the boat and Reg stated he would sit at the stern of the boat because there is more room and I could sit at the bow. No problem. I arranged all the equipment into some form of order - bags, nets and drogue. Eventually, we were ready for the off.

As I settled down I noticed quite a number of boats were already motoring out into the middle of the lake and heading towards their preferred fishing area. We, on the other hand, were still sitting motionless. Why? We all know that the outboard engine on these small fishing boats is located at the stern and if a person volunteers to sit beside that engine then surely that suggests the person volunteering to sit at the stern at least knows how to operate the engine as such. Wrong!

"Kipper," that's me, "How do you work this ********* thing?"

Oh my God, I thought. Fortunately, just as Reg said this the fishery manager of the time, Bill Martindale, just happened to be passing the boat,

"That's not a problem son," said he.

Over the next few minutes Reg duly received instruction and tuition on how to start and control the old Seagull engine. Well, it saved me from being disturbed and resetting all the equipment lying around the boat to swap places with him. Good on you Bill!

Within a few minutes we were up and sailing, leaving the harbour and quayside, which in reality is just a shingle beach. Motoring at a fair rate of knots towards the top end of the lake, Reg sitting like Captain Capable at the helm with a great big broad smile. We sailed past Inchmahome Island, skirted Dog Island and went towards the Mallin shore which was to be our initial choice of fishing area.

The lake supported reasonable conditions and things appeared to be progressing well.

I said to Reg, "right here will do us fine, you can stop anytime."

No response.

"Right Reg, stop."

Still no response.

"Reg, STOP before we run aground."

"I would stop if I could. How do you stop the bloody thing?" he shouted.

Bill Martindale had shown Reg how to start and steer, but had not given instruction of how to stop the engine.

I couldn't stop laughing, so jokingly I said, "for Christ sake Reg, you're an engineer, work it out! Just turn the fuel shut-off valve."

"Where the **** is that?"

Still laughing, I carefully started to make my way to the stern of the boat to help this big damsel in distress when all of a sudden the engine cut.

"Well done! I take it you found the fuel shut-off valve?"

"Fuel shut off valve? Did I ****, I pulled off the plug lead."

Some engineer! Unorthodox, but it worked. At least it stopped us from running aground, that and turning the rudder anyway. Finally, we settled down to cast a line.

*Lunch for Reg - no wonder he's smiling - it's my whisky!*

We fished for a few hours without success (no change there then) and by this time it was approaching lunch time.

We found a sheltered spot out of the breeze and had lunch. The photograph says it all.

Well-fed and watered, we were ready to do battle again. Even though weather and overhead conditions appeared favourable, the trout were proving to be a bit of a challenge but, to be fair, Menteith can sometimes be like that for me. That's part of the lake's attraction, that and the beautiful scenery of course. Anyway, it is said "success comes to those that wait," and in this case it actually turned out to be very true. It wasn't until the last three quarters of an hour before the fish decided to play and success came to yours truly and luckily I managed a couple before the end of the session.

"Right Reg, times up, start the engine, we'll need to head back to harbour." At least by now he knew the three "S's" of boatmanship – start, steer, stop - quick learner this man.

I have so many memories of Johnnie Walker Angling Club I could write a book!

# Personal Statistics and Closing Comments

I stated right at the very beginning of this book that I described myself not as a prolific angler, but just an everyday "Joe Bloggs" angler.

This fact is probably supported when one looks at my lifetime results, in terms of actual number of fish landed. What I will say is, the ones recorded within the diaries are those fish that did comply with legal or local minimum takeable limits. Over and above those recorded there were many, many, many smaller fish hooked and landed throughout the years, each and every one giving a degree of satisfaction, even if it was just to admire the form and condition of these beautiful little fish or to know that your river was producing successful natural breeding and these were the future. I just did not have the notion to record the size of young trout or salmon. Every one of these small fish (along with many of the larger fish) were carefully returned unharmed to the river, as I said, these little gems were our future. In addition to the fish successfully landed, there were many others, probably hundreds over the years, which were hooked and lost, a fact in my opinion which happened to me far too often, but that's fishing! Man against beast, some you win some you lose, it's all part of the attraction.

The following pages give some idea of the kind of statistical success I have been fortunate enough to have experienced throughout my angling life with over 90 per cent of my time and success being spent on the banks of the Rivers Irvine and Annick Water.

## Fish Totals

| Year | Salmon | Sea Trout | Brown Trout | Rainbow Trout | Brook /Blue | Total | Notes |
|------|--------|-----------|-------------|---------------|-------------|-------|-------|
| | | | Species | | | | |
| 1970 | ? | 1 | ? | N/A | N/A | 1 | 9" Limit |
| 1971 | NIL | 3 | 41 | N/A | N/A | 44 | 9" Limit |
| 1972 | 1 | 1 | 6 | N/A | N/A | 8 | 9" Limit |
| 1973 | NIL | 1 | 5 | N/A | N/A | 6 | 9" Limit |
| 1974 | NIL | 1 | 13 | N/A | N/A | 14 | 9" Limit |
| 1975 | NIL | 4 | 1 | N/A | N/A | 5 | 9" Limit |
| 1976 | NIL | NIL | 10 | N/A | N/A | 10 | 9" Limit |
| 1977 | NIL | 2 | 11 | N/A | N/A | 13 | 9" Limit |
| 1978 | 1 | 5 | 10 | N/A | N/A | 16 | 9" Limit |
| 1979 | NIL | 2 | 2 | N/A | N/A | 4 | 10" Limit |
| 1980 | NIL | 2 | 4 | N/A | N/A | 6 | 10" Limit |
| 1981 | NIL | NIL | 11 | N/A | N/A | 11 | 9" Limit |
| 1982 | 1 | 1 | 7 | N/A | N/A | 9 | 9" Limit |
| 1983 | 1 | NIL | 10 | N/A | N/A | 11 | 9" Limit |
| 1984 | NIL | 2 | 5 | N/A | N/A | 7 | 9" Limit |
| 1985 | 1 | NIL | 7 | N/A | N/A | 8 | 9" Limit |
| 1986 | 2 | 3 | 14 | N/A | N/A | 19 | 9" Limit |
| 1987 | NIL | 9 | 6 | N/A | N/A | 15 | 9" Limit |
| 1988 | 2 | 5 | 14 | N/A | N/A | 21 | 9" Limit |
| 1989 | 4 | 6 | 20 | N/A | N/A | 30 | 9" Limit |
| 1990 | NIL | 9 | 20 | 5 | N/A | 34 | 9" Limit |

*Personal Statistics and Closing Comments*

| 1991 | NIL | NIL | 13 | 2 | N/A | 15 | 9" Limit |
|---|---|---|---|---|---|---|---|
| 1992 | 1 | 3 | 7 | 4 | N/A | 15 | 9" Limit |
| 1993 | 1 | 1 | 104 | 35 | 7 | 148 | 9" Limit |
| 1994 | NIL | NIL | 16 | 15 | NIL | 31 | 9" Limit |
| 1995 | 1 | 1 | 29 | 35 | NIL | 66 | 9" Limit |
| 1996 | 1 | 1 | 29 | 39 | NIL | 70 | 9" Limit |
| 1997 | NIL | 1 | 59 | 49 | 2 | 111 | 9" Limit |
| 1998 | 2 | 6 | 53 | 20 | NIL | 81 | 10" Limit |
| 1999 | NIL | 1 | 45 | 34 | NIL | 80 | 10" Limit |
| 2000 | 1 | 2 | 37 | 43 | NIL | 83 | 10" Limit |
| 2001 | 0 | NIL | 7 | 27 | Nil | 34 | 10" Limit |
| 2002 | 3 | 4 | 20 | 36 | Nil | 63 | 10" Limit |
| 2003 | 1 | NIL | 0 | 18 | 1 | 20 | 10" Limit |
| 2004 | 4 | NIL | 13 | 20 | Nil | 37 | 10" Limit |
| 2005 | NIL | 1 | 25 | 17 | Nil | 43 | 10" Limit |
| 2006 | NIL | 2 | 9 | 17 | Nil | 28 | 10" Limit |
| 2007 | 3 | 3 | 12 | 20 | 5 | 43 | 10" Limit |
| 2008 | 3 | 2 | 16 | 19 | 1 | 41 | 10" Limit |
| 2009 | 5 | 2 | 13 | 13 | NIL | 33 | 10" Limit |
| 2010 | 9 | NIL | 22 | 13 | 1 | 45 | 10" Limit |
| 2011 | 5 | 2 | 10 | 19 | 19 | 55 | 10" Limit |
| 2012 | 3 | 1 | 12 | 20 | * | 36 | 10" Limit |
| 2013 | 0 | 0 | 12 | 27 | | 39 | 10" Limit |
| 2014 | 2 | 1 | 14 | 19 | | 36 | 10" Limit |
| 2015 | 3 | 1 | 5 | 6 | | 15 | 10" Limit |
| | 61 | 92 | 799 | 572 | 36 | 1560 | 1560 |

Average catch per outing - 2.7 fish.

*2012 – Amalgamated Blues and Rainbows.

Salmon Caught

| No. | Month | Season | Length | Girth | Gender | Weight | Method | Description of bait/lure or fly etc. | Venue & Location |
|---|---|---|---|---|---|---|---|---|---|
| 1 | 24-Jun | 1972 | 20" | ? | Cock | 3 Lb 0oz | Spin | No. 2 Silver Mepp | River Irvine – Bogie Bridge pool |
| 2 | 4-Oct | 1978 | 34" | ? | Cock | 9 Lb 8oz | Spin | Blue & Silver Devon | River Irvine – No. 11 pool – Tail |
| 3 | 27-Aug | 1982 | 28" | 13" | Hen | 7 Lb 8oz | Spin | No. 1 Silver Mepp | River Irvine – No. 11 pool – Tail |
| 4 | 14-Oct | 1983 | 26.5" | ? | Hen | 5 Lb 10oz | Fly | Blue Doctor | River Irvine – Top pool Galston |
| 5 | 9-Sep | 1985 | 23.5" | ? | Cock | 4Lb 0oz | Fly | Grouse & Gold | River Irvine – Ford-side pool |
| 6 | 31-Oct | 1986 | 21.75" | ? | Hen | 3 Lb 7oz | Worm | Worm | River Irvine – Grougar pool – Hurlford |
| 7 | 24-Oct | 1986 | 23" | ? | Cock | 3lb 4oz | Fly | Garry Dog | River Irvine – Firestation Pool Newmilns |
| 8 | 2-Apr | 1988 | 31" | 15" | Hen (spr) | 8lb 15.5oz | Worm | Worm | River Annick – Above Viaduct ,Annick Lodge |
| 9 | 15-Sep | 1988 | 24.5" | 11.25" | Cock | 4lb 2oz | Fly | Peter Ross (14) | River Irvine – Ford-side pool (Tailend) |
| 10 | 17-Aug | 1989 | 24" | 11" | Hen | 3lb 12oz | Fly | Thunder & Lightning (10) | River Irvine – Ford-side pool (Tailend) |
| 11 | 26-Aug | 1989 | 27.25" | ? | Cock | 6lb 12oz | Fly | Peter Ross (10) | River Irvine – No.11 Stream |
| 12 | 28-Aug | 1989 | 30.5" | 16.25" | Cock | 10Lb 0oz | Fly | Thunder & Lightning (10) | River Irvine – No.11 Stream |
| 13 | 18-Sep | 1989 | 25.5" | 12.5" | Hen | 5Ls 0oz | Fly | Thunder & Lightning (8) | River Cree – Picture-house pool |
| 14 | 5-Sep | 1992 | 28" | 12" | Cock | 6lb oz | Fly | Silver Invicta (14) | River Irvine – Bogie Bridge Stream |
| 15 | 13-Sep | 1993 | 27" | 12" | Hen | 5Lb 14oz | Spin | Silver Toby | River Irvine – Scaffolding below Holmes Bridge |
| 16 | 18-Oct | 1995 | 28" | 13" | Hen | 6Lb 14oz | Fly | Red body/yellow wing Tube Fly | River Urr – Chappleton Pool |

| # | Date | Year | | | Sex | Weight | Method | Fly/Lure | Location |
|---|------|------|---|---|-----|--------|--------|----------|----------|
| 17 | 11-Nov | 1996 | 36.5" | 16.5" | Cock | 13Lb 8oz | Fly | Ally's Shrimp | River Irvine – Sandy bend pool Drybridge (Tailend) |
| 18 | 28-Jul | 1998 | 25.5" | 13" | Cock | 6Lb 0oz | Fly | Peter Ross (14) | River Irvine – Willow flat/stream |
| 19 | 26-Aug | 1998 | 24.5" | 12" | Hen | 4Lb 10oz | Fly | Pearly Wickhams (14) | River Irvine – Stream below Red Bridge |
| 20 | 23-Nov | 2000 | ? | ? | Hen | Approx 8Lb | Fly | Commet – Waddington | River Teviot – Fish returned |
| 21 | 13-Aug | 2002 | 23.25" | ? | Hen | 4Lb 0oz | Fly | Dunkeld | River Alness – Beat 2? |
| 22 | 20-Aug | 2002 | 22.5" | ? | Hen | 3Lb 4oz | Fly | Dunkeld | River Irvine – No. 11 pool (Tail) |
| 23 | 16-Oct | 2002 | 25.5" | ? | Hen | 5Lb 4oz. | Fly | Ally's shrimp – (10) | River irvine – No. 11 pool (Head) |
| 24 | 18-Aug | 2003 | ? | ? | Cock | 5Lb 8oz | Fly | Butcher (12) | River South Esk – Breadalbane |
| 25 | 9-Aug | 2004 | ? | ? | Cock | 3Lb 4oz | Fly | Stoat Tail (10) | River South Esk – Flat Lie |
| 26 | 29-Sep | 2004 | 26" | 12.5" | Hen | 6Lb 2oz | Fly | Stoat Tail (10) – Double | River Irvine – Willow flat/stream |
| 27 | 8-Oct | 2004 | 26.5" | ? | Cock | 5Lb 12oz | Fly | Jeannie (12) – Treble | River Irvine – Top side Red Bridge. |
| 28 | 18-Oct | 2004 | ? | ? | Hen | Approx 8Lb | Fly | Thunder & Lightning (10) | River Irvine – No. 11 pool (Tail) – Fresh Fish – Fish returned |
| 29 | 22-Sep | 2007 | 24.6" | 12.2" | cock | 5Lb 0oz | Fly | Ally's Shrimp (12) | River Irvine – Bogie Bridge Stream |
| 30 | 11-Oct | 2007 | 27" | ? | Hen | 6lbs 14onz | Fly | Ally's Shrimp (12) | River Irvine – No.11 Pool – (head) – Just below Carmel mouth. |
| 31 | 3-Nov | 2007 | ? | ? | Cock | Approx. 8lb | Fly | Home designed Jeanie Hairwing(12) | River Irvine – Top side of Red Bridge. – Reddish – Fish returned |
| 32 | 13-Sep | 2008 | 23 | | Hen | 3Lb 8oz | Fly | Gold bodied Tosh (12) – Black & yellow | River Irvine – Willow Flat/Stream |
| 33 | 6-Oct | 2008 | 26" | ? | Hen | 5Lb 12oz | Spin | Blue & Silver Devon | River Irvine – No. 11 Pool – (head) – Just Below Carmel Mouth |

| No. | Date | Year | Length | ? | Cock/Hen | Weight | Spin/Fly | Fly | Location |
|---|---|---|---|---|---|---|---|---|---|
| 34 | 6-Oct | 2008 | ? | ? | Cock | Approx. 4 Lb | Spin | Blue & Silver Devon | River Irvine – Top side of Red Bridge – Slightly coloured, Fish returned. |
| 35 | 5-Sep | 2009 | ? | ? | Hen | Approx 6Lb | Fly | Silver Thunder Stoat (10 treble) | River Irvine – No. 11 Pool – (head) – Just Below Carmel Mouth |
| 36 | 5-Sep | 2009 | 23" | ? | Hen | 3Lb 6oz | Fly | Silver Thunder Stoat (10 treble) | River Irvine – Top side Red Bridge. |
| 37 | 2-Oct | 2009 | 23.5" | 12 | Hen | 4lb 4oz | Fly | Yellow Dog (12 Treble) | River Irvine – No11 pool (tailend) |
| 38 | 5-Oct | 2009 | 26" | 13 | Hen | 5Lb 12oz | Fly | Silver Stoat (Size 12 Treble) | River Irvine – Willow Flat/Stream |
| 39 | 10-Oct | 2009 | 23" | 12 | Hen | 4Lb 4oz | Fly | Invicta (Size 10) | River Irvine – No. 11 Pool (head) |
| 40 | 26-Aug | 2010 | 24.5" | ? | Hen | 4Lb 12oz | Fly | Hairy Mary Varient (Gold bodied) – (Size 12 treble) | River Irvine – No. 11 Stream |
| 41 | 16-Sep | 2010 | 23" | ? | Cock | 3Lb 4oz | Fly | Hairy Mary Varient (Gold bodied) – (Size 12 treble) | River Irvine – Tail of Red Bridge pool |
| 42 | 17-Sep | 2010 | ? | ? | Cock | Approx. 3:04lbs | Fly | Hairy Mary Varient (Gold bodied) – (Size 12 treble) | River Irvine – Bogie Bridge Stream – Sea liced bar of silver – Fish returned |
| 43 | 17-Sep | 2010 | 26 | ? | Cock | 5lbs 13onz | Fly | Hairy Mary Varient (Gold bodied) – (Size 12 treble) | River Irvine – Bogie Bridge Stream – Sea Liced bar of silver |
| 44 | 21-Sep | 2010 | ? | ? | Cock | Approx. 3Lb | Fly | Hairy Mary Varient (Gold bodied) – (Size 12 treble) | River Irvine – Top side Red Bridge. – Slightly coloured. – Fish returned. |
| 45 | 24-Sep | 2010 | ? | ? | Cock | Scales 4:08lbs | Fly | Black & Yellow (Size 10-Treble) | River Irvine – Red Bridge Streams – Fish returned |
| 46 | 25-Sep | 2010 | 25.5" | ? | Hen | 5lbs 7onz | Fly | Black & Yellow (Size 10-Treble) | River Irvine – No.11, Carmel Lye |
| 47 | 25-Sep | 2010 | 25? | ? | Hen | Scales 5:04Lb | Fly | Hairy Mary Varient (Gold bodied) – (Size 12 treble) | River Irvine – No.11 Tail Lye – Fish returned |

| # | Date | Year | | | | | | Fly | Location / Comments |
|---|------|------|----|----|------|------|-----|-----|---------------------|
| 48 | 05-Oct | 2010 | 26" | | Cock | 5Lb 3oz | Fly | Yellow Dog (12 Treble) | River Irvine – Wires Pool |
| 49 | 24-Jun | 2011 | 29" | 13.7" | Hen | 7Lb 12oz | Fly | Black & Yellow (Size 10-Treble) | River Irvine – No. 11 Stream |
| 50 | 16-Sep | 2011 | 23" | | Cock | 3Lb 7oz | Fly | Gold bodied Wickhams (Size 10 Single hook) | River Irvine – Willow flat/stream |
| 51 | 16-Sep | 2011 | 24.5" | | Hen | 4Lb 12oz | Fly | Gold bodied Wickhams (Size 10 Single hook) | River Irvine – Tail of Red Bridge pool |
| 52 | 24-Sep | 2011 | ? | ? | Cock | App. 4Lb | Fly | Emerald Stoat tail varient – (Size 10 treble) | River Irvine – Top side Red Bridge. – Fish returned |
| 53 | 23-Oct | 2011 | 33.5" | 17" | Hen | 10Lb 14oz | Fly | Hairy Mary Varient (Gold bodied) – (Size 12 treble) | River Irvine – Red Bridge Streams |
| 54 | 06-Oct | 2012 | 23" | ? | Hen | 3Lb 8oz | Fly | Munro Killer – (Size 12 Treble) – Dropper | River Irvine – Bogie Bridge stream – tail lye |
| 55 | 06-Oct | 2012 | ? | ? | Cock | Approx 6Lb 8oz | Fly | Thunder & Lightning – (Size 10 Single) – Dropper | River Irvine – Willow Flat, Hymalayan Balsom – Fish Returned. |
| 56 | 15-Oct | 2012 | ? | ? | Hen | Approx 6Lb 8oz | Fly | Red Tag Silver Stoat Tail – (Size 10 single) – Dropper | River Ayr – Muirkirk AC – Swing Bridge – Below Water meetings – Fish Returned |
| 57 | 18-Aug | 2014 | 32" | 15.75" | Hen | 10Lb 8oz | Fly | Silver Butcher – (Size 10 Single hook) | River Irvine – Willow Flat stream (hole). |
| 58 | 07-Oct | 2014 | 23.5" | ? | Hen | 4Lb 2oz | Fly | Pearly bodied Thunder stoat – (Size 10 treble) | River Irvine – Willow Flat stream (hole). – exact same lye as above. |
| 59 | 30-Jul | 2015 | 30" | 14.12" | Hen | 8Lb 12oz | Fly | Silver bodied – Black & Yellow (Size 10-Treble) | River Irvine – No. 11 Stream |
| 60 | 28-Aug | 2015 | 34.5" | ? | Hen | 15Lb 8oz. | Fly | Gold Bodied – Black & Yellow (Size 10 – Treble) | River Irvine – Willow Flat (Kippers) |

| 61 | 28-Aug | 2015 | 24" | ? | Cock | 4Lb 8oz | Fly | Gold Bodied – Black & Yellow (Size 10 – Treble) | River Irvine – No11 Stream. – Fish Returned |

updated – 02/09/15

| % age | Returned | | |
|---|---|---|---|
| 15.6 | 5 | Hen | 35 |
| 24.0 | 6 | Cock | 26 |
| 19.2 | 11 | | 61 |

| |
|---|
| Fly – 53 – 86.2% |
| Spin- – 6- – 10.3% |
| Worm – 2- – 3.4% |

Photograph available.

Fish returned

**Salmon Length to Weight Ratio**

| Length | Weight | C/H | Quantity | Average | Mid-Length | Weight in onz |
|--------|--------|-----|----------|---------|-----------|---------------|
| 20- 23" | 3lbs 0onz | C | | | | |
| | 3lbs 0onz | C | | | | |
| | 3lbs 4onz | H | | | | |
| | 3lbs 4onz | H | | | | |
| | 3lbs 4onz | C | | | | |
| | 3lbs 8onz | H | 12 | 3lbs 5onz | 21.5" | 632 |
| | 3lbs 6onz | H | | | | |
| | 3lbs 4onz | C | | | | |
| | 3lbs 4onz | C | | | | |
| | 3lbs 7onz | C | | | | |
| | 3lbs 8onz | H | | | | |
| | 3lbs 7onz | C | | | | |
| 23"- 25" | 4lbs 0onz | C | | | | |
| | 4lbs 2onz | C | | | | |
| | 3lbs 12onz | H | | | | |
| | 4lbs 10onz | H | | | | |
| | 4lbs 0onz | H | | | | |
| | 4lbs 12onz | H | | | | |
| | 5lbs 0onz | C | 14 | 4lbs 5onz | 24" | 962 |
| | 4lbs 0onz | C | | | | |
| | 4lbs 4onz | H | | | | |
| | 4lbs 4onz | H | | | | |
| | 4lbs 8onz | H | | | | |
| | 4lbs 12onz | H | | | | |
| | 4lbs 0onz | C | | | | |
| | 4lbs 2onz | H | | | | |

351

| | | | | | | | |
|---|---|---|---|---|---|---|---|
| 25"- 27" | 5lbs 10onz | H | | | | | |
| | 5lbs 0onz | H | | | | | |
| | 6lbs 0onz | C | | | | | |
| | 5lbs 4onz | H | | | | | |
| | 5lbs 8onz | C | | | | | |
| | 6lbs 2onz | H | | | | | |
| | 5lbs 12onz | C | | | | | |
| | 5lbs 13onz | | | | | | |
| | 6lbs 14onz | H | 17 | 5lbs 13onz | 26" | 1573 | |
| | 5lbs 12onz | H | | | | | |
| | 6lbs 0onz | H | | | | | |
| | 5lbs 12onz | H | | | | | |
| | 5lbs 7onz | H | | | | | |
| | 5lbs 4onz | H | | | | | |
| | 5lbs 3onz | C | | | | | |
| | 6lbs 8onz | C | | | | | |
| | 6lbs 8onz | H | | | | | |
| 27"- 29" | 7lbs 8onz | H | | | | | |
| | 6lbs 12 onz | C | | | | | |
| | 6lbs 0onz | C | 6 | 6lbs 13onz | 28" | 652 | |
| | 5lbs 14onz | H | | | | | |
| | 6lbs 14onz | H | | | | | |
| | 7lbs 12onz | H | | | | | |
| 29"- 31" | 10lbs 0onz | C | | | | | |
| | 8lbs 0onz | H | | | | | |
| | 8lbs 0onz | H | 5 | 8lbs 8onz | 30" | 544 | |
| | 8lbs 0onz | C | | | | | |
| | 8Lb 12oz | H | | | | | |
| 31"- 33" | 8lbs 15onz | H | 2 | 9lbs 11onz | 32" | 311 | |
| | 10lbs 8onz | H | | | | | |
| 33"- 35" | 9lbs 8onz | C | 2 | 10lbs 3onz | 34" | 326 | |
| | 10lbs 14onz | H | | | | | |
| 35"- 37" | 13lbs 8onz | C | 1 | 13lbs 8onz | 36" | 216 | |
| | | | | 994/8 = 124.25/16= | | 3526 | |

|   |    |         |
|---|----|---------|
|   | 59 | 7lbs 8onz |
| H | 33 |         |
| C | 25 |         |

Caught on the Rver Irvine- but not club waters

Other club waters

## Length/Girth & Weight Relationsip (Calculation)

|    | Girth | Length | % Ratio |
|----|-------|--------|---------|
| 1  | 13    | 28     | 46.4    |
| 2  | 15    | 31     | 48.3    |
| 3  | 11.25 | 24.5   | 45.8    |
| 4  | 11    | 24     | 45.8    |
| 5  | 16.25 | 30.5   | 53.3    |
| 6  | 12.5  | 25.5   | 48      |
| 7  | 12    | 28     | 42.8    |
| 8  | 12    | 27     | 44.4    |
| 9  | 13    | 28     | 46.4    |
| 10 | 16.25 | 36.5   | 45.2    |
| 11 | 13    | 25.5   | 51.2    |
| 12 | 12    | 24.5   | 48.9    |
| 13 | 12.5  | 26     | 48.1    |
| 14 | 12.2  | 24.6   | 49.6    |
| 15 | 12    | 23.5   | 51      |
|    |       |        | 715.2   |
|    |       |        | 47.7    |

| Length (inch) | Approx weight. |
|---------------|----------------|
| 20  | 3 lbs 0onz   |
| 21.5| 3 lbs 5onz   |
| 22  | 3 lbs 8onz   |
| 23  | 3 lbs 12onz  |
| 24  | 4 lbs 5onz   |
| 25  | 5lbs 0onz    |
| 26  | 5 lbs 12onz  |
| 27  | 6 lbs 0onz   |
| 28  | 6 lbs 13onz  |
| 29  | 8 lbs 0onz   |
| 30  | 8lbs 8onz    |
| 31  | 10 lbs 0onz  |
| 32  | 9lbs 11onz   |
| 33  | 11lbs 4onz   |
| 34  | 10lbs 3onz   |
| 35  | 12 lbs 12onz |
| 36  | 13lbs 8onz   |

## Example 1

Girth = 14.5"

Calculated Lentgh = 14.5 / 47.4 x 100

30"

Est. Weight - 9lbs

## Example 2

Length = 27.75"
Girth = 13.125"
Est Weight = 6.75lbs - 7lbs

## Example 3 - Actual Fish (cock)

Length 27.25"
Weight - 6lbs 12onz
Calc Girth = 12.9"

**Best Month Table**

| | Jan | Feb | Mar | Apr | May | Jun | Jul | Aug | Sep | Oct | Nov | Dec | Total | Returned |
|---|---|---|---|---|---|---|---|---|---|---|---|---|---|---|
| Cock | | | | | | 1 | 1 | 4 | 11 | 6 | 2 | | 25 | 2 |
| Hen | | | | 1 | | 1 | 1 | 6 | 9 | 13 | 1 | | 32 | 3 |
| | 0 | 0 | 0 | 1 | 0 | 2 | 2 | 10 | 20 | 19 | 3 | 0 | 57 | 5 |

| Method | No. of fish | Percentage |
|---|---|---|
| Fly | 53 | 86.0 |
| Spinning | 6 | 10.2 |
| Worm | 2 | 3.8 |
| Total | 61 | 100.0 |

Updated 02/09/15

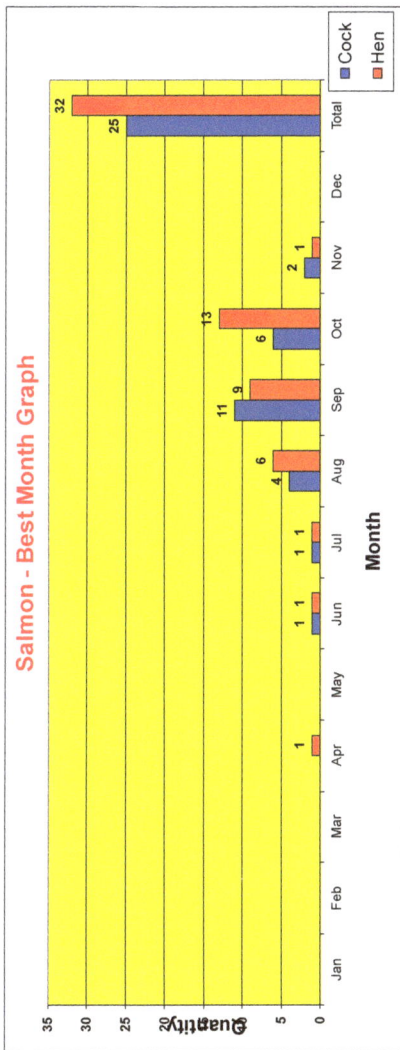

Salmon - Best Month Graph

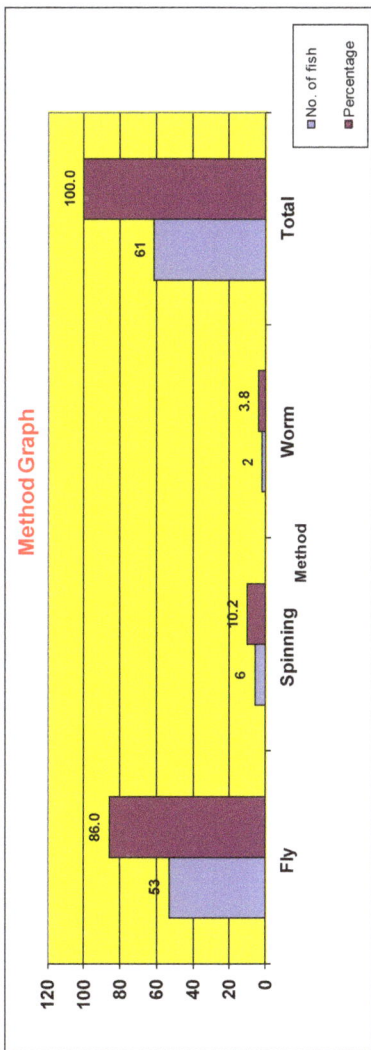

Method Graph

## A True Fisherman's Tail

### Salmon - Method groups

| Group 1 – Fly (Single hook) | | Group 2 – Fly (Small Treble hook) | |
|---|---|---|---|
| Dunkeld/Cinamon & Gold | 3 | Hairy Mary/ Blue Charm | 7 |
| Peter Ross | 3 | Jeanie/Tosh (black & yellow) | 9 |
| Wickams | 3 | Stoat Tails | 6 |
| Invicta | 2 | Thunder & Lightning | 5 |
| Butcher | 2 | Ally's Shrimp | 4 |
| Thunder & Lightning | 1 | Gary (yellow) Dog | 3 |
| Silver Stoat Tail | 1 | Blue Doctor | 1 |
| Sub-Total | 15 | Emerald Stoat | 1 |
| | | Sub-Total | 36 |

| Group 3 - Fly (Tube & Waddington) | | Group 4 - Spinning | |
|---|---|---|---|
| Orange & Yellow | 1 | Blue & Silver Devon | 3 |
| Commet | 1 | Silver Mepp | 2 |
| Sub-Total | 2 | Silver Toby | 1 |
| | | Sub-Total | 6 |

| Group 5 – Bait | | | |
|---|---|---|---|
| Worm | 2 | **Grand Total** | **61** |

Updated – 31/07/15

356

## Salmon Caught - Time of Month.

| | 1 | 2 | 3 | 4 | 5 | 6 | 7 | 8 | 9 | 10 | 11 | 12 | 13 | 14 | 15 | 16 | 17 | 18 | 19 | 20 | 21 | 22 | 23 | 24 | 25 | 26 | 27 | 28 | 29 | 30 | 31 | | |
|---|---|---|---|---|---|---|---|---|---|---|---|---|---|---|---|---|---|---|---|---|---|---|---|---|---|---|---|---|---|---|---|---|---|
| April | | 1 | | | | | | | | | | | | | | | | | | | | | | | | | | | | | | 1 | April |
| June | | | | | | | | | | | | | | | | | | | | | | | | 2 | | | | | | | | 2 | June |
| July | | | | | | | | | | | | | | 1 | | | | | | | | | | | | | | | | 1 | | 2 | July |
| August | | | | | | | | | | | | 1 | 2 | | 1 | 2 | 1 | | 1 | | 1 | | | | 1 | 2 | 1 | | | | | 13 | August |
| Sept | | | | | | | | 1 | 1 | | | | | 1 | 1 | 1 | 2 | 1 | | | | 2 | 1 | 2 | 2 | 1 | | 3 | 1 | | | 20 | Sept |
| Oct | | | 1 | 1 | 3 | 4 | 1 | 1 | | 1 | 1 | | | | | | | | | 1 | | 1 | 1 | 1 | | | | 1 | | | 1 | 20 | Oct |
| Nov | | | 1 | | | | | | | 1 | 1 | | | | | | | | | | | | | | | | | | | | | 3 | Nov |
| | 0 | 2 | 1 | 1 | 5 | 4 | 1 | 2 | 1 | 2 | 0 | 3 | 1 | 2 | 4 | 3 | 4 | 1 | 1 | 1 | 1 | 2 | 5 | 3 | 2 | 1 | 1 | 4 | 1 | 1 | 1 | 3 | 61 |
| | | | Week 1 | | | | | | | Week 2 | | | | | | | Week 3 | | | | | | | Week 4 | | | | | | Last days | | | |
| | | | 14 | | | | | | | 10 | | | | | | | 16 | | | | | | | 18 | | | | | | 3 | | | |

Updated - 02/09/15

**Most productive time of month**

| | | |
|---|---|---|
| August | 17th / 28th. | 9 |
| September | 13th. / 25th. | 12 |
| October | 2nd. - 18th. | 14 |

## Salmon caught on Fly

| | |
|---|---|
| Ally's Shrimp | 4 |
| Butcher | 2 |
| Blue Doctor | 1 |
| Commet (Waddington) | 1 |
| Dunkeld/Cinnamon & Gold | 3 |
| Garry Dog | 3 |
| Hairy Mary/Blue Charm | 7 |
| Invicta/Wickhams | 5 |
| Jeanie/Black Mariah | 2 |
| Peter Ross | 3 |
| Red & Yellow Tube | 1 |
| Stoats Tails | 8 |
| Thunder & Lightning/Munro Killer | 6 |
| Tosh (Black & Yellow) | 7 |

53

Updated – 02/09/15

## Spinning

| | |
|---|---|
| Blue & Silver Devon | 3 |
| Silver Mepp | 2 |
| Silver Toby | 1 |

| Worm | 2 |
|---|---|

8

61

# Salmon – Location caught

## River Irvine – DAC waters

| | | |
|---|---|---|
| Bogie Bridge Pool | 1 | |
| Bogie Bridge Stream | 5 | 6 |
| No. 11 Head | 5 | |
| No. 11 Pool | 1 | |
| No. 11 Tail | 6 | |
| No. 11 Stream | 6 | 18 |
| Willow Stream/Flat | 9 | |
| Red Bridge – Above | 6 | 15 |
| Red Bridge Pool – tail | 2 | |
| Red Bridge – Stream (Fordside) | 5 | |
| Wires Pool | 2 | 9 |
| Holmes Flat | 1 | 1 |
| Sandy Bend Pool – Tail (Drybridge) | 1 | 1 |

50

## Other Locations

| | | |
|---|---|---|
| River Alness | Beat 2 | 1 |
| River Annick | Viaduct – Annick Lodge | 1 |
| River Ayr | Muirkirk water – Water meetings | 1 |
| River Cree | Picture house pool | 1 |
| River Irvine | Galston/ Newmilns – Fire station pool | 1 |
| River Irvine | Galston Gowf club pool | 1 |
| River Irvine | Hurlford/Galston – Grougar pool | 1 |
| River South Esk | Breadalbane pool | 1 |
| River South Esk | Flat Lye | 1 |
| River Teviot | Name of pool not known | 1 |
| River Urr | Chappelton pool | 1 |

11

Updated – 02/09/15

Total    61

| Salmon Qty | |
|---|---|
| 1970 | ? |
| 1971 | NIL |
| 1972 | 1 |
| 1973 | NIL |
| 1974 | NIL |
| 1975 | NIL |

| | |
|---|---|
| 1976 | NIL |
| 1977 | NIL |
| 1978 | 1 |
| 1979 | NIL |
| 1980 | NIL |
| 1981 | NIL |
| 1982 | 1 |

| | |
|---|---|
| 1983 | 1 |
| 1984 | NIL |
| 1985 | 1 |
| 1986 | 2 |
| 1987 | NIL |
| 1988 | 2 |
| 1989 | 4 |

| | |
|---|---|
| 1990 | NIL |
| 1991 | NIL |
| 1992 | 1 |
| 1993 | 1 |
| 1994 | NIL |
| 1995 | 1 |
| 1996 | 1 |

| | |
|---|---|
| 1997 | NIL |
| 1998 | 2 |
| 1999 | NIL |
| 2000 | 1 |
| 2001 | NIL |
| 2002 | 3 |
| 2003 | 1 |

| | |
|---|---|
| 2004 | 4 |
| 2005 | 0 |
| 2006 | 0 |
| 2007 | 3 |
| 2008 | 3 |
| 2009 | 5 |
| 2010 | 9 |

| | |
|---|---|
| 2011 | 5 |
| 2012 | 3 |
| 2013 | 0 |
| 2014 | 2 |
| 2015 | 3 |
| 2016 | |
| 2017 | |

Salmon Qty

360

## Heaviest Fish

| YEAR | SALMON | SEA TROUT | BROWN TROUT | RAINBOW TROUT | BROOK TROUT Blue Trout |
|------|--------|-----------|-------------|---------------|------------------------|
| | | | **Species** | | |
| 1970 | | 12 onz | | | |
| 1971 | | 1 lbs 12 onz | 12 onz | | |
| 1972 | 3lbs 0 onz | 2lbs 8 onz | 10 onz | | |
| 1973 | | 6 onz | 8 onz | | |
| 1974 | | 14 onz | 8 onz | | |
| 1975 | | 10 onz | 2 lbs 9 onz | | |
| 1976 | | | 12 onz | | |
| 1977 | | 1 lbs 0 onz | 1 lbs 2 onz | | |
| 1978 | 9 lbs 8 onz | 2 lbs 10 onz | 10 onz | | |
| 1979 | | 3 lbs 12 onz | 8 onz | | |
| 1980 | | 1 lbs 8 onz | 14 onz | | |
| 1981 | | | 14 onz | | |
| 1982 | 7 lbs 8 onz | 8.5 onz | 13 onz | | |
| 1983 | 5 lbs 12 onz | | 12 onz | | |
| 1984 | | 1 lbs 3 onz | 12.5 onz | | |
| 1985 | 4 lbs 0 onz | | 1 lbs 2 onz | | |
| 1986 | 3 lbs 7 onz | 14 onz | 1 lbs 8 onz | | |
| 1987 | | 11 onz | 7.5 onz | | |
| 1988 | 9 lbs 0 onz | 12 onz | 8.5 onz | | |
| 1989 | 10 lbs 0 onz | 13 onz | 15 onz | | |
| 1990 | | 1 lbs 10 onz | 1 lbs 1.5 onz | 2 lbs 12 onz | |
| 1991 | | | 13.5 onz | 12 onz | |
| 1992 | 6 lbs 0 onz | 10 onz | 11 onz | 1 lbs 12 onz | |
| 1993 | 5 lbs 14 onz | 10 onz | 1 lbs 12 onz | 2 lbs 3 onz | 2 lbs 1 onz |
| 1994 | | | 2 lbs 8 onz | 2 lbs 2 onz | |
| 1995 | 6 lbs 14 onz | 2 lbs 8 onz | 3 lbs 14 onz | 2 lbs 0 onz | |
| 1996 | 13 lbs 8 onz | 10 onz | 1 lbs 11 onz | 2 lbs 5 onz | |
| 1997 | | 1 lbs 12 onz | 2 lbs 8 onz | 2 lbs 14 onz | 14 onz |
| 1998 | 6 lbs 0 onz | 1 lbs 4 onz | 1 lbs 6 onz | 5 lbs 12 onz | |
| 1999 | | 1 lbs 2 onz | 2 lbs 3 onz | 3 lbs 2 onz | |

*A True Fisherman's Tail*

| | | | | | | |
|---|---|---|---|---|---|---|
| **2000** | 8 lbs 0 onz | 8 onz | 1 lbs 2 onz | 4 lbs 2onz | | |
| **2001** | 0 | 0 | 1 lbs. 0 onz | 3 lbs. 12 onz. | | |
| **2002** | 5 lbs 4 onz | 12 onz | 2 lbs 9 onz | 7 lbs 13 onz | | |
| **2003** | 5 lbs 8 onz | n/a | n/a | 5 lbs 4 onz | | |
| **2004** | 8 lbs app | 0 | 1 lbs 4onz | 4 lbs 13onz | | |
| **2005** | 0 | 14onz | 1 lbs 0onz | 4 lbs 8onz | | Steelhead = 4 lbs 0 onz |
| **2006** | 0 | 1 lbs 0onz | 1 lbs 0onz | 4lbs 8onz | | |
| **2007** | 8lbs approx | | | | | Blue Trout = 1 lbs 12 onz |
| **2008** | 5lbs 12 onz | App 1lbs 4onz | App 1lbs 8onz | 3 lbs 12 onz | 1 lbs 4 onz | |
| **2009** | 6lbs 0 onz | App. 1lbs 0onz | App 1lbs 4onz | 3 lbs 7onz | | |
| **2010** | 5lbs 13 onz | 0 | 10onz | 3 lbs 10 onz | 2 lbs 1 onz | |
| **2011** | 10 lbs 14 onz | 12onz | 1lbs 8onz | 4 lbs 0 onz | 3 lbs 0 onz | |
| **2012** | 6 lbs 8 onz | 10onz | 2lbs | 4 lbs 8 onz | | |
| **2013** | 0 | 0 | 1lbs | 5 lbs | | |
| **2014** | 10 lbs 8 onz. | 14 onz | | 3 lbs 13onz | | |
| **2015** | | | | | | |
| **2016** | | | | | | |
| **2017** | | | | | | |
| **2018** | | | | | | |
| **2019** | | | | | | |
| **2020** | | | | | | |

Steelhead = 4 lbs 0 onz

| | | | | Average Weight | | | |
|------|------------|------------|------------|------------|------------|------------|------------|
| YEAR | SALMON | SEA TROUT | BROWN TROUT | RAINBOW TROUT | BROOK TROUT | STEEL-HEAD | BLUE TROUT |
| 1970 | ? | 10.0 onz | ? | N/A | N/A | | |
| 1971 | nil | 17.0 onz | 7.0 onz | N/A | N/A | | |
| 1972 | 3.0 lbs | 40.0 onz | 8.1 onz | N/A | N/A | | |
| 1973 | nil | 6.0 onz | 8.0 onz | N/A | N/A | | |
| 1974 | nil | 14.0 onz | 8.0 onz | N/A | N/A | | |
| 1975 | nil | 7.75 onz | 41 .0 onz | N/A | N/A | | |
| 1976 | nil | nil | 12.0 onz | N/A | N/A | | |
| 1977 | nil | 14.0 onz | 9.2 onz | N/A | N/A | | |
| 1978 | 9 lbs 7 onz | 16.0 onz | 6.0 onz | N/A | N/A | | |
| 1979 | nil | 44.0 onz | 6.5 onz | N/A | N/A | | |
| 1980 | nil | 23.0 onz | 10.0 onz | N/A | N/A | | |
| 1981 | nil | nil | 6.6 onz | N/A | N/A | | |
| 1982 | 7 lbs 7 onz | 8.5 onz | 7.1 onz | N/A | N/A | | |
| 1983 | 5 lbs 10 onz | nil | 6.7 onz | N/A | N/A | | |
| 1984 | nil | 15.0 onz | 9.0 onz | N/A | N/A | | |
| 1985 | 4 lbs 0 onz | nil | 9.1 onz | N/A | N/A | | |
| 1986 | 3 lbs 5.5 onz | 10.0 onz | 9.0 onz | N/A | N/A | | |
| 1987 | nil | 8.0 onz | 6.5 onz | N/A | N/A | | |
| 1988 | 9 lbs 0 onz | 12.0 onz | 8.5 onz | N/A | N/A | | |
| 1989 | 6 lbs 6 onz | 9.4 onz | 7.7 onz | N/A | N/A | | |
| 1990 | nil | 12.0 onz | 7.5 onz | 28 onz | nil | | |
| 1991 | nil | nil | 7.5 onz | 11.0 onz | nil | | |
| 1992 | 6 lbs 0 onz | 8.3 onz | 7.5 onz | 23.0 onz | nil | | |
| 1993 | 5 lbs 14 onz | 10.0 onz | 7.4 onz | 20 onz | 22.5 onz | | |
| 1994 | nil | nil | 13.75 onz | 18.5 onz | nil | | |
| 1995 | 6 lbs 14 onz | 40.0 onz | 10.7 onz | 22.5 onz | nil | | |
| 1996 | 13 lbs 8 onz | 10.0 onz | 7.6 onz | 20.5 onz | nil | | |
| 1997 | nil | 28.0 onz | 9.6 onz | 24.0 onz | 14.0 onz | | |
| 1998 | 5 lbs 5 onz | 13.5 onz | 9.3 onz | 34.0 onz | nil | 3 lbs 2.5 onz | 1 lbs 8 ONZ |
| 1999 | nil | 18.0 onz | 11.2 onz | 30.5 onz | nil | | |
| 2000 | 8 lbs 0onz | 8.0 onz | 9.5 onz | 26.0 onz | nil | | 1 lbs 4 onz |

| 2001 | nil | nil | 9.5onz | 32.0 onz | | | |
|------|-----|-----|--------|----------|--|--|--|
| 2002 | 4lbs 3onz | 10onz | 8onz | 28onz | | | |
| 2003 | 3lbs 8onz | nil | | 52.5onz | | | 2lbs 14onz |
| 2004 | 5lbs 8onz | nil | 9.5onz | 34onz | | | |
| 2005 | Nil | 14onz | 10onz | 40onz | | | |
| 2006 | Nil | 14onz | 15.5onz | 44onz | | | |
| 2007 | 6lbs 10onz | 1lbs 6onz | 10onz | 35onz | | | 2lbs 9onz |
| 2008 | 4lbs 8onz | 1lbs 0onz | 11onz | 39onz | | | 1lbs 4onz |
| 2009 | 4lbs 6onz | 12onz | 12onz | 38onz | | | |
| 2010 | 4lbs 8onz | nil | 6onz | 34onz | | | |
| 2011 | 6lbs 3onz | 11onz | 10onz | 45onz | | | |
| 2012 | 5lbs 5onz | 8onz | 9onz | 38onz | | | |
| 2013 | Nil | | | | | | |
| 2014 | | | | | | | |
| 2015 | | | | | | | |

# Dreghorn Angling Club

| History of Stocking | | | | | | | |
|------|-------|---------|------|------|-------|------|----------|
| YEAR | MONTH | SPECIES | SIZE | QTY | TOTAL | COST | COMMENTS |
| 1966 | | Brown Trout | 4" | 4,000 | 4,000 | £138.18/1d | |
| 1967 | | Brown Trout | 4" | 4,000 | 8,000 | £130.10/- | |
| 1968 | | Brown Trout | 4" | 4,000 | 12,000 | £138.18/- | |
| 1969 | | Brown Trout | 4" | 4,000 | 16,000 | £134.10/- | |
| 1970 | | Brown Trout | 4" | 2,000 | 18,000 | £70.10/- | |
| 1971 | | Brown Trout | 4" | 4,000 | 22,000 | £201.50 | |
| 1972 | | NIL | NIL | NIL | NIL | NIL | |
| 1973 | | NIL | NIL | NIL | NIL | NIL | |
| 1974 | | Brown Trout | 9" | 500 | 22,500 | £142.15 | |
| 1975 | | Brown Trout | 9" | 500 | 23,000 | £182.84 | |
| 1976 | | Brown Trout | 9" | 500 | 23,500 | £182.84 | |
| 1977 | | Brown Trout | 4" | 6,000 | 29,500 | £390.00 | |
| 1977 | | Brown Trout | 11" | 4,200 | 33,700 | £1,133.00 | |

| 1978 | | Brown Trout | 4" | 4,000 | 37,700 | £260.00 | |
|------|------|-------------|------|-------|--------|---------|---|
| 1978 | | Brown Trout | 11" | 1,000 | 38,700 | £663.00 | |
| 1979 | | Brown Trout | 4" | 4,000 | 42,700 | ? | |
| 1979 | | Brown Trout | 4" | 5,000 | 47,700 | ? | |
| 1980 | | Brown Trout | 9" | 1,160 | 48,860 | £715.00 | |
| 1981 | FEB | Brook Trout | 7" | 500 | 49360 | ? | |
| 1981 | FEB | Brown Trout | 7" | 2,000 | 51,360 | | |
| 1981 | NOV | Brown Trout | 9" | 500 | 51,860 | ? | |
| 1981 | NOV | Brown Trout | 9" | 900 | 52,760 | | Joint Stocking |
| 1982 | NIL | NIL | NIL | NIL | NIL | NIL | |
| 1983 | FEB | Brown Trout | 11" | 150 | 52,910 | ? | |
| 1983 | FEB | Brown Trout | 9" | 500 | 53,410 | ? | |
| 1983 | FEB | Brown Trout | 5" | 1,000 | 54,410 | ? | |
| 1983 | FEB | Brown Trout | 9" | 1,000 | 55,410 | £575.00 ea. | Joint Stocking |
| 1983 | FEB | Brown Trout | 5" | 2,000 | 57,410 | | Joint Stocking |
| 1983 | NOV | Brown Trout | 9" | 1,400 | 58,810 | ? | |
| 1983 | NOV | Brown Trout | 5" | 1,000 | 59,810 | £1,534.15 | |
| 1984 | NIL | NIL | NIL | NIL | NIL | NIL | |
| 1985 | FEB | Brown Trout | 9"-10" | 500 | 60,310 | ? | |
| 1985 | FEB | Brown Trout | 5"- 6" | 500 | 60,810 | ? | |
| 1985 | DEC | Brown Trout | 9"-10" | 500 | 61,310 | ? | |
| 1985 | DEC. | Brown Trout | 5" | 1,000 | 62,310 | ? | |
| 1985 | DEC. | Brown Trout | 12" | 100 | 62,410 | ? | |
| 1986 | NIL | NIL | NIL | NIL | NIL | NIL | |
| 1987 | FEB | Brown Trout | 9" | 500 | 62,910 | ? | |
| 1987 | FEB | Brown Trout | 5" | 1000 | 63,910 | ? | |
| 1987 | FEB | Brown Trout | 12" | 150 | 64,060 | ? | |
| 1988 | FEB | Brown Trout | 10" | 600 | 64,660 | ? | |
| 1989 | FEB | Brown Trout | 12" | 800 | 65,460 | ? | |
| 1989 | FEB | Brown Trout | 9" | 200 | 65,660 | ? | |
| 1989 | FEB | Brown Trout | 5" | 500 | 66,160 | ? | |
| 1990 | FEB | Brown Trout | 10" | 1200 | 67,360 | | |
| 1990 | FEB | Brown Trout | 6" | 1000 | 68,360 | | |
| 1990 | FEB | Brown Trout | 2 lbs | 20 | 68,380 | | |
| 1991 | FEB | Brown Trout | 10" | 800 | 69,180 | | |

| | | | | | | | |
|---|---|---|---|---|---|---|---|
| 1991 | FEB | Brown Trout | 2 lbs | 10 | 69,190 | | |
| 1992 | FEB | Brown Trout | 6" | 350 | 69,540 | * | |
| 1992 | FEB | Brown Trout | 10" | 1000 | 70,540 | *£1,791.80 | |
| 1993 | MAR | Brown Trout | 9/10" | 1000 | 71,540 | * | |
| 1993 | MAR | Brown Trout | 1/1.5 lbs | 100 | 71,640 | * | |
| 1993 | MAR | Brown Trout | 2 lbs. | 10 | 71,650 | * £1904.75 | |
| 1994 | FEB | Brown Trout | 4" | 600 | 72,250 | | |
| 1994 | FEB | Brown Trout | 10/12" | 500 | 72,750 | | |
| 1995 | MAR | Brown Trout | 10/12" | 900 | 73,650 | | |
| 1995 | JUN | Brown Trout | 10/12" | 350 | 74,000 | £500 | CDC/DREG |
| 1996 | MAR | Brown Trout | 10/11" | 500 | 74,500 | * | |
| 1996 | MAR | Brown Trout | 5/7" | 100 | 74,600 | * £965.00 | |
| 1997 | MAR | Brown Trout | 10" | 450 | 75,050 | * | |
| 1997 | MAR | Brown Trout | 6" | 200 | 75,250 | *£900.00 | |
| 1998 | MAR | Brown Trout | 11/12" | 520 | 75,770 | £1,000.00 | |
| 1999 | FEB | Brown Trout | 10/12" | 500 | 76,270 | £900.00 | |
| 1999 | JUN | Brown Trout | 12/16" | 350 | 76,570 | £750.00 | NAC/DREG |
| 2000 | FEB | Brown Trout | 10"/12" | 380 | 76,950 | | |
| 2001 | FEB | Brown Trout | 11- 13" | 420 | 77370 | £1,100.00 | |
| 2002 | FEB | Brown Trout | 12- 13" | 500 | 77870 | | |
| 2003 | Feb | Brown Trout | 10"-12" | 500 | 78370 | | |
| 2004 | Feb | Brown Trout | 10"-12" | 530 | 78900 | | |
| 2005 | Feb | Brown Trout | 10"-12" | 514 | 79414 | £1,200.00 | |
| 2006 | Mar | Brown Trout | 10"-12" | 500 | 79914 | £1,400.00 | |
| 2006 | Jul | Brown Trout | 12"-14" | 100 | 80014 | £315.00 | |
| 2007 | Mar | Brown Trout | 11"-13" | 500 | 80514 | £1,400.00 | |
| 2008 | Mar | Brown Trout | 11"-14" | 476 | 80990 | £1,400.00 | |
| 2009 | Mar | Brown Trout | 11"-14" | 445 | 81435 | £1,400.00 | |
| 2010 | Feb | Brown Trout | 11"-13" | 630 | 82065 | £2,000.00 | |
| 2011 | Feb | Brown Trout | 11"-13" | 340 | 82405 | £1,106.00 | |

| 2011 | May | Brown Trout | 12"-14" | 240 | 82645 | | |
| 2012 | 25th Feb | Brown Trout | 12"-14" | 450 | 83095 | £1,499.00 | |
| 2013 | 15th March | Brown Trout | 12"-14" | 450 | 83545 | £1,498.00 | |
| 2014 | 15th March | Brown Trout | 12"-14" | 430 | 83975 | £1,500.00 | |
| 2015 | 14th March | Brown Trout | 12"-14" | 430 | 84405 | £1,527.00 | |
| 2016 | | | | | 84405 | | |

# Venues Fished by Catgory

| | Rivers | | Wild Loch/fishery | | Small Fishery/Res. | |
|---|---|---|---|---|---|---|
| 1 | Alness | 4 | Ardgowan | 4 | Annbank | 1 |
| 2 | Annan | 5 | Awe | 4 | Arranview | 1 |
| 3 | Annick | 4 | Brack | 4 | Bowden Springs Fishery | 2 |
| 4 | Avon | 3 | Bradan | 4 | Burnfoot Res. | 4 |
| 5 | Ayr | 4 | Buidhie | 3 | Burns Fishery (Tarbolton) | 3 |
| 6 | Black Water of Dee | 2 | Butterstone | 3 | Cowans Law | 2 |
| 7 | Bladnoch | 1 | Carron Dam | 4 | Coyle Water | 3 |
| 8 | Carron | 4 | Chon | 3 | Craufurdland | 3 |
| 9 | Clyde | 5 | Clatteringshaws Res. | 2 | Dalvennan | 2 |
| 10 | Cree | 5 | Craigendunton Res. | 3 | Drum Fishery | 2 |
| 11 | Doon | 3 | Doon | 4 | Fintalla Loch | 2 |
| 12 | Earn | 3 | Dornal | 4 | Glenburn Res./ Fairlie Moor | 3 |
| 13 | Eden | 5 | Drumlangford | 2 | Howwood | 4 |
| 14 | Ewe ( Estuary) | 1 | Earlston | 2 | Kilchrist Fishery | 1 |
| 15 | Forth | 3 | Earn | 2 | Loch Heathe- Glen Clova | 2 |
| 16 | Garnock | 4 | Fad | 5 | Middleton | 2 |
| 17 | Girvan | 3 | Fitty | 3 | Northcraig Res. | 1 |
| 18 | Irvine | 4 | Fruid | 2 | Orchil Fishery | 3 |
| 19 | Ken | 5 | Garve | 3 | Raithe Res. (Prestwick) | 3 |
| 20 | Kyle of Sutherland, Bonar Bridge | 3 | Harelaw Dam | 3 | Regal Fishery Drumclog | 3 |

| 21 | Leven | 2 | Hillend Res. | 2 | Rough Loch | 1 |
|----|-------|---|--------------|---|------------|---|
| 22 | Lune | 3 | Invar (Galloway) | 3 | Solway Fishery | 2 |
| 23 | Nith | 4 | Ken | 1 | Springwater Fishery | 3 |
| 24 | Ribble | 3 | Kirriereoch | 3 | Stable Lakes | 2 |
| 25 | South Esk | 5 | Lake of Menteith | 5 | Swanswater | 2 |
| 26 | Spey | 4 | Leven | 3 | Troon Res. | 3 |
| 27 | Stinchar | 3 | Linlithgow | 3 | Unknown Lochan – J Pape | 3 |
| 28 | Teith | 3 | Lubnaig | 3 | Unknown Lochan – Crocketford | 2 |
| 29 | Teviot | 5 | Muirhead Res. (Largs) | 3 | Waterside Fishery | 1 |
| 30 | Tummell | 4 | Northird Res. | 5 | Morton Castle – Drumlanrigg | 4 |
| 31 | Tweed | 4 | Ochiltree | 3 | Achagour | 2 |
| 32 | Urr | 4 | Pinbraid | 3 | | |
| 33 | Wyllie | 4 | Pinwhapple Resevoir. | 3 | | |
| 34 | | | Portmore | 4 | | |
| 35 | | | Roscobie | 3 | | |
| 36 | | | Soulseat | 2 | | |
| 37 | | | Tay | 2 | | |
| 38 | | | Vennichar | 3 | | |
| 39 | | | Penwhapple Resevoir | 3 | | |

| Total – 103 Different Venues. |
|---|
| As of May 2015 |

1. Wouldn't be bothered if never fished again.

2. Nice to have fished but wouldn't go out my way to fish again.

3. Always willing to fish on occasion.

4. Impressed and enjoyed fishing — would like to fish regularly.

5. Would always fish at every opportunity.

# Returns

| Year | Metod Success rate (%) | | | | Percentage | | Club Returns | | |
|---|---|---|---|---|---|---|---|---|---|
| | Spinning | Worm | Fly | Nat. Minnow | Takeable fish ret'd | Takeable fish ret'd Club waters | Ret's as per AGM Salmon | Ret's as per AGM S/Trout | Ret's as per AGM B/Trout |
| 1970 | | | | | | | | | |
| 1971 | 7 | 64 | 28 | | 17 | | | | |
| 1972 | 25 | 37.5 | 37.5 | | 16.5 | | | | |
| 1973 | 50 | 17 | 33 | | 40 | | | | |
| 1974 | 28.5 | 57 | 14.5 | | 38.5 | | | | |
| 1975 | 80 | 20 | nil | | nil | | | | |
| 1976 | 40 | nil | 60 | | 10 | | | | |
| 1977 | 85 | 7.5 | 7.5 | | nil | | | | |
| 1978 | 25 | 44 | 31 | | 60 | | | | |
| 1979 | nil | 50 | 50 | | nil | | | | |
| 1980 | 33.5 | nil | 66.5 | | nil | | | | |
| 1981 | 18 | 9 | 9 | 64 | 36 | | 15 | 102 | |
| 1982 | 33 | 11 | 44 | 11 | 28.5 | | 10 | 69 | |
| 1983 | 27 | 18 | 54 | nil | 40 | | 39 | 106 | |
| 1984 | 28 | 28 | 14 | 28 | 20 | | 27 | 145 | |
| 1985 | 25 | 25 | 37.5 | 12.5 | 43 | | 61 | 228 | |
| 1986 | 11 | 26 | 21 | 42 | 50 | | 14 | 98 | |
| 1987 | nil | 73 | 27 | nil | 50 | | 15 | 301 | |
| 1988 | 10 | 43 | 33 | 14 | 50 | | 33 | 232 | |
| 1989 | 6.5 | 3.5 | 76.5 | 13.5 | 40 | | 143 | 211 | |
| 1990 | 12 | 20 | 68 | nil | 50 | | 45 | 145 | |
| 1991 | 31 | nil | 69 | nil | 54 | | 27 | 44 | |
| 1992 | nil | 53.5 | 46.5 | nil | 20 | | 51 | 51 | 587 |
| 1993 | 0.5 | 5 | 94.5 | | 64 | 27 | 44 | 28 | 431 |
| 1994 | 10 | 3 | 87 | | 37 | 71 | 34 | 15 | 112 |
| 1995 | nil | 4.5 | 95.5 | | 41 | 100 | 6 | 16 | 453 |
| 1996 | 4.5 | 1.5 | 94 | | 39 | 60 | 6 | 12 | 261 |
| 1997 | nil | 1 | 99 | | 42.5 | 81 | 4 | 7 | |

| | | | | | | | | | |
|------|-----|-----|------|-----|-----|-----|--------|------|-----|
| **1998** | 1 | 3.5 | 95.5 | | 59 | 66 | 40 | 23 | 283 |
| **1999** | 9 | 1 | 90 | | 59 | 100 | 6 | 11 | 194 |
| **2000** | 3.5 | nil | 96.5 | nil | 49 | 100 | 38 | 10 | 196 |
| **2001** | | | | | | | | | |
| **2002** | | | | | | | 34 | 4 | |
| **2003** | | | | | | | | | |
| **2004** | | | | | | | | | |
| **2005** | | | | | | | | | |
| **2006** | | | | | | | 20 | 2 | 118 |
| **2007** | | | | | | | 36 | 4 | 100 |
| **2008** | | | | | | | 33 | 10 | 150 |
| **2009** | | | | | | | 26 | 4 | 128 |
| **2010** | | | | | | | 33 | 3 | 21 |
| **2011** | | | | | | | 17 | 2 | 85 |
| **2012** | | | | | | | 14 | 17 | 185 |
| **2013** | | | | | | | 17(12) | 9 | 93 |
| **2014** | | | | | | | 20 | 41 ? | 199 | One man 36?
| **2015** | | | | | | | 25+3 | 4 | 117 |

## Dreghorn Angling Club - Membership Details.

| Year | Total club members |
|------|------|
| 1984 | 467 |
| 1985 | 330 |
| 1986 | 334 |
| 1987 | 332 |
| 1988 | 313 |
| 1989 | 362 |
| 1990 | 365 |
| 1991 | 341 |
| 1992 | 290 |

| Year | Members |
|------|------|
| 1993 | 293 |
| 1994 | 271 |
| 1995 | 224 |
| 1996 | 229 |
| 1997 | 201 |
| 1998 | 209 |
| 1999 | 198 |
| 2000 | 209 |
| 2001 | 197 |
| 2002 | 252 |
| 2003 | 318 |

| Year | Members |
|------|------|
| 2004 | 251 |
| 2005 | 297 |
| 2006 | 267 |
| 2007 | 284 |
| 2008 | 282 |
| 2009 | 308 |
| 2010 | 276 |
| 2011 | 319 |
| 2012 | 278 |
| 2013 | 268 |
| 2014 | |

| Year | Position | Term (yrs) |
|------|----------|------------|
| 1966 -1972 | Junior member. | 6 |
| 1973 - 1975 | Adult member. | 3 |
| 1976 -1978 | Vice- President. | 3 |
| 1979 -1984 | President | 6 |
| 1985 | Committee member. | 1 |
| 1986 - 1987 | Unwarrented bailiff / Club member. | 2 |
| 1988 - 1991 | Warrented bailiff / Committee member / Auditor. | 4 |
| 1992 - 2002 | Committee member / Auditor. | 12 |
| 2003 - 2016 | Treasurer | 13 |
| | | 50 |

| | Ret's as per AGM Salmon | Ret's as per AGM S/Trout | Ret's as per AGM B/Trout |
|---|---|---|---|
| **1981** | 15 | 102 | |
| **1982** | 10 | 69 | |
| **1983** | 39 | 106 | |
| **1984** | 27 | 145 | |
| **1985** | 61 | 228 | |
| **1986** | 14 | 98 | |
| **1987** | 15 | 301 | |
| **1988** | 33 | 232 | |
| **1989** | 143 | 211 | |
| **1990** | 45 | 145 | |
| **1991** | 27 | 44 | |
| **1992** | 51 | 51 | 587 |
| **1993** | 44 | 28 | 431 |
| **1994** | 34 | 15 | 112 |
| **1995** | 6 | 16 | 453 |
| **1996** | 6 | 12 | 261 |
| **1997** | 4 | 7 | |
| **1998** | 40 | 23 | 283 |
| **1999** | 6 | 11 | 194 |
| **2000** | 38 | 10 | 196 |
| **2001** | 51 | 2 | 143 |
| **2002** | 34 | 4 | 164 |
| **2003** | 12 | 2 | 24 |
| **2004** | 36 | 2 | 127 |
| **2005** | 22 | 5 | 117 |
| **2006** | 20 | 2 | 118 |
| **2007** | 36 | 4 | 100 |
| **2008** | 33 | 10 | 150 |
| **2009** | 26 | 4 | 128 |
| **2010** | 33 | 3 | 21 |
| **2011** | 17 | 2 | 85 |
| **2012** | 14 | 17 | 185 |
| **2013** | 29 | 9 | 93 |
| **2014** | 20 | 16 | 199 |
| **2015** | 28 | 4 | 117 |

| Year | Ret's as per AGM Salmon |
|---|---|
| 2015 | 28 |
| 2014 | 20 |
| 2013 | 29 |
| 2012 | 14 |
| 2011 | 17 |
| 2010 | 33 |
| 2009 | 26 |
| 2008 | 33 |
| 2007 | 36 |
| 2006 | 20 |
| 2005 | 22 |
| 2004 | 36 |
| 2003 | 12 |
| 2002 | 34 |
| 2001 | 51 |
| 2000 | 38 |
| 1999 | 6 |
| 1998 | 40 |
| 1997 | 4 |
| 1996 | 6 |
| 1995 | 33 |
| 1994 | 15 |
| 1993 | 44 |
| 1992 | 51 |
| 1991 | 27 |
| 1990 | 45 |
| 1989 | 143 |
| 1988 | 33 |
| 1987 | 15 |
| 1986 | 14 |
| 1985 | 61 |
| 1984 | 27 |
| 1983 | 39 |
| 1982 | 10 |
| 1981 | 15 |

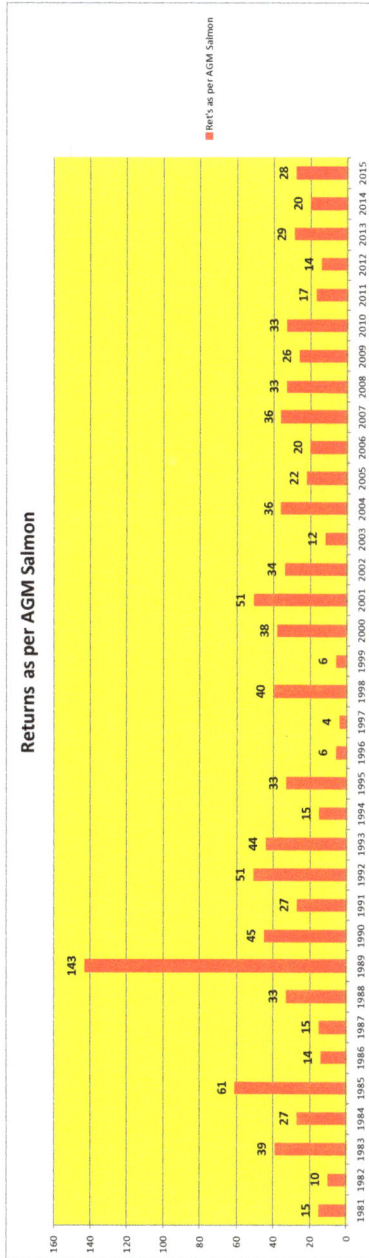

Returns as per AGM Salmon

| Year | Ret's as per AGM Sea Trout |
|------|------|
| 2015 | 4 |
| 2014 | 16 |
| 2013 | 9 |
| 2012 | 17 |
| 2011 | 2 |
| 2010 | 3 |
| 2009 | 4 |
| 2008 | 10 |
| 2007 | 4 |
| 2006 | 2 |
| 2005 | 5 |
| 2004 | 2 |
| 2003 | 2 |
| 2002 | 4 |
| 2001 | 2 |
| 2000 | 10 |
| 1999 | 11 |
| 1998 | 23 |
| 1997 | 4 |
| 1996 | 12 |
| 1995 | 16 |
| 1994 | 15 |
| 1993 | 28 |
| 1992 | 51 |
| 1991 | 44 |
| 1990 | 145 |
| 1989 | 211 |
| 1988 | 232 |
| 1987 | 301 |
| 1986 | 98 |
| 1985 | 228 |
| 1984 | 145 |
| 1983 | 106 |
| 1982 | 69 |
| 1981 | 102 |

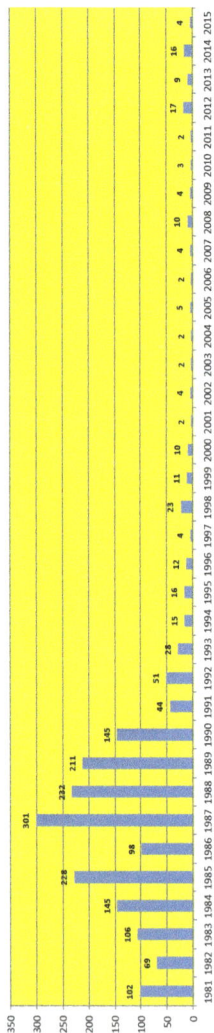

Ret's as per AGM Sea Trout

Yearly averages - Salmon

1981 - 1988 -- 8yrs --- 25.5 Salmon

1990 - 1999 - 10yrs --- 26.3 Salmon

2000 - 2010 --- 10yr ---- 30.8 Salmon

2010 -- 2015 -- 6yrs --- 23.5 Salmon

2000 - 2015 --- 16 yrs --- 27.15 Salmon

# SALMON - LENGTH AND WEIGHT

**Length/Weight Ratio - Estimated**

| | Imperial (Inches) | Metric (mm) | Keith's - Avg. Weight (based on personal record of salmon caught.) | Sturdie Scale River DEE (Estimate) |
|---|---|---|---|---|
| Length | 21.5" | 546 | 3lbs 5oz | |
| | 24" | 610 | 4lbs 5oz | 5lbs 8oz |
| | 26" | 660 | 5lbs 13oz | 7lbs 3oz |
| | 28" | 710 | 6lbs 13oz | 9lbs 1oz |
| | 30" | 762 | 8lbs 8oz | 10lbs 9oz |
| | 32" | 812 | 9lbs 11oz | 12lbs 8oz |
| | 34" | 864 | 10lbs 3oz | 15lbs 7oz |
| | 36" | 915 | 13lbs 0oz | 18lbs 6oz |

With reference to the table above:

How can one be so accurate when guessing the actual weight of a salmon? Compare the difference between the two columns on the right of the table. Why should there be such a difference?

I believe there is no absolute definitive way of accurately knowing the weight of a salmon without actually weighing the fish on calibrated scales. There are too many variants to consider. I believe the best one can do is to give a best estimate, an estimate usually based on experiences gained by long-term monitoring, observation, measuring and weighing and knowing your local environment.

Myself personally, over the years I have been guilty of slightly under estimating the weight of larger-type fish (usually not by much I may add – but underestimate I do). How anyone can put a specific accurate figure on the weight of a salmon defeats me, even the estimated figures in the table above have quite a large variance between what I have factually experienced and what the figures from the Sturdie Scale details from the River Dee show. It doesn't surprise me. I mentioned earlier about the variants which need to be considered.

**For example:**

- The type of river or the environment in which the fish is found.
- Is it a cock or hen fish? (Hen fish full of eggs.)
- How long has the fish been in the river since leaving the sea? How long has the fish been fasting for?
- Is it fresh off the tide? Or right in the upper reaches of the river?
- Length, girth, condition etc. etc.

In 2015 I was lucky enough to land a lovely fresh hen fish with a length of 34.5 inches, weighing in at 15.08 lbs. With reference to the table, the Dee estimate is very accurate, but would it have been as accurate later in the fish's journey? Like a lot of things in life there's much truth in the old saying, "There's no substitute for experience."

There have been many changes over the years since I first started fishing with the worm (as every boy did at that time) to the type of fishing in which I now partake. My own personal skill level has improved from being virtually self-taught, to learning by trial and error through mistakes, and for the few people who did point me in the right direction – I wholeheartedly thank them and am very much indebted to them.

I have experienced angling for wild brown trout with worm, then progressing to using spinning methods and similar techniques, moving into fly fishing and even being fortunate enough to have experienced a degree of success fishing for sea trout before their demise in my local river (refer to appendix 8).

Being introduced to fishing for rainbow trout during the nineties and ultimately fishing for the "King of Fish," the salmon, although pound for pound I reckon sea trout are the ultimate in fighting experience. I sincerely hope the sea trout can recover to the numbers they once were during the times where, in reality, I was too young and inexperienced to appreciate true success when fishing for sea trout.

Then, of course, there is the illegal method of poaching, even these methods and techniques have changed over the years. During my early years, most of the poaching methods which were adopted on my local river were performed by either gaffing fish as they ascended the local dams and weirs or snigling with rod and heavy sink lines with a team of big bare hooks ripped through the salmon lies. Poaching methods advanced to using fine mesh nylon gill nets and Cyanide poisoning was also rife during the late eighties and early nineties. No wonder the stocks of fish were depleting at such an alarming rate.

Obviously, I am not naive enough to totally blame poaching for the demise of stocks, but I have a firm belief it is certainly one of the main contributors.

I stated that when I was young I spent most of my time on the river bank, how times change? Today I'm lucky if I manage time to fish for brown trout at all. I also have to carefully pre-plan outings well in advance if I want to fish for rainbow trout and even then, it's usually only for a few hours rather than a full day session.

As the season advances into August and the back-end fishing for salmon arrives, I always seem to be fighting the clock, especially as the autumn evenings begin to draw-in. What's happened to my fishing time? I honestly thought as one got older, one would have more time on their hands - how wrong I was!

My only saving grace throughout the past ten years or so, and considering the restricted amount of opportunity I now get to fish, is that comparing the ratio of number of fish actually caught to the number of visits I pay to the waterside, I am fortunate enough to manage an average of about 2.5 fish for every outing. This return may not satisfy everyone, but I make no apology when I say I'm quite happy with that. "There's more to fishing than catching fish."

I sincerely hope you, the reader, have enjoyed reading the contents of this book and have managed to relate some of my experiences to those of your own. If you have, then I believe I have achieved my objective. Angling has provided me with so many unforgettable and happy memories and recollections.

It only leaves me to wish all anglers everywhere "tight lines" and wish you all the very best for the future.

Enjoy your angling, respect your quarry and love your environment.

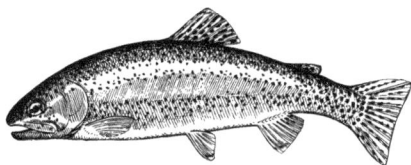

# FISHERMAN'S LAMENT

*Sometimes o'er early*

*Sometimes o'er late*

*Sometimes na water*

*Sometimes a spate*

*Sometimes o'er dirty*

*Some o'er clear*

*Ther's aye something Wrang*

*When a'm fishin' here???*

*Amen.*